D0846023

Public Opinion & Collective Action

Public Opinion & Collective Action

The Boston School Desegregation Conflict

With a Foreword by Arthur L. Stinchcombe

D. Garth Taylor

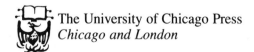 The University of Chicago Press
Chicago and London

D. Garth Taylor is associate professor of political
science at the University of Chicago. He is the coauthor
of *Paths of Neighborhood Change: Race and Crime in
Urban America,* also published by the University of
Chicago Press.

The University of Chicago Press, Chicago 60637
The University of Chicago Press, Ltd., London
© 1986 by The University of Chicago
All rights reserved. Published 1986
Printed in the United States of America
95 94 93 92 91 90 89 88 87 86   5 4 3 2 1

Library of Congress Cataloging-in-Publication Data

Taylor, D. Garth.
  Public opinion & collective action.

  Bibliography: p.
  Includes index.
    1. School integration—Massachusetts—Boston—
Public opinion.   2. Racism—Massachusetts—Boston.
3. Boston (Mass.)—Race relations—Public opinion.
4. Public opinion—Massachusetts—Boston.   I. Title.
II. Title: Public opinion and collective action.
LC214.23.B67T39   1986   370.19′342   86-4359
ISBN 0-226-79155-6

Contents

Foreword

It is an inherent problem with democracy, the "Madisonian" problem, that democracy for one group often means oppression for another. Madison, being a conservative, was particularly interested in how majorities of the poor might oppress minorities of the rich. Government actions that have bad consequences for black people bring up the Madisonian problem for liberals and radicals, that the majority of the better off may oppress, and often have oppressed, the minorities of the poor.

A crucial determinant of exactly how this happens is the structure of jurisdictions of local, state and federal governments. The majority of the North and West in the sixties had a different opinion than the white majorities of many Southern states about who should vote, how Southern schools should be organized, whether the law could be used to segregate restaurants and hotels, and the like. The determination of exactly which questions were under the jurisdiction of the state in race relations, what kinds of laws states had a right to pass and enforce, determined *which* majorities had the right to "oppress" *which* minorities; could Northern and Western whites and blacks take away the jurisdiction from the "democratic" majorities of Southern states, so that they could not maintain the system of Jim Crow?

"Which majorities?" has been a crucial problem in the busing controversy. D. Garth Taylor shows here that the great majority of white Bostonians are not racist on most questions but that a great majority of the nonracist majority is against busing in Boston. The Massachusetts state government, presumably representing the majority of the people of the state, passed laws requiring that Boston achieve racial balance in their schools, and the federal government (though not through its representative institutions in the Congress and the presidency) imposed a determination by court order that this had to be done by busing. There was no other practical way.

Although no doubt a majority of white Americans oppose busing in Northern school districts to achieve racial balance, the majority also want to live under a constitution that protects the rights of minorities, and at least a large minority prefer a rule of law to a pure rule of majorities. The nonrepresentative character of the court decisions on busing, therefore, at the very least poses a serious problem about how to run a democracy. The question of whether Boston should get to run its own schools, as decided by Boston democratic politics, thus represents a core problem in democratic theory, the question of jurisdictions of majorities.

Taylor has a fascinating analysis of the way this problem came to be posed in Boston. His analysis of the development of the "doctrine of voluntary compliance" in Chapter 2 shows how the legal tradition had opposing themes, some of which justified resistance to legal means, busing in particular, to achieve goals that the majority of the white public believes in, a nonracist society and a nonracist school system. In several chapters he traces how the traditions of Boston resistance to the Massachusetts government's habit of taking over municipal functions and powers, and Catholic resistance to Protestant-controlled public schools and defense of the right to run parochial schools, created traditions and structures of institutional leadership that made it easy to raise the question of "Which majorities?" during the busing controversy.

In a delicate survey analysis of wonderful panel data from several Boston white neighborhoods, collected due to the scientific foresight and under the management of Michael Ross, he shows how symbolic and social ties to these Boston political institutions and Catholic ethnic leaderships fed into the organization of the protest against busing.

The key thing Taylor demonstrates is that many white people who thought that blacks had been unfairly dealt with by American society, and who thought they ought to be treated better, nevertheless thought that they were being unfairly dealt with in the attempt to remedy this unfairness by busing. The right to run their own school system the way they thought wise was being taken away from them, and policies were being introduced that they thought damaged them. And it reminded them of the way Protestant Massachusetts had treated Catholic Boston in a long dispute about which majorities counted.

The reason for giving such a detailed summary of the argument here is not to take credit for it but to set the stage for arguing that this is an example of how detailed and sophisticated social science knowledge, knowledge backed when possible by numbers, can deepen the way we address value questions. It shows that although fanatics make a lot of the noise and get a lot of TV coverage, behind them, in important social movements, are a lot of reasonable folks confronted with a true dilemma. Most of us believe that sometimes power has to be taken away (if it can be done) from majorities to achieve higher values, such as justice for black people in America. But most of us want to be extremely cautious about doing that, because we do not want democracy lightly treated.

When basic values like justice and democracy come into conflict, then it becomes extremely important to understand exactly what is going on, exactly what it is that makes the majority think they are being treated unjustly, exactly what traditions support and which undermine the attempt to implement a more just alternative for black people, and exactly which ones provide a vigorous support of democracy. For we still want a vigorous democracy in Boston, whatever our opinion about the protests against busing that that democratic tradition led to.

Our value choices in situations like that in Boston are not simple, and oversimplifying them to a conflict between racist fanatics and reasonable rational judges does not deepen our capacity to live in a democratic, but just, society. I believe that this book by D. Garth Taylor does deepen that capacity.

Arthur L. Stinchcombe
Northwestern University

Preface

This book examines a number of problems in contemporary American racial politics: How has white American racism changed in recent years? Why has increased public tolerance for interracial contact not led to support for desegregation and affirmative action? When and why do public protests against desegregation become widespread?

By analyzing the public reaction to school desegregation in Boston in the middle 1970s, with some comparisons to other cities and to national survey data, this book shows that white Americans now predominantly reject a doctrine of racial superiority that was widespread even a generation ago, and yet they refuse to accept requirements for racial change. The result is an uneasy doctrine of "voluntary compliance," justified by beliefs about unfairness and harm caused by desegregation, that is the basis of white American racial ideology today. The analysis in this book shows how leaders of government, leaders of community institutions, and media shape (and often reinforce) the doctrine of voluntary compliance as they try to influence public reactions to desegregation while maintaining their position in the community.

The findings in this book address a number of new theories of public opinion, political leadership, social movements, and political mobilization. Separate chapters focus specifically on the theory of American racial attitudes, the theory of perceived injustice as an antecedent to mobilization, the theory of political entrepreneurship, the theory of the spiral of silence, and the theory of goal-directed versus "irrational" participation in collective action.

Most chapters make heavy use of a panel survey of Boston neighborhood residents in the 1970s, superbly designed by J. Michael

Ross, and administered, for the most part, by the National Opinion Research Center. The first, and most important, acknowledgment that must be made is to Dr. Ross. Without his efforts this book, literally, could not have been written. His energy and talent are evident in the extremely high quality and comprehensiveness of the survey data.

My involvement with the data began when Dr. Ross asked me to become a principal investigator to analyze the survey data and to write a report for the granting agencies. Joining me as an investigator on this project was Professor Arthur Stinchcombe. Together, we wrote a report titled "The Boston School Desegregation Controversy" and submitted it to the National Institute of Education (Taylor and Stinchcombe 1979). I owe great thanks to Professor Stinchcombe for his collaboration on the 1979 report and also, more important, for his colleagueship over the years. I have come to believe that professional coauthorship is the second most intimate relationship there is. A public acknowledgment of the interaction, such as this one, seems an understatement. It is, however, the way such collaborations are celebrated in the academy.

In addition to the survey data, I have also made extensive use of historical and contextual information about the city of Boston and about other cities experiencing similar kinds of difficulties with desegregation. Much of this information was gathered while I was a research associate at the Institute for Research on Poverty at Madison, Wisconsin. Thanks are due to that organization and especially to Professor Karl Taeuber for gifts of time and support that gave me the opportunity to think about how historical and contextual information ought to be used to clarify and amplify empirical patterns from survey data. I also owe special thanks to James Hannon, at the time a graduate student in the Sociology Department at Madison, for making available to me his M.A. thesis on the role of the Catholic church during the Boston crisis.

Others who must be specially acknowledged for taking an active and helpful interest in this project are Professors Benjamin Page and Gary Orfield. Each has read numerous parts of the manuscript (sometimes several drafts) and freely shared insights, reactions, and suggestions for change.

A number of colleagues read the 1979 project report and offered reactions that substantially improved this book. The list includes

Ronald Henderson, Kenneth Prewitt, Stephen Weatherford, Gunnar Myrdal, Robert Crain, and Seymour Martin Lipset.

Many colleagues responded to my calls for guidance and read early drafts of this book, or individual chapters, and replied with important suggestions that I tried to take into account. This list includes James A. Davis, Christine Rossell, Eleanor Singer, William Gamson, Elisabeth Noelle-Neumann, Mark Granovetter, John McCarthy, Doris Graber, Joe Spaeth, Charles Whitney, Ellen Wartella, Sandra Ball-Rokeach, Norman Bradburn, Jack McLeod, Sheldon Stryker, Howard Schuman, Chris Achen, Lawrence Bobo, Edward Hamburg, Tahi Motl, Andrew Shapiro, Esther Fuchs, Robert Shapiro, and Bert Useem.

I owe a debt to students who have worked on this project. These people interacted with the substantive material and also provided capable assistance in managing the complexities of the historical and empirical research. This list includes (in historical order) Stephen Garry, Bruce Peterson, Douglas Dow, and Roland Anglin. I also owe a debt of gratitude to my University of Chicago students who read early drafts of this material in my course "Survey Analysis of Collective Political Action."

In every case I have been grateful for the advice and assistance offered to me. Whether we have agreed or disagreed, the lines of thought developed during interactions with my readers and critics have been stimulating for me and I hope for them as well.

This book is primarily an analysis of the Boston school desegregation controversy, but I believe it has relevance for understanding racial issues in any American city. By almost any historical standard the events in Boston were extreme. But it is only from examination of extreme cases that it is possible to study the dynamics of conflict as these dynamics change from the low to the moderate to the extreme level. My goal is to explain the extremity of the conflict in Boston in a systematic way. I hope that from this exercise reactions to desegregation in other cities and in other decades can be better understood and better managed as well.

Introduction

No man will treat with indifference the principle of
race. It is the key of history.

Benjamin Disraeli

1 | The Boston School Desegregation Conflict

Some Boston Landmarks

In 1869 Massachusetts enacted the first law in America authorizing expenditure of public funds to transport children to and from school. This law changed the nature of public schooling in America by codifying the intention of the state to make universal access to education not only a right but also a practical possibility for its citizens.

In 1974 Federal Circuit Court Judge Arthur Garrity ruled that the public schools in Boston were illegally segregated and that public funds must be spent to transport both black and white children for the purpose of integration. This decision also affected the nature of public schooling in America. It was one of the first times a Northern school board was found guilty of segregative actions by a federal court. In terms of the percentage of pupils mandatorily reassigned, Judge Garrity's plan was, at the time, the most extensive plan for desegregation ever implemented. The public reaction to the decision was one of the first instances of massive, violent resistance to school desegregation in the North. The Boston public schools were ultimately desegregated. The controversy there, however, has strengthened white opposition to mandatory desegregation in other cities and in American national politics since that time.

The extremity of the response makes the experience in Boston a valuable case for studying the dynamics of community conflict: the process of mobilization and the beliefs that are most strongly related to protest cannot be effectively studied in communities where the opposition remains unorganized or politically mute. This book does not suggest, however, that what happened in Boston is representative of what happened or what will happen in other American cities undergoing mandatory school desegregation. The history and demography of the city, the prior organization and sophistication of the antibusing forces, the type of plan implemented, and the enrollment change after desegregation make the reaction to mandatory desegregation more extreme in Boston than in any other Northern city. In most cities undergoing school desegregation, a more peaceful transition is more likely. Even places experiencing comparative difficulty, such as Louisville, Kentucky have been calm compared to Boston.

The first part of this book analyzes the popular beliefs—opinions, attitudes, what Myrdal calls "moral valuations"—that currently justify, in the minds of American citizens, opposition to mandatory desegregation. These beliefs are deeply rooted in American legal and social history. Past judicial decisions, past legislative actions, and past election results provide precedent and justification for those who argue that mandatory change is socially harmful and unjust, is contrary to our national traditions, and is likely to be declared illegal in the future. Compliance with desegregation policy should be, in the popular mind at the present time, voluntary instead of mandatory. Part One analyzes current beliefs about desegregation as independent social facts and the method by which they "enter directly into the causal mechanism of interracial relations" (Myrdal 1944).

Because the popular beliefs justifying opposition to mandatory desegregation are so widespread, there is a nearly unanimous level of opposition to busing in Boston and in every other American city that has been surveyed. The high level of opposition to busing, however, does not always lead to protest and conflict when desegregation is required. For the grievances of individuals to find expression in a community response, other circumstances must aid what Rule and Tilly call "the transition from uncoordinated individual dissatisfactions to collective assaults on the holders of power" (1975, p. 50). Part Two of this book analyzes the political processes that determine whether public dissatisfaction with busing remains a matter of uncoordinated, individual discontent, or whether it develops into a collective assault on mandatory desegregation.

The remainder of this chapter is devoted to an overview of the book, a description of the sources of information analyzed, and a number of comments about the methodology employed for making statistical and historical inferences.

Chapter Topics in Part One

Chapter 2 is a discussion of American history and racial ideology during the years preceding the Boston school desegregation controversy. The "Doctrine of Voluntary Compliance"—the belief that segregation is illegal but that desegregation is voluntary—is discussed as a core concept shaping Americans' understanding of their constitutional rights and responsibilities in the area of race relations. The roots of this belief are found in legal opinions, legislative actions, and political pronouncements, from every geographic region of the country dating back to Reconstruction. Americans who act on this belief do so with the faith that they are acting within the legal traditions of the society. The forces that came into conflict over this belief in Boston—the civil rights movement and the "voluntary compliance" movement—are examined.

Chapters 3 and 4 examine Boston neighborhood residents' beliefs about race relations and desegregation, and the relation of these beliefs to antibusing protest. Myrdal describes many American beliefs about race relations and the law as "rationalizations" because these beliefs make tolerance of segregation seem appropriate, reasonable, constitutionally necessary and, therefore, "rational." Chapters 3 and 4 examine American beliefs that, in this sense, "rationalize" antibusing protest: racism, and perceived injustice to whites.

"Racism," as the term is used in this book and as it is usually employed in social science discussion, means a belief in white supremacy. A racist is someone who believes that blacks are inferior. A racist believes that, because of this, it is justifiable and even necessary to erect barriers preventing participation in activities that imply social equality between the races. This view is discussed in Chapter 2 as the "doctrine of social inequality."

Chapter 3 shows that the reaction against school desegregation in Boston and other Northern cities came at a time when white opinion was moving away from support for white supremacist ideals, legally mandated discrimination, and the doctrine of social inequality. White supremacists were, of course, prominent during the Boston crisis, and Chapter 3 shows that those who maintain racist views about the inferiority of blacks are more likely than those who do not to join in antibusing protest. But the most striking finding from Chapter 3 is the high level of opposition to busing, and willingness to protest, among the majority of Boston neighborhood residents who could not be counted as supremacists or racists by any other social science criterion. Most Boston neighborhood residents rationalize support for protest against desegregation with reasons that do not have to do directly with white supremacy.

Instead, the principal rationale for desegregation protest in Boston is perceived injustice and perceived social harm. When the doctrine of voluntary compliance is challenged by a court order for mandatory desegregation, Americans believe that an injustice is being done to the democratic system of government and that social harm is threatened for the community. Woodward's argument concentrates on perceived injustice and social harm as the reasons for opposition to school desegregation in the North:

> Once it appeared that the courts were going to move against . . . school segregation in northern cities . . . many of the old southern arguments reemerged, this time from northern mouths, those of liberals included: desegregation promoted racial conflict and disorder in schools; it was of doubtful benefit to black students anyway and many blacks did not want it; it destroyed neighborhood schools and neighborhoods; it was impossible in cities with growing black majorities in schools without busing, and that was too costly, counter-productive and politically disastrous. (Woodward 1974, pp. 216–217)

The belief that mandatory busing is unfair and socially harmful is referred to in Chapter 4 as an "injustice frame of reference" (Gamson et al. 1982). The injustice frame is the principal rationalization for opposition to desegregation. It is because the busing issue is viewed this way that the majority of Americans who do not favor white supremacy are opposed, nevertheless, to mandatory desegregation.

The evidence I have seen from a large number of surveys suggests that the injustice frame of reference is widespread. Most of the residents of most American communities believe mandatory busing is unjust and socially harmful. The reason one community erupts into conflict and another does not when ordered to desegregate is not because the perception of injustice is greater in one than in the other. Rather, a cluster of causes that can, at this point, be summarized as "local political circumstances" determine the extent of conflict a community will experience over school desegregation. The injustice frame, in other words, is a necessary but not sufficient condition for antibusing mobilization. Without the widespread perception of injustice there would not be antibusing mobilization. The fact that there is a widespread perception of injustice provides a constituency that can be mobilized into antibusing protest when local political circumstances encourage or allow this to happen. The political circumstances that facilitate mobilization are the topics in Part Two of this book.

Chapter Topics in Part Two

In some communities the injustice believed to accompany mandatory school desegregation aggravates other long-standing community cleavages and political conflicts. The imposition of school desegregation in the deep South aroused sentiments supporting the pre–Civil War doctrine of nullification. The imposition of Judge Garrity's decision in Boston aggravated a conflict over administration of city services that had divided religious and ethnic groups in the state for more than a century. The history of the Yankee-immigrant conflict over administration of city resources is introduced in Chapter 4. The relevance of this for the policies of Boston Cardinal Humberto Medeiros and the Catholic church are analyzed in Chapter 5. The implications for political leaders responsible for implementing the court order, such as Boston Mayor Kevin White, are analyzed in Chapter 6.

The antibusing forces in a community are more likely to be successful when they are able to make use of preexisting community organizations and community resources to facilitate mobilization. Chapter 5 shows that, in spite of the intentions of Cardinal Medeiros and other leaders, some of the Catholic church's resources as a community organization—networks of membership, communication, and leadership—helped amplify the opinions and actions of antibusing protesters.

Chapter 6 analyzes the situation of local elected political leaders when they are legally required to implement an unpopular policy. In the American system of government, the responsibility for enforcing school desegregation falls to elected officials at the local level of government. I describe this in Chapter 6 as the principal of decentralized enforcement. Given the unpopularity of mandatory desegregation, the only way local officials can fulfill their legal responsibilities and stay in office is to rely on the courts, higher public officials, and other community leaders to associate themselves with a rigid requirement to go along with the mandates of the court order. In the language of one famous analysis of Southern school desegregation, these officials must be willing to play a "scapegoat" role—to be a focus for opposition and a rallying point for convincing the public of the imminence of the policy and the need for compliance—to ease the pressures on local officials who have the immediate responsibility to enforce the law (Peltason 1961). (Peltason does not use the term "scapegoat" in its precise, lexical denotation, but deference to the acuity of his analysis and subsequent use of the term in the literature argues for keeping the word.) In Boston Judge Garrity took a scapegoat role, but other community leaders and politicians did not.

Awareness of a division between the community and "outside" forces who seek to impose an unpopular policy can, itself, contribute to the likelihood of antibusing conflict. The grounding of the Boston school desegregation controversy in the Yankee-immigrant struggle over governance of the city was already discussed in connection with Chapter 5. But even in communities that have not experienced a Yankee-immigrant conflict, perception of widespread opposition between the community and outside authorities can close off options for a peaceful resolution to the problem. Chapter 7 explores the reasons for this relationship. Three theories linking perception of cohesive community discontent with increased willingness to protest are studied. The findings link earlier macrolevel observations about the effects of media and political leadership with microlevel theories of willingness to protest. Pronouncements by public leaders, media biases that present one side of the question, conversational networks that reinforce antibusing views, and any other factor that increases the perception of widespread opposition to desegregation also increases the likelihood that those who are opposed to busing will join in protests.

There is a tendency for the factors discussed in Part Two to cumulate into a shared public sense that gains may possibly be realized from protest and that one's contribution may be important in achieving those gains. This shared public sense can be loosely described as a view that the benefits outweigh the costs of protest. A closer analysis shows, however, that the benefits and costs weighed by individuals are not as precisely calculable or as tangible as the rhetoric of a purely economic model of protest would suggest. For instance, very few people who protest do so because they believe it will end busing. In fact, the overwhelming majority are convinced that this goal will never be achieved. Those who join in antibusing protest primarily do so because they believe it is likely to result in a nonspecifiable but positive gain, in an indefinite but reasonable length of time. Chapter 8 reviews the evidence for this theory of protest participation and discusses the importance of the sense of injustice, the aggravation of longstanding patterns of community cleavage, the abdication of the scapegoat role by political leadership, and other factors discussed in Parts One and Two in light of this theory of protest.

Chapter 9 is a summary and evaluation of the major issues addressed in this book. Does the record in Boston suggest that desegregation is a failure as a social policy? To what extent is the Boston experience typical, representative, or predictive of the reaction to mandatory desegregation in other American cities? Finally, what is the significance of the Boston experience for American desegregation politics in the decade since Judge Garrity's order?

Survey Data

Each chapter in this book draws upon data from a five-wave panel survey of residents of the Boston metropolitan area conducted between October 1973 and July 1975 by the National Opinion Research Center (Ross 1976; Taylor and Stinchcombe 1977).

Five interviews over a 22-month period were attempted with 631 residents of the Boston area. The data collection began eight months before the initial court order mandating desegregation (June 1974) and ended in July 1975 after a controversial first year of implementation of the "Phase I" plan. The timing of each wave of the survey relative to some of the other events surrounding Judge Garrity's order is shown in table 1.1.

The survey was designed to achieve a sample of white adult residents in six Boston neighborhoods and one Boston suburb. The neighborhoods were chosen to represent a variety of community cir-

Table 1.1   *A Brief Chronology of the Boston School Desegregation Controversy*

8/65 The Massachusetts Legislature enacts the Racial Imbalance Act (RIA) with the most stringent school integration requirements of any major city in the nation. School boards must take affirmative action against racial imbalance by redistricting, pupil reassignment, strategic placement of new schools and busing. Strong enforcement sanctions.

3/72 The local chapter of the NAACP sues in Judge Arthur Garrity's Federal Court before alleging government discrimination in creating and maintaining a segregated public school system.

6/73 Massachusetts State Board of Education recommends enforcing the RIA in Boston by busing 19,000 students (of 83,000 total) to reduce the number of racially imbalanced schools to 42 (from 61).

10/73 WAVE 1 INTERVIEWS COMPLETED FOR THE BOSTON STUDY

4/74 Massachusetts State Supreme Court calls for implementation of the plan proposed by the State Board of Education (6/73) in Autumn, 1974.

4/74 WAVE 2 INTERVIEWS COMPLETED FOR THE BOSTON STUDY

5/74 School assignments for the State Board plan are made public.

6/74 Judge Garrity decision (3/72) calls for implementation of the plan proposed by the State Board (Phase I) in Autumn, 1974 and calls for a plan for full desegregation for Autumn, 1975 (Phase II).

7/74 WAVE 3 INTERVIEWS COMPLETED FOR THE BOSTON STUDY

9/74 School opens. During the first few months there is an estimated 12 percent drop in enrollment and episodic violence.

10/74 State Governor assigns State police to patrol Boston schools.

11/74 WAVE 4 INTERVIEWS COMPLETED FOR THE BOSTON SCHOOL STUDY

12/74 Boston school board votes not to file a Phase II plan (6/74).

12/74 Judge Garrity threatens Boston school board with receivership.

2/75 Judge Garrity announces court-appointed panel to design Phase II.

5/75 Judge Garrity announces Phase II plan. Public school attendance dropped an estimated 27 percent during the 1974/75 school year.

7/75 WAVE 5 INTERVIEWS COMPLETED FOR THE BOSTON STUDY

cumstances, while controlling for factors that might make the analysis of reaction to court-implemented desegregation contingent on the analysis of other aspects of the urban process, such as fears about immanent racial change in the community. Each neighborhood met the following criteria:

1. Neighborhoods are racially stable. All sampling points are in census tracts that are at least 98 percent white and not adjacent to predominantly black tracts.
2. Ethnic enclaves—i.e., census tracts with more than 50 percent foreign stock—are excluded from the sample.
3. Tracts are included only if they contain a mix of public and parochial school attendance. Tracts with less than half or more than three fourths of children attending public schools are excluded.
4. Neighborhoods are residentially stable and of median social status. Sampling points are in tracts where most have lived in the same housing unit for at least five years and are near the median in education and family income.

In addition to the six neighborhoods chosen for analysis, comparable interview data were collected in one Boston suburb to act as a "control group"—residents of a comparable urban landscape who were not directly affected by Judge Garrity's order. The findings in this book do not depend on control comparisons, so the survey analysis is restricted to questionnaire data from the six neighborhoods.[1]

Within each neighborhood a stratified sampling procedure was used to obtain proportionally representative samples of parents with children in the public schools, parents with children in private or parochial schools, and married adults between 23 and 50 years of age with no children between 3 and 16 years of age. The intended sample size for each neighborhood varied between about 70 and 100 cases. Response rates fluctuated by wave and by neighborhood. The lowest response rate for any wave, however, was a respectable 79 percent. The lowest average response rate for any neighborhood, across waves, was 77 percent.

The neighborhoods in this study vary somewhat on socio-

---

1. The neighborhoods are Jamaica Plain, Roslindale, South Dorchester, Hyde Park, West Roxbury, and East Boston.

economic characteristics, on some measures of orientation to Judge Garrity's order, and on certain measures of racial tolerance. However, for the questions addressed in this book—the dynamics of public reaction, the causes of willingness to contribute to antibusing actions—neighborhood variations, at least for the sample of neighborhoods considered here, are not a significant explanatory factor. Therefore, the tabulations in this book combine results for the different neighborhoods. The language of the analysis makes clear, however, that the results only describe the dynamics in these particular neighborhoods. No claim is made that the data are a self-weighting sample of adult white residents in Boston.

The five-wave survey of Boston neighborhood residents is one of the most extensive empirical bases ever collected for analyzing the dynamics of individual participation in a community conflict. Nevertheless, there are limitations to the data. Because of concerns about the patience of respondents, and limitations of funding, it is not possible to ask all questions that might be of interest in a survey wave, nor is it possible to repeat all questions of interest in each wave of the survey. In addition, issues evolve during a community crisis: topics and issues become salient during the later stages of a conflict that could not have been anticipated during earlier times or during the initial design phases of the study. As a result, not all tables presented here show results for all waves of the panel survey. In every table the survey wave can be found by noting at the foot of the table the number for the question analyzed and then turning to the Appendix where exact wordings and waves are shown. In addition, for any table where data for more than one wave are used, the waves are specifically noted in the table as well as in the Appendix.

Additional Narrative Material

Each chapter makes use of additional narrative material concerning the history and events surrounding Judge Garrity's order. This information comes primarily from my studies of newspapers, television news reports, and other observations and interviews made during and after the Boston school desegregation conflict. Other histories of this conflict have been published (Richard, Knox, and Oliphant 1975; Dentler and Scott 1981; Hillson 1977; Hannon 1980; U.S. Commission on Civil Rights 1975). Crain et al. (1968) discuss the history of school desegregation in Boston, using the pseudonym

"Bay City." Some of the historical information analyzed here is also presented in a more extensive time line published by Stinchcombe and Taylor (1980).

In some chapters the nonsurvey information—the historical, observational, and narrative material—provide critical evidence supporting the interpretations drawn from the survey data. In fact, part of my reason for writing this book is to show how to expand the scope of information that survey analysts can use to make a social science argument. Some social scientists believe that the only kinds of conclusions that can be drawn in studies that use a lot of survey data are statistically precise repetitions of table findings. I do not agree. I believe there is a responsibility to integrate the results from multiple sources of information to place the results from any single source in context.

For instance, Chapter 5 presents data (table 5.5) showing that those who respect Boston's Cardinal Medeiros are more likely to agree with his position on desegregation. Of course, looking at the table alone, one cannot tell whether (a) respect for a leader causes agreement with his or her mandates, (b) the causality flows in the opposite direction, or (c) whether respect and agreement are simply attitudes that occur together because of life experiences. The observation that data alone cannot provide evidence of causal direction is one of the first rules of research taught in any quality methods course.

How does one make causal inferences, then? Some argue that causal inferences are never justified. According to this view, a researcher may only adopt a scientific-sounding language of "correlation and covariation" and leave to the reader, the policymaker, or someone else the responsibility for drawing a causal conclusion. In my opinion this passes the buck. The researcher is almost always in a better position than the reader to consider the full range of theory and evidence available and to guide the reader over the leap from the data and the rules of statistical inference to the goal of theoretical understanding and substantive knowledge.

In the case at hand, historical and observational evidence show that the cardinal intended to influence the public. In addition, the survey data show public perception of the cardinal's attempt to influence the public. Finally, the theory of political entrepreneurship is an independent, analytic framework describing how influence attempts by public leaders are likely to be effective. When there is corroborative evidence about the intent to cause a reaction, when there is public perception of steps taken to bring the reaction about, and when there is an independent theoretical base for postulating the effect of an action, then the burden of proof is met for moving beyond a discussion of covariation in the data and drawing, instead, conclusions of likely causal impact.

Statistical Analysis

The statistical results in this book are presented so as to make the argument accessible to any reader, regardless of the level of methodological training. All of the principal results are illustrated with percentage tables and procedures for causal analysis based on percentage difference statistics. The tables are organized so that by noting the original sample sizes and the distributions on key variables, such as attitude toward busing and religion, it is possible to construct the sample size and cell frequencies for each table.

The Boston sample for each wave of the survey analyzed here (approximately 550 respondents) is somewhat smaller than the number of cases normally used in today's studies of social phenomena. Given the sampling errors for most of the percentages, and formulas that assume no sources of error other than those arising from simple random sampling, a difference of about 7 or 8 percent is required before individual percentage differences calculated from the tables in this book can be said to be statistically significant.

Although all of the tables present simple percentage calculations, most of the findings reported in this book were originally derived from more elaborate statistical models. For instance, the conclusion in Chapter 4 about the importance of perceived injustice as a cause of antibusing protest is based on four LISREL-style multiple-indicator models. Model I, also used in Chapter 3, analyzes protest as a function of racism and has 9 equations. Model II, showing that the effect of racism continues even after controlling for strength of antibusing opinion, has 11 equations, 9 of which are similar in form but not exactly the same as Model I. Model III, showing that the effect of racism is greatly lessened after controlling for perceived injustice (and maintaining the control for strength of antibusing opinion), has 21 equations. Model IV, showing that the results are not significantly affected when religion (the topic of analysis in Chapter 5) is controlled, has 22 equations, 21 of which are similar

to but not exactly the same as Model III. This gives 63 equations
that were analyzed in connection with Chapter 4. Other chapters are
based on analyses of similar magnitude.

A complete discussion of the technical details, at a level of
documentation acceptable to the technically minded reader, would
more than double the length of the manuscript. It would also make
the book much more exclusively an advanced technical and statistical treatise. The importance of, and contribution of, the nonsurvey sources of information would be overlooked or diminished.
Furthermore, I am not even persuaded that the multiple-equation
models provide significant amounts of additional evidence beyond
what can be shown with a careful consideration of the materials that
are presented here. The footnotes in each chapter explain the kinds
of issues addressed by the more elaborate statistical models and how
the findings from these models support the analyses presented in this
book. For further pursuit on these issues, interested readers are in-
vited to consult other publications based on these data (Taylor and
Stinchcombe 1977; Stinchcombe and Taylor 1980) or to communi-
cate with the author directly.

Some of the tables report results using parallel measures that
would be considered multiple indicators of a single latent variable.
For instance, table 5.7 shows religious differences on seven different
measures of perceived public opposition to busing and the court
order. Four percentage differences are individually significant using
the 7–8 percent criterion (7%, 9%, 10%, and 18%), one comparison is a difference of means which is more than twice its standard error (and therefore individually significant), but two percentage differences are not individually significant even though they are
in the hypothesized direction (5%, 6%). What is the appropriate decision rule for determining the significance of the overall pattern
in the table, given that some of the individual results conflict? In
the multiple indicator model (which adjusts for unreliabilities) the
result is highly significant, yielding no difficulty for interpretation.
There is no simple formula, however, for reworking the results in a
complex percentage table to determine what the significance levels
would be in a multiple indicator framework. To deal with this problem, I would suggest the following rule for inferring overall significance levels from complex tables when the simple 7–8 percent rule
yields conflicting results: when most of the comparisons in a table

are significant, then it is accurate to describe the overall pattern of results as significant as long as almost all of the remaining comparisons are in the right direction. Fortunately, there are very few instances when it is necessary to even address this issue. In almost every table the interpretation of results is unambiguously the same under any of the usual procedures for determining significance.

One
Desegregation Beliefs and Protest

We don't have to appeal to fanatics. They're on our side anyway.

Robert Patterson, Executive Secretary
Citizens Councils of Alabama

2 | American Racial Ideology and the Boston Conflict

Historical Perspective on American Race Doctrine

Since the time of the Emancipation Proclamation, the conflict over school desegregation and the legal status of black Americans has been embroiled in doctrinal disputes central to the hearts and minds of the American public. The first dispute involves a distinction between legally defined "civil rights" and what I will refer to as the "doctrine of social inequality."

Civil rights are rights to life, liberty, and the pursuit of happiness specifically guaranteed under the Constitution. Demands for civil rights, as those rights are defined at any historical moment, are viewed by Americans as legitimate. The objection most often made to any extension of black rights or any increased use of the police power of the state to protect black rights is that such changes are not required to protect blacks' civil rights but are actually attempts to effect social equality. The demand for social equality is not accepted as legitimate. It requires whites to ignore differences in ability or attainment between themselves and blacks. Legal changes that force mixing between blacks and whites in what at the historical moment are considered to be "social" settings are particularly suspect. Blacks are not, in general, believed to have the social preparation for those interactions, nor have they earned the right for such encounters through their own efforts at economic, social, and educational advancement. The doctrine of social inequality is the keystone of white supremacist thought.

Sensitivity to this doctrine was once extremely strong in American society, even among those who were otherwise strong advocates of black civil rights. For instance, Abraham Lincoln in a public speech in 1858 spoke in favor of ending slavery and extending certain civil rights to blacks, but he carefully drew a line between civil rights and social equality:

> I will say then that I am not, nor ever have been in favor of bringing about in any way the social and political equality of white and black races [applause]—that I am not nor ever have been in favor of making voters or jurors of Negroes, nor of qualifying them to hold public office, nor to intermarry with white people, and I will say in addition to this that there is a physical difference between the black and white races which I believe will for ever forbid the two races living together on terms of social and political equality. And inasmuch as they cannot so live, while they do remain together there must be the position of superior and inferior, and I as much as any other man am in favor of having the superior position assigned to the white race. (See Sandburg 1926, chap. 112 ff.)

For all but the most recent decades in the life of the American republic, attending desegregated public schools has not been demanded by law or supported by public opinion as a civil right. Rather, schools were considered to be within the realm protected by the doctrine of social inequality.

The second great dispute in school desegregation and civil rights law is whether the behavioral changes required of whites to safeguard black civil rights shall be voluntary or mandatory. This issue in its early historical manifestations was closely tied to the first. That is, one of the arguments against governmental procedures for mandatory compliance was that the rights in question were not actually civil rights but, rather, disguised attempts to force social equality. In the recent American past, however, from approximately the time of the Truman era, the issue of mandatory versus voluntary compliance has taken a life separate from the issue of civil rights versus the doctrine of social inequality. Beginning around the time of the Truman administration, most Americans began to abandon white supremacist ideals and accept a definition of blacks' civil rights that, by historical comparisons, was expansive. But at the same time most Americans, most political leaders, and even a great many lawmakers and judges persisted in the conviction that enforcement of these rights should not be mandatory. This belief will be referred to as the doctrine of voluntary compliance.

The next several paragraphs examine the process by which black attendance in desegregated public schools came to be defined as a civil right rather than an illegitimate attack on the doctrine of social inequality. Following this, the doctrinal debate over mandatory versus voluntary compliance is then explained in more detail.

School Desegregation and the Doctrine of Social Inequality

The Civil Rights Act of 1875, the last plank of Reconstruction passed under the enforcement provision of the Fourteenth Amendment, expanded the definition of "civil rights" to include equal access to public accommodations, public transportation, public entertainment and jury participation. This list went well beyond what would have been considered appropriate even a generation earlier— at, for instance, the time of the speech by Abraham Lincoln cited earlier. Desegregated schools, however, were not recognized as a civil right in this act. During this period of American history the Constitution had been amended three times and dozens of supporting bills had been passed by Congress to guarantee black freedom, equality, and the vote. But supporters of black rights did not add desegregated education to the list of protected civil rights. Why not?

Richard Kluger, in his remarkable history of desegregation law, argues that, because of the rudimentary nature of the public school system during the time, desegregation did not seem a critical issue (Kluger 1975, p. 50). The reason for the omission of desegregated education from the list of guaranteed civil rights goes deeper than this, however. The reason is that desegregated education crossed the consensually defined boundary between civil rights and social equality at that time.

The progressive philosophy of race during the time of Reconstruction might be described as compassionate paternalism. Blacks were generally regarded as inferior, but many who held this view did not necessarily agree that inferiors ought to be ostracized or publicly humiliated (Woodward 1974, p. 48). During this time white allies supported justice for blacks, provided the proposed remedy stopped short of any intermingling, actual or potential, of the two races—this being the commonly understood boundary for social equality at the time (Ashmore 1982, p. 69).

During Reconstruction, the first high-water mark for the legal status of blacks in America, there was not enough support to widen the definition of civil rights to include desegregated schooling. After the Compromise of 1876—when Southerners supported presidential candidate Rutherford B. Hayes in the electoral college in exchange for Republican promises to support economic development and end Reconstruction (Franklin 1961)—the distinction between civil rights and social equality was the entering wedge for a retrenchment and repeal of most black rights achieved in the earlier era. The Supreme Court's famous 1896 opinion allowing segregated public transportation in the case of *Plessy v. Ferguson* began by invoking the old distinction between civil rights and social equality:

> The [Fourteenth] amendment . . . could not have been intended to abolish distinctions based upon color, or to enforce social, as distinguished from political equality, or a commingling of the two races upon terms unsatisfactory to either. . . . [Therefore] laws permitting, or even requiring [racial] separation in places where [the races] are liable to be brought into contact do not necessarily imply the inferiority of either race to the other.

The court argued that laws recognizing social inequality are legal and that Americans have a constitutional right to codify social distance and social inequality into law. The doctrine of social inequality became the law of the land.

The court then specifically referred to segregated schooling as an appropriate, legal codification of social inequality that provided a historical precedent for determining when and how "civil rights" could be limited in other areas as well:

> The most common instance of this is connected with the establishment of separate schools for white and colored children, which has been held to be a valid exercise of the legislative power even by the courts of states where the political rights of the colored have been longest and most earnestly enforced.

Schools were ineluctably in the realm of the private, even though schooling may be paid for by public moneys and provided as a matter of public law. The doctrine of social inequality, as applied to schools, was so widely accepted that black access to desegregated schools simply was not a justiciable issue for another half century. Supreme Court Justice Felix Frankfurter noted, during the discussion of the *Brown v. Board of Education* case in 1954,

> To outlaw segregation would demolish the long-standing prerogatives of 21 state legislatures. . . . In all likelihood the framers of the [Fourteenth] Amendment had not intended to outlaw segregation [in the public schools.] . . . Neither contemporary nor subsequent courts nor state legislatures had interpreted the amendment as proscribing the practice.

A related application of the doctrine of social inequality was the legal support for racially segregated neighborhoods. After 1910 "enmeshing ghetto laws" were enacted in Northern cities to designate separate blocks for blacks and for whites. In 1917 the Supreme Court ruled in *Buchanan v. Worley* that, under the Fourteenth Amendment, city governments could not enforce such laws. However, in 1926 the Supreme Court unanimously ruled in favor of restrictive mortgage covenants limiting access of blacks as well as other unpopular minorities such as Asians, Turks, Jews, Catholics and non-Caucasians to "white" neighborhoods by stipulating that a homeowner could not re-sell his or her property to a member of one or more of these groups (Vose 1959). The Supreme Court's opinion in *Corrigan v. Buckley* held that nothing in the Constitution prevents parties "from entering into contracts respecting the control and disposition of their own property."

The belief in the value of codifying social inequality was so complete that, following the *Corrigan v. Buckley* decision, federal, state, and local governments accepted segregated housing as a socially stabilizing policy. The Federal Housing Administration for two generations insisted on this arrangement as a condition for granting mortgage insurance (Abrams 1955). This is one reason why the often-made distinction between de jure school segregation (that required by state law or school board procedures) and one type of de facto school segregation (that arising because of neighborhood segregation) tends to break down when a broader, historical view is taken of the full range of relevant issues.

Segregated cities and segregated schools were established as a matter of social policy in America. The policy was meant to reflect the just codification of social inequality. Blacks' civil rights, as defined at any historical moment, were still subject to protection by government. However, when demands for justice touched on areas protected by the doctrine of social inequality—i.e., areas involving interracial social contact—the legal issues are appropriately summarized in an 1877 editorial in the *Springfield Republican:* "No remedy whatever exists against moral intimidation and race prejudice."

The Second Reconstruction and Black Civil Rights

The repressive consensus regarding black Americans' rights did not hold. From the 1940s to the late 1960s, a period dubbed the "Second Reconstruction" by C. Vann Woodward, the definition of blacks' civil rights again widened, at the expense of realms of experience once protected under the doctrine of social inequality.

The Second Reconstruction took place because of demographic, economic, and political changes that altered the balance of power between blacks and whites in American society. Some of the changes since the First Reconstruction that made the American political structure more vulnerable to black demands and increased the resources available to blacks for challenging the status quo are:

1. the decline of cotton farming, the plantation system of agriculture and consequently, of social control of blacks in the South (Baron 1971; Cash 1941; Ashmore 1982);
2. the massive redistribution of the nation's black population toward Northern cities (Fligstein 1981; Henri 1975);
3. the strengthening of the black organizational and economic base in Northern cities (Drake and Clayton 1963);
4. increased black voting strength in Northern cities as well as in other electorally "key" areas in the South (Berman 1970; Moon 1948; Key 1949; Bartley and Graham 1975; Daniel 1969; Abney 1974; Bullock 1975; Preston, Henderson, and Puryear 1982; Lawson 1976; Piven and Cloward 1979);
5. the expansion of black employment opportunities and increased political sophistication among blacks during World War I and World War II (Ashmore 1982);
6. international political tensions that drew attention to America's conflict between democratic values and segregationist practice, particularly the specter of large numbers of black soldiers fighting to end fascism in Europe only to return to

Jim Crow practices at home (Berman 1970; Kluger 1975); and,
7. strengthening of black churches, black colleges, and chapters of the NAACP in the urban South (McAdam 1982).

After the black civil rights movement achieved some visible signs of success in the early 1960s it gained further strength from financial contributions and leadership support from whites (McAdam 1982, p. 148). After initial movement successes, white public opinion in almost every part of the country changed toward a greater tolerance of, receptivity to, and even demand for black civil rights (Taylor, Sheatsley, and Greeley 1978).

During the Second Reconstruction two great ideas took hold that altered the legal basis for blacks' civil rights. First, American law directly challenged white supremacist thought and the doctrine of social inequality. The Supreme Court experimented with the theory that this doctrine amounted to little else than a justification for trapping blacks in a hierarchy of caste that produced outcomes aberrant to democratic values. Second, after undermining the doctrine of social inequality, the Supreme Court asserted a number of years later that not only must whites give up their rights to segregation but that in certain realms previously considered protected from race mixing, compliance was mandatory, not voluntary. The principal decisions in the evolution of the law are summarized in later parts of this chapter.

The keystone of the Second Reconstruction was the Supreme Court's reversal of the doctrine of social inequality in its famous 1954 decision in *Brown v. Board of Education*. The NAACP strategy for attacking the doctrine of social inequality in this case produced a new role for professional social scientists. Expert witnesses testified on the nature of caste systems, the cumulative effects of discrimination and poverty, and the web of institutional discrimination creating housing segregation, barriers to social advancement, and ghettoization of neighborhoods and schools.[1] This strategy re-

1. On behalf of the NAACP, Kenneth Clark, Isidor Chein, and Stuart Cook prepared a 4,000-word summation of the state of social-scientific knowledge of segregation and its effects at the time of the trial of *Brown v. Board of Education*. This statement is available in published form (Clark 1953). The statement was signed by 35 prominent social scientists, including Jerome Bruner, David Krech,

vived the "Brandeis brief"—a blend of law and applied social research named after Louis Brandeis who, in 1908, defended the 10-hour working day (against demands for more) on the grounds of health and public welfare in the case of *Muller v. Oregon.*

The goal of the NAACP strategy was to discredit the view that segregation is justified because of the doctrine of social inequality and that there should be no remedy against moral intimidation and prejudice in the field of public education. The NAACP argued that acts of segregation acquire a new significance when they are endowed with the compulsory conformity and the majesty of the law. Victims of such laws suffer special harms as they attempt to become educated and enter society. Therefore, separate educational facilities can never be equal.

The Supreme Court had given its opinion once before on this specific argument in the 1896 case of *Plessy v. Ferguson:*

> We consider the underlying fallacy of the plaintiff's argument to consist in the assumption that the enforced separation of the two races stamps the colored race with a badge of inferiority. If this be so, it is not by reason of anything found in the act, but solely because the colored race chooses to put that construction upon it.

The negative effects of legally sanctioned discrimination, if any, are, according to Supreme Court opinion in *Plessy v. Ferguson,* exclusively in the mind of the victim and under his or her control.

The 1896 precedent supporting the doctrine of social inequality was the basis for school board responses to the NAACP's Brandeis brief in the case of *Brown v. Board of Education.* John W. Davis, solicitor general under Woodrow Wilson, United States Representative, Democratic party candidate for president of the United States in 1924, and the attorney representing South Carolina at the *Brown v. Board of Education* trial, argued:

Robert Redfield, Otto Klineberg, M. Brewster Smith, Alfred McLung Lee, Floyd Allport, Daniel Katz, Theodore Newcomb, Robin Williams, Gordon Allport, Samuel Stouffer, Robert Merton, R. N. MacIver, Paul Lazarsfeld, Hadley Cantril, Arnold Rose, and Allison Davis.

Working on a more recent case, Karl Taeuber and Gary Orfield prepared an updated discussion of social scientific knowledge on discrimination and its effects, particularly addressing issues of housing discrimination and school segregation (Taeuber et al. 1980).

I think I have never read a drearier lot of testimony than that furnished by the so-called educational and psychological experts. . . . [That testimony] deals entirely with legislative policy and does not tread on constitutional right. . . . That evidence in and of itself is of slight weight and in conflict with the opinion of other and better informed sources.

In 1954, however, the Supreme Court did not agree. Its opinion in *Brown v. Board of Education* declared:

Segregation of white and colored children in public schools has a detrimental effect upon the colored children. The impact is greater when it has the sanction of the law; for the policy of separating the races is usually interpreted as denoting the inferiority of the Negro group. A sense of inferiority affects the motivation of a child to learn. Segregation with the sanction of the law, therefore, has a tendency to retard the educational and mental development of Negro children and to deprive them of some of the benefits they would receive in a racially integrated school system.

This opinion overturned all legal requirements for segregated public schooling, and did so in a way that eliminated the constitutional basis for the doctrine of social inequality in all realms, thus breaking the back of the Jim Crow system and hastening the decline of white supremacist thought in America (Woodward 1974; Rist 1980).

At the time the decision was announced, some viewed it negatively because of its attack on the doctrine of social inequality. Immediately after the decision, James Reston wrote:

Relying more on the social scientists than on legal precedents . . . the Court insisted on equality of the mind and heart rather than on equal school facilities.

On March 12, 1956, more than 100 congressmen from 11 states of the old Confederacy signed a statement called the Southern Manifesto that stated:

The Court's unwarranted decision is a clear abuse of judicial power which substitutes the Justices' personal political and social ideas for the established law of the land. . . . [We pledge] to use all lawful means to bring about a reversal of this decision which is contrary to the Constitution.

Many of the signers of the Southern Manifesto believed the Supreme Court was misled by Communist writers into making a decision based on sociology and contrary to law. Judge Armistead Dobie, of the Fourth Federal Circuit Court of Appeals (South Carolina) warned the nation specifically about Gunnar Myrdal whom the judge declared to be a "foreign Communistic anthropologist."

The argument in favor of the doctrine of social inequality and against the court's "social scientific" opinion is still occasionally heard in American politics. George Wallace presented himself as the self-proclaimed spokesman for the "little people" against the "theorists." Richard Nixon, in a message to Congress in 1972, described busing as a "symbol of social engineering on the basis of abstractions."

But the evidence shows that, by the time of the *Brown v. Board of Education* decision, the American public was ready to give up the doctrine of social inequality and legally mandated segregation. Within 10 years after the decision, American public opinion showed a widespread acceptance of the Supreme Court's position in favor of black access to a number of situations previously protected by the doctrine, including the right to attend desegregated public schools (Taylor, Sheatsley, and Greeley 1978). In the words of Martin Luther King:

> For the vast majority of white Americans, the decade 1955 to 1965 has been a struggle to treat the Negro with a degree of decency. . . . White America was ready to demand that the Negro should be spared the lash of brutality and coarse degradation. (King 1967, p. 3)

Within a few years after the *Brown v. Board of Education* decision, the struggle over school desegregation implementation stopped being a debate over whether the policy is legal and began to be a debate over whether compliance with the policy is mandatory. The doctrine of social inequality is now all but dead in America. The doctrine of voluntary compliance lives on. It is the basis for public debates, legislative attacks on desegregation policy, and even a great many judicial opinions from the time of the *Brown v. Board of Education* decision to the present.

Origins of the Doctrine of Voluntary Compliance

The doctrine of voluntary compliance was part of American politics well before the Supreme Court's decision in *Brown v. Board of Education*. The first articulation of this doctrine as national policy occurred in response to the Fair Employment Practices Commission (FEPC) during the waning moments of the Truman administration (Kesselman 1947; Ruchames 1953). The Supreme Court's decision in *Brown v. Board of Education* occurred at a time when political coalitions and a national consensus favoring voluntary compliance with the FEPC had already been built. The conflict over implementation of *Brown* expanded the debate to include not just job discrimination but also school and neighborhood integration.

The demographic, economic and political changes that would alter the balance of power between blacks and whites in America were well in evidence by the time of the Truman administration. Shifts in black voting patterns in the 1936 and 1940 presidential elections had established them as part of the Democratic coalition. President Roosevelt rarely supported or endorsed civil rights legislation but did respond to black political pressure by authorizing a civil rights section in the Department of Justice in 1939 and creating the Fair Employment Practices Commission by executive order in 1941 (Kirby 1980). After that, demographic and economic realities conspired to increase black political strength. Between 1941 and 1946 one million blacks migrated to Northern cities, diluting the strength of previous voting blocs and providing a potential margin of victory for the Democratic party in close national elections (see references cited earlier).

The black vote became central to Democratic party strategy. The early predictions for the 1948 election were that Truman would lose by a landslide (Mosteller et al. 1949). Truman's hope during the 1948 presidential campaign was to hold together the Roosevelt coalition by appealing to labor and urban minorities (Ross 1968). As part of this strategy, the 1948 Democratic party convention adopted a strong civil rights plank written by Hubert Humphrey. This was done with the support of city bosses who feared that unless explicit provisions were made to hold the black vote they would not only lose the national election but state and local Democratic candidates would also go down in the landslide (Berman 1970, p. 112).

The Democratic party's 1948 civil rights plank, accepted by a margin of 651.5 to 582.5, read:

> We call upon the Congress to support our President in guaranteeing these basic and fundamental principles: The right of full and equal political participation, the right to equal opportunity of employment, the right to security of persons, and the right of equal treatment in the service and defense of our Nation.

This is the paragraph that caused half the Alabama delegation and all of the Mississippi delegation to walk out of the convention. The Southern delegates who remained did so in spite of the platform. They supported Georgia Senator Richard Russell over Truman for the presidential nomination by a margin of 263 to 13. After the convention Truman called Congress into a special session to enact laws supporting mandatory enforcement of the rights listed in the platform.

There is some question as to whether Truman actually expected laws requiring mandatory enforcement of civil rights to ever be passed or whether this was a symbolic gesture to appeal to black voters (Berman 1970; Ashmore 1982, p. 121). In his political career, however, Truman repeatedly called for mandatory enforcement. In a radio-broadcast speech to an NAACP rally at the Lincoln Memorial in June 1947, he declared:

> The extension of civil rights today means, not protection of the people against the government, but protection of the people by government. . . . We cannot, any longer, await the growth of a will to action in the slowest state or the most backward community. Our national government must show the way. . . . Our case for democracy [in the cold war] should be as strong as we can make it. It should rest on practical evidence that we have been able to put our own house in order.

The argument linking civil rights and anticommunism was once a well-traveled road. In December 1952 the United States attorney general submitted a brief supporting the NAACP position in *Brown v. Board of Education* that argued:

Racial discrimination furnishes grist for the Communist propaganda mills and it raises doubts even among friendly nations as to the intensity of our devotion to the democratic faith. . . . [It] remains a source of constant embarrassment to this government in the day-to-day conduct of its foreign relations; and it jeopardizes the effective maintenance of our moral leadership of the free and democratic nations of the world.

A decade later the attorney general Robert Kennedy applauded the enrollment of Hamilton Holmes and Charlayne Hunter Gault, the first black students admitted to the University of Georgia, because it would "without question aid and assist the fight against communist political infiltration and guerilla warfare." Even Richard Nixon explored the strength of cold war fear as an antidote to racial prejudice. In defending his party's 1960 civil rights platform he argued that providing justice for minorities would take away from "the Communist leaders any arguments against America and what she stands for."

Some of Truman's actions were more than symbolic. During the special congressional session called during the summer of 1948, he issued his executive order desegregating the armed services and another executive order strengthening FEPC actions by creating the Fair Employment Board of the Civil Services Commission.

These events—Truman's support for mandatory enforcement of civil rights legislation, the 1948 Democratic party platform on civil rights, and Truman's executive orders on civil rights—stimulated a reaction. Those who stood to lose the most set about the task of building a national coalition and a national consensus favoring the doctrine of voluntary compliance.

In July 1948, after the walkout at the Democratic party convention, the States' Rights Jeffersonian Democratic party (Dixiecrats) held its founding convention in Birmingham, Alabama. They nominated South Carolina Governor Strom Thurmond for president and Mississippi Governor Fielding Wright for vice-president. This party's platform made clear where it stood on the question of mandatory enforcement of civil rights:

[We oppose] meddling outsiders dedicated to the destruction of states' rights, the regulation of business, and ultimately to the Communist ideal of total regimentation of people of all races and creeds.

The Dixiecrat party lost the election, receiving about 2.5 percent of the popular vote and 39 (of 531) electoral votes in the 1948 election.

The real Dixiecrat victory came a year later. Truman's proposals for mandatory enforcement of civil rights did not become law. In fact, the bulk of Truman's civil rights program failed in Congress when a coalition of conservative Southern Democrats and conservative Republicans from all areas of the country changed Senate procedures governing filibuster and cloture.

In exchange for support on the filibuster, Southerners agreed to support conservative Republicans and vote against repeal of the Taft-Hartley Act. This exchange is a modern instance of the tendency in Southern politics, persuasively analyzed by W. C. Cash, to sublimate class conflict to the race issue. Cash argues that the plantation system degraded the economic position and the capacity for organization of white laborers. But white labor accepted this because of their favored position in the moral order of white supremacy.

> [The plantation system] elevated this common white to a position comparable to that of, say, the Doric knight of ancient Sparta. Not only was he not exploited directly, he himself was made by extension a member of the dominant class—was lodged solidly on a tremendous superiority, which, however much the blacks in the "big house" might sneer at him, and however much their masters might privately agree with them, he would never publicly lose. Come what might, he would always be a white man. And before that vast and capacious distinction, all others were foreshortened, dwarfed, and all but obliterated. (Cash 1941, p. 40)

The outcome was, in Cash's words, "the almost complete disappearance of economic and social focus on the part of the masses" (p. 40). The link between prosperity and security, independence, or social esteem was not as great as in the North. The drive to confront the owners of capital because of a desire for economic advancement, as opposed to advancement in the cause of white supremacy, was not as intense.

The national consensus favoring the doctrine of voluntary compliance with civil rights legislation was established by the time of the 1952 presidential election. By this time a coalition of Southerners and Republicans already constituted a conservative majority against mandatory compliance. The leadership of the Southern movement to prevent Truman's nomination in 1952 now included such powerful and important figures as Senator Harry Byrd of Virginia and Governor James F. Byrnes of South Carolina. In 1951 South Dakota Republican Senator Karl Mundt proposed a third party uniting Republicans and Southern Democrats to nominate, it was rumored, a Taft-Byrd or an Eisenhower-Russell ticket. Senator Mundt thought this coalition was essential "not only for the Republican party and our two party system but also for the most effective fight possible against communism in America." Mundt's vision was not realized, although prominent Southern Democrats such as South Carolina Governor James F. Byrnes and Louisiana Governor Robert F. Kennon supported the Republican candidate for president.

In 1952 both the Democratic and the Republican candidates for president opposed mandatory enforcement of the FEPC. Thus, the doctrine of voluntary compliance became the national consensus, not to be challenged in major political debate. The 1952 Democratic party platform favored steps "effectively to secure civil rights," but presidential candidate Adlai Stevenson spoke otherwise. At a press conference in August 1952 the Illinois governor made it clear that he did not favor "compulsory" FEPC legislation. Nor did he support the platform proposal to reinstate majority cloture—a step that would end the hold of the Southern/Republican bloc over civil rights legislation. He said it was his impression that "it would be a very dangerous thing indeed to limit debate in a parliamentary body in a democracy."

The 1952 Republican Party civil rights plank appealed to state's rights advocates, reminded them that discrimination was illegal, but suggested that mandatory enforcement would make government more bureaucratic, creating more harm than good:

> It is the primary responsibility of each state to order and control its own domestic institutions. . . . However, we believe that the Federal government should take supplemental action within its Constitutional jurisdiction to oppose discrimination against race, religion or national origin. We will prove our good faith by . . . enacting federal legislation to further just and equitable treatment in the area of discriminatory employment practices. Federal action should not duplicate state efforts to end such practices; should not set up another huge bureaucracy.

In a press conference in June 1952, Republican presidential candidate Eisenhower made clear the difference between declaring discrimination to be illegal and the "radical" policy of mandatory integration:

> I do not believe that we can cure all of the evils in men's hearts by law and when you get to compulsory action of certain specific phases of this thing I really believe we can do more than make it a Federally compulsory thing.

The Texas war hero later suggested what more could be done: he would favor passage of FEPC laws in each of the 48 states (an unlikely event).

School Desegregation and the Doctrine of Voluntary Compliance

The Supreme Court was faced, in 1954, with the need to fashion a procedure for implementing the civil rights it had recognized in *Brown v. Board of Education*. The policy for implementing *Brown* had to take into account the public unpopularity of mandatory desegregation, the political coalition that had already been built against mandatory implementation, and the national political consensus already achieved on this issue by major parties not to support it. For several years the Supreme Court, and many others who were, otherwise, strong advocates of black civil rights, resolved this problem by accepting the doctrine of voluntary compliance as if it were a principle of law.

The Court ordered a separate hearing on implementation, referred to as *Brown v. Board of Education II*. A study was conducted for this hearing by Kenneth Clark to determine the feasibility of mandatory desegregation in the face of public opposition. This report, introduced as evidence and published as a special edition of the *Journal of Social Issues* (Clark 1953) argued that changes of action, heart, and mind are most likely to occur when people believe there is no effective alternative. The court was not convinced that this condition could be met. Therefore, the Supreme Court's opinion in *Brown v. Board of Education II* did not call for immediate, mandatory implementation of school desegregation:

To effectuate [this decision] may call for elimination of a variety of obstacles. . . . Once . . . a start has been made, [lower] courts may find that additional time is necessary to carry out the ruling in an effective manner. . . . To that end, the courts may consider problems related to administration, arising from the physical condition of the school plant, the school transportation system, personnel, revision of school districts and attendance areas into compact units to achieve a system of determining admission to the public schools on a nonracial basis, and revision of local laws and regulations which may be necessary in solving the foregoing problems.

The tactical decision by the court in *Brown II* did not explicitly say that compliance with desegregation was voluntary. It left open, however, the question of when mandatory compliance was to occur. This loophole was not lost on Georgia Lieutenant Governor Ernest Vandiver who declared: "A reasonable time can be construed as one year or two hundred. . . . Thank God we've got good Federal judges."

Within two or three years after the *Brown* decision, American law more or less reflected the consensus in American opinion that segregation is illegal but that desegregation is voluntary. The legal basis for the doctrine of voluntary compliance was Federal Judge John Parker's 1955 ruling that the *Brown* decision does not require integration, it merely forbids discrimination. Parker's ruling declared that so-called freedom-of-choice plans are acceptable ways to implement the *Brown* decision in South Carolina:

If the schools . . . are open to children of all races, no violation of the Constitution is involved even though children of different races voluntarily attend different schools, as they attend different churches. . . . The Constitution, in other words, does not require integration. It merely forbids discrimination. It does not forbid such discrimination as occurs as the result of voluntary action. It merely forbids the use of governmental power to enforce segregation (quoted in Kluger 1975, pp. 751–752).

Freedom of choice plans, which purportedly made the school system "color blind," in fact produced very little desegregation in public schools. For 15 years after the *Brown v. Board of Education* decision there were no signs of significant change in most states of the Deep South and only limited signs of change in the border states.[2] For this reason Martin Luther King, writing in 1967, observed that "the Supreme Court decisions on school desegregation, which we described at the time as historic, have not made history."

The Attack on Voluntary Compliance

If Lyndon Johnson had not won a landslide in the election in 1964, and if he had not carried with him 38 new Democratic seats in the House and enjoyed a more than two to one Senate majority, American school desegregation policy would never have advanced much beyond the doctrine of voluntary compliance (Sundquist 1968). During the first few years of the Johnson administration crucial actions by Congress and the Executive (and not, let it be emphasized, by the Judiciary) caused a wholesale change in the level of desegregated schooling. Under the Civil Rights Act of 1964, certification of desegregation by the Office of Education of the U.S. Department of Health, Education and Welfare was required before federal moneys were available for a school district. Under aggressive HEW leadership, the act was also interpreted as a basis for threatening a cutoff of funds in order to promote desegregation. In 1968, HEW initiated 28 community reviews—including one in Boston—to see if school desegregation guidelines were being met. The act also authorized the U.S. attorney general to initiate lawsuits on behalf of black children for the desegregation of school districts.

Although the act did not specifically require busing, it was often the case that the only way a school district could escape HEW sanctions was to implement some type of transportation plan (Rodgers and Bullock 1976; Cataldo et al. 1978). As noted in Chapter 3, the apparent contradiction between the intent and the implementation of the 1964 Civil Rights Act is sometimes produced as evidence for the argument that mandatory school desegregation is not a legal policy.

The passage of the 1964 Civil Rights Act and the implementation of its provisions by HEW and the Department of Justice challenged the doctrine of voluntary compliance, as it had been im-

---

2. A list of significant studies of desegregation implementation would include: Bartley 1969; Crain et al. 1968; Muse 1961; Orfield 1969; Peltason 1961; Sarratt 1966; Wakefield 1960; Weinberg 1977.

plemented by school boards across the nation. The willingness of government to pursue desegregation as a national policy, the continued pressure from civil rights groups, and the specter of ghetto disturbances after the middle 1960s created an environment where the Supreme Court was willing to take a more aggressive position against the doctrine of voluntary compliance than it had in the years immediately following *Brown v. Board of Education.*

The doctrine of social inequality was killed when the Supreme Court declared separate facilities to be inherently unequal. The effects of the doctrine of voluntary compliance cannot be rooted out by such a simple mechanism. The only way to disabuse people of the notion that they do not have to attend desegregated schools is to (1) tell them they must, and then (2) measure the amount of desegregation actually present and employ sanctions to require compliance when behavior falls below expectations.

The Supreme Court's 1968 decision in *Green v. County School Board of New Kent County, Virginia* began the attack on the doctrine of voluntary compliance by specifically eliminating South Carolina Federal Circuit Judge Parker's theory of freedom of choice as an acceptable principle guiding school desegregation implementation. The court ruled that school systems have "an affirmative duty to take whatever steps might be necessary to convert to a [racially] unitary system in which racial discrimination would be eliminated root and branch." Plans were now required by law that gerrymandered school zones, closed some majority black schools, paired and clustered majority black with majority white schools, and/or built new schools in a pattern that would increase integration.

As cases came to trial from different locations, it became clear that the steps mentioned in the previous paragraph would not always be enough to produce significant changes in the level of public school segregation. The problem was the pattern of residential segregation in American cities. Governmental action had inordinately contributed to this pattern with policies promoting racially restrictive mortgage covenants and racial isolation as a means for neighborhood stabilization. As the Court had once supported the doctrine of social inequality in its *Plessy v. Ferguson* decision, it had once endorsed these policies as well in its 1926 decision in *Corrigan v. Buckley.* Pupil transportation was the only foreseeable remedy for this pattern of discrimination.

In 1971 the Supreme Court ruled in *Swann v. Charlotte-*

Mecklenburg Board of Education that, all things being equal, it was desirable to assign pupils to schools nearest their homes, but "all things are not equal in a system that has been deliberately constructed to maintain and enforce segregation." It was not enough now for such a community to come forward with a "racially neutral" assignment plan based on existing residential patterns that in themselves had developed around segregated schools in the past, because "such plans may fail to counteract the continuing effects of past school segregation." The court began to take notice of the interaction between segregative school board practices and other governmental actions segregating housing (as well as other aspects of community life) as a cause of segregation in the schools. The supposed difference between de jure and de facto segregation became less distinct: segregation was segregation, whether caused by state law, school board actions, or federally mandated policies of restrictive neighborhood zoning. The court, in this case, also ruled that busing might be necessary to meet legal requirements for desegregation.

After the *Swann* decision, school desegregation in the South proceeded at a hasty rather than a deliberate speed. The combination of aggressive enforcement by HEW and the Department of Justice and a Supreme Court decision affirming the use of busing was highly effective. Black concentration in predominantly minority schools in the South dropped from 81 percent in 1968 to 55 percent in 1972 (Orfield 1983, pp. 53–58).

Without federal coercion, segregation would not have been reduced (Wirt 1970, p. 290; Rodgers and Bullock 1976, p. 45). The results seem to support those agreeing with Roscoe Pound's dictum: "Law makes habits, it does not wait for them to grow."

Political Strategy during the Second Reconstruction

American public opinion has never given up the doctrine of voluntary compliance. During the years following the Truman administration the coalition that formed to block mandatory enforcement of fair employment practices legislation became the servant of this point of view in national politics.

The coalition was in temporary disarray during the Johnson presidency. It was not able to block the significant changes in civil rights law between 1964 and 1968 that constitute the high-water mark of the Second Reconstruction (Sundquist 1968; Woodward 1974; Orfield 1978). But the coalition was never weak. It had changed Senate rules to permit filibuster blockages of civil rights legislation since the 1940s. It temporarily gained control of the national Republican party when Ronald Reagan successfully nominated Barry Goldwater to be the party's presidential candidate in 1964. Goldwater received 39 percent of the popular vote and 52 of 538 electoral votes—all from Southern states. Even though Goldwater lost in 1964, two years later the Democrats lost 47 seats in the House of Representatives, the largest Democratic House loss since the repudiation of Woodrow Wilson's policies in 1920.

The nomination of Goldwater in 1964 and the results of the House races in 1966 were interpreted as evidence of widespread opinion change—"backlash"—among whites (Brink and Harris 1967; Killian 1975; Lubell 1964). But most studies of American public opinion that use carefully constructed trend data lead to a different conclusion (Taylor, Sheatsley, and Greeley 1978; Taylor 1979; Greeley 1980). There is little evidence of prosegregation opinion change during this time.

A more accurate interpretation of the Goldwater phenomenon, the 1966 House elections, and political changes since that time is that the majority of American public opinion was, and is, opposed to discrimination but also opposes mandatory desegregation. The public will favors the doctrine of voluntary compliance. The coalition against mandatory enforcement of fair employment practices legislation, begun in the 1940s and always a significant political factor since then, seeks ways to embody the national expression of that will. When the issue of mandatory enforcement is salient, and when the political choices are clear-cut, then the ordinary processes of national electoral competition will favor those who support the doctrine of voluntary compliance over those who do not. The Goldwater phenomenon and the House races of 1966 represent attempts to redefine and reposition political strategy to make the choices more clear-cut so that the coalition opposed to mandatory desegregation can reap the benefits of national majority support.

In the 1968 presidential election, Richard Nixon won with 43 percent of the national vote. George Wallace received 14 percent support and 46 of 538 electoral votes. After this election, Nixon took bold steps to clear the field—i.e., to make the Republican party unambiguously the heir of the anti-FEPC coalition and the legitimate spokesman for the majority will on the doctrine of voluntary compliance. He began by attacking HEW and Justice Department policies that had successfully forced desegregation in a number of school districts in the South and border states. After a few years of the Nixon administration, it was no longer a sure thing that threatened federal aid cutoffs and Justice Department prosecutions would actually occur (Panetta and Gall 1971; Orfield 1978).

When the Supreme Court attacked freedom of choice plans and the doctrine of voluntary compliance in the *Green* decision, Nixon declared his support for the principle of "an open society which does not have to be homogeneous or even fully integrated and where it is natural and right that we have Italian or Irish or Negro or Norwegian neighborhoods." He then requested the Justice Department to draft a constitutional amendment that would nullify the Court's decision. The proposed amendment was written by Assistant Attorney General William Rehnquist. As a clerk to Supreme Court Justice Robert Jackson in the early 1950s, Rehnquist had defended the exclusion of blacks from Democratic party political clubs in Texas (thus denying the right to participate effectively in elections) in a memo, arguing:

> The Constitution does not prevent the majority from banding together, nor does it attaint success in this effort. It is about time the Court faced the fact that the white people in the South don't like the colored people; the Constitution restrains them from effecting this dislike through state action, but it most assuredly did not appoint the Court as a sociological watchdog to rear up every time private discrimination rears up its admittedly ugly head. To the extent that this decision advances the frontier of state action and 'social gain,' it pushes back the frontier of freedom of association and majority rule.

Years later, speaking against a 1967 ordinance desegregating the Phoenix, Arizona, public schools, Rehnquist argued in favor of the doctrine of voluntary compliance: "We are no more dedicated to an integrated society than we are to a segregated society." By the time of the Boston school conflict Nixon had successfully nominated Rehnquist to the Supreme Court.

Table 2.1   *Percent Black Students in Predominantly Minority Schools: 1968–1980*

	1968	1972	1976	1980
South	81	55	55	57
Northeast	67	70	73	80
Rest of United States	74	70	66	65

Note: Based on figures reported by Orfield 1983, pp. 53–58.

Northern School Desegregation

Since 1971 public schools in the South have been more integrated than public schools in the North. Table 2.1 shows the percent of black students in predominantly minority schools in the South and in other regions of the country in 1968, 1972, 1976, and 1980.

Between 1968 and 1972 black enrollment in predominantly minority schools declined from 81 percent to 55 percent in the South. The change was nowhere near as great outside the South. In fact, in the Northeast the trend was in the opposite direction: toward greater segregation. In Boston, for instance, black enrollment in predominantly minority schools was 77 percent in 1968 and 82 percent in 1972, making it more segregated than any major city south of Washington D.C.

In 1973, a year before Judge Garrity's decision, the Court ruled for the first time that the *Brown* ruling applied to Northern cities as well. In *Keyes v. Denver, Colorado School District No. 1*, the Court found:

1. The Denver school board had taken intentionally segregative actions in a meaningful portion of a school system, creating a presumption that all segregated schooling within the system was not adventitious; and therefore,
2. As with *Swann*, past segregative practices obliged the school district to go well beyond racially "neutral" plans in the future—i.e., busing, if necessary to achieve desegregation, must be used.

The Boston Court Order

The lawsuit resulting in Judge Garrity's decree was filed in March 1972, after the *Swann* decision approving the use of busing, if necessary, but before the *Keyes* decision extending desegregation northward. I have never learned whether there was a conscious NAACP strategy to make Boston one of the early Northern cases. The Massachusetts State law mandating public school desegregation, the Racial Imbalance Act (RIA), was the most stringent law of its kind in the nation. Moreover, the judiciary in Boston and in Massachusetts may have indicated its interest in enforcing the RIA. These factors may have made Massachusetts a likely site for early NAACP action.

A second reason for early NAACP action in Boston may have been the extreme resistance to school desegregation by Boston neighborhood residents and community leaders. The expanded powers of HEW under the 1964 Civil Rights Act were felt almost immediately in Boston. Almost every year from 1966 on state or federal assistance was withheld from the Boston school system because of the Boston school board's policy prohibiting busing as a means for achieving integration (thereby making compliance with the RIA impossible). But, because of the political skills of the Boston school board and, eventually, because of the weakening of HEW enforcement after the 1968 election, threats to withhold assistance did not have much effect. Each year the Boston school board responded to the withholding of funds with counterlitigation that often resulted in compromise and delay in implementation of the RIA.

Federal Circuit Judge Arthur Garrity's order to desegregate the Boston public schools in *Morgan v. Hennigan* was announced in June 1974. Careful analyses of the legal issues and findings of fact in the Boston case have been published by Abrams (1975) and Dentler and Scott (1981). Table 1.1, presented in Chapter 1 to show the timing of the panel waves for the Boston neighborhood survey also shows a brief chronology of events surrounding the court order.

Judge Garrity ordered that citywide desegregation proceed in two stages. During the first year, referred to as Phase I, the Boston school board was ordered to implement a plan designed a year earlier during legal proceedings in a different, state-level court of justice. In terms of the percentage of students mandatorily reassigned, this was one of the more extensive plans ever implemented in an

American city. At the time of Judge Garrity's order the Phase I plan had already been delayed once because the state-level proceedings, based on enforcement of the RIA, were under appeal.

The Boston public schools opened under Judge Garrity's Phase I order in September 1974. The city had not trained school employees or prepared school facilities adequately for desegregation. Phase I implementation was accompanied by extensive boycotts, a high level of community violence directed against the court order, and a high level of noncooperation by the school board. Judge Garrity's enforcement strategy included an escalation of the court's authority into areas where community organizations and community leaders would normally be expected to shape a positive public reaction. The court created community organizations for overseeing desegregation implementation and created expert panels with community representation for designing the Phase II implementation plan and other changes. Phase II was the most extensive two-way busing plan ever implemented in an American city. Threats of receivership did little to stimulate a positive response by the Boston school board. Finally there was a court takeover of the operation of the schools during the period of Phase II implementation. By a combination of legal and persuasive techniques, the court stimulated the mayor to order more comprehensive city planning for Phase II implementation than had been done for Phase I.

The remaining chapters in Part I of this book explore the doctrine of social inequality and the doctrine of voluntary compliance as the "moral valuations" (Myrdal 1944) guiding public reactions to the court order in Boston and in other American cities. Part II of this book explores the particular features of the political process that contribute to antibusing mobilization, given the prevailing moral valuations in the constituency.

3 | Racism and Protest

The Current Status of White Supremacist Opinion

Most of the people living in Boston in the early 1970s grew up when white supremacy was a nearly universal racial view in this country. White supremacy was, for instance, accepted as scientific fact in the 1910 edition of the *Encyclopedia Britannica:* " . . . the negro would appear to stand on a lower evolutionary plane than the white man, and to be more closely related to the highest anthropoids."

The *Brown v. Board of Education* lawsuits reached the Supreme Court because lower courts had recognized white supremacy as the rule in American law and public opinion. In 1951 a Federal Circuit Court of Appeals refused to desegregate the public schools in Charleston, South Carolina, saying:

> It is a late day to say that such segregation is violative of fundamental constitutional rights. . . . If conditions have changed so that segregation is no longer wise, this is a matter for the legislatures and not the courts. The members of the judiciary have no more right to read their ideas of sociology into the Constitution than their ideas of economics.

In the early years after *Brown,* separation of the races was still defended at high levels on the grounds of white supremacy. Federal Circuit Court Judge T. Whitfield Davidson refused to desegregate the Dallas, Texas, schools in 1959 because:

> As long as [the Negro] begins imitating his white brother he is not at his best. . . . The white man has a right to maintain his racial integ-

44

rity. . . . Integrated schools . . . would lead . . . to an amalgamation of the races. . . . In no clime and in no nation have the races ever amalgamated that it has not been to the disadvantage of both. . . . We will [therefore] not name any date or issue any order. . . . The School Board should further study this question and perhaps take further action, maybe an election.

Most of the people living in Boston in the early 1970s grew up when white supremacy and separation of the races were justified by fears of miscegenation and violence. The New Orleans school board's brief against desegregation after *Brown II* declared:

Integration . . . would endanger the health and morals of white children. . . . A large segment of our Negro population has little or no sense of morality . . . to intermingle them with the white children in our public schools could well corrupt the minds and hearts of the white children to their lifelong and perhaps eternal injury.

Cole Blease, governor of South Carolina, long ago defended the practice of lynching by arguing: "Whenever the Constitution comes between me and the virtue of the white women of the South, I say to hell with the Constitution." Lynching was not a federal crime, and therefore not the subject of vigorous prosecution until Truman's presidency (Raper 1969; Berman 1970).

It is remarkable, in light of this history, that Boston neighborhood residents almost unanimously reject the idea that separation of the races is legal—that whites have a right to segregated neighborhoods and/or that small amounts of school desegregation are unacceptable. The survey data suggest, in fact, that the rejection of the doctrine of social inequality is more complete in Boston than in other comparable American cities. The data are tabulated in table 3.1, which shows public opinion in Boston neighborhoods on a number of questions normally used by survey rearchers to measure racism, prejudice and intolerance of integration.[1]

1. Few researchers would argue that all of these items are unidimensional measures of support for white supremacy. I agree that some of the items involve extra care in interpretation, as the subsequent analysis in this chapter shows. Since these items are frequently used in national studies of racial attitudes, I present them all here for comparative purposes.

Table 3.1   *Racial Attitudes in Boston Neighborhoods and in Comparable American Cities*

	Boston Neighborhoods	New England/ Snowbelt Cities
Percent agreeing whites have a right to segregated neighborhoods	12	43
Percent objecting if a family member brings black friend to dinner	19	20
Percent agreeing blacks should not push where not wanted	45	63
Percent objecting to school integration:		
object 10%	12	7
object 0%–50%	48	30
Percent favoring integration separation or something between:		
Integration:		
Wave 1	11	
Wave 5	8	
In between:		
Wave 1	46	
Wave 5	52	
Percent opposed to two-way busing for desegregation:		
Wave 1	86	
Wave 2	90	
Wave 3	89	80
Wave 4	87	
Wave 5	91	

Note: Question wordings: see Appendix 1 for Boston survey, nos. 1–5; see Davis and Smith (1983) for General Social Survey.

Boston data are combined from samples of white residents of six Boston neighborhoods. New England and Snowbelt city data are for white respondents in General Social Surveys conducted between 1973 and 1977.

Table 3.1 also shows parallel results for white central city residents in Standard Metropolitan Statistical Areas (SMSAs) in the Northeast and the Midwest.[2] The parallel results are calculated from the General Social Survey (GSS), a national study of American public opinion conducted nearly every year since 1972 (Davis and Smith 1983). The national data combine results for surveys conducted between 1973 and 1977, roughly corresponding to the period just before, during, and after data collection in Boston.[3] The GSS questions are nearly identical in wording to those asked in the Boston survey. One question in the Boston survey about preference for integration, separation, or "something in between" is not asked in the GSS, so parallel data are not available.

The first row of figures shows the percent who agree with the statement that "white people have the right to keep blacks out of their neighborhood and blacks should respect that right." Only 12 percent in the Boston sample agree. In the parallel national sample 43 percent agree.[4] The second row shows the percent who would object "if a member of [the] family wanted to bring a black friend home to dinner." About 20 percent in the Boston sample and the GSS sample say they would object. The third row shows the percent who agree with the statement that "blacks should not push themselves where they are not wanted." In the Boston neighborhood sample 45 percent agree with this statement, while in the parallel sample of white neighborhood residents 63 percent agree. The fourth row shows that 12 percent in Boston and 7 percent in comparable American cities would object to sending their children to an integrated school that was up to 10 percent black.

The findings so far suggest that the average Boston resident (and the average American by the early 1970s) did not believe that a barrier should be constructed separating the races, to be kept unbroken

2. U.S. Bureau of the Census definitions of central city, SMSA, and region are used.

3. As noted in Chapter 1, the sample design makes the Boston neighborhood survey not strictly comparable with results from other national, regional, or city surveys. Therefore, this chapter primarily discusses the Boston results, with only impressionistic comparisons to the national data.

4. There are approximately 1,000 respondents in the GSS sample and 500 in the Boston neighborhood survey. If it is assumed there is no bias from differences in sampling procedures and no further correction factors are used, differences greater than about 5 percent are statistically significant at the .05 level.

by even token or symbolic acts of desegregation. This may not seem like a tremendously hospitable statement. We should remember, however, that in almost every school district desegregated by court order during the 1950s and the early 1960s, holding the line of apartheid was one of the critical issues motivating protest (Orfield 1969; Rodgers and Bullock 1972, p. 14). As recently as 10 years before the time the data shown in table 3.1 were collected, white endorsement of apartheid and preference for segregation on each of the questions so far examined was much greater (Taylor, Sheatsley, and Greeley 1978; Taylor 1979; Schuman, Steeh, and Bobo 1983). Sometime during the Second Reconstruction, as the data in table 3.1 illustrate, stringent insistence on white supremacy and separation of the races became the minority opinion in America. More- over, for at least some of the measures considered here, Boston neighborhood residents are distinctly more receptive to the idea of racial integration than the parallel sample of neighborhood residents from comparable American cities.

The question arises, at this point, of whether we can have confi- dence in what the survey data tell us about the racial attitudes of the American public, and Boston neighborhood residents in particular. Some may ask, "Aren't answers to these kinds of survey questions really reflections of the politeness of survey respondents who do not want to appear racist in an interview situation?" What evidence is there that these survey questions measure anything significant?

When I began studying American racial attitudes, I felt some of these concerns about the meaningfulness of the survey measures. My observations while traveling to a large number of urban and rural areas, visiting Northern and Southern parts of the country, and hearing Americans of all age groups discuss their views about race, however, have given me much more faith that the patterns revealed by the survey data are meaningful and interpretable as they stand. The differences that one observes today in racial attitudes by age, by education, by region, and by size of place are also shown in the sur- vey data. (All patterns appear in the expected direction in the GSS data; the Boston differences by age and education are the same as the GSS findings.) It is not possible to perform a similar experiment with time—i.e., we cannot roll back the clock and measure our im- pressions of the past against the present. Survey data from the past, however, tell us that there has been a change. The difference in racial attitudes between now and 10–15 years ago is of a similar magnitude to the difference between the North and the South or between the young and the old today. Therefore, the time trends, as measured in the survey data, seem plausible to me as well.

Why is the North, and especially Boston, less in favor of the doctrine of social inequality? And why is this increasingly the case in the last few decades?

The etiquette of race relations in the North was never as firmly rooted in white supremacy and the doctrine of social inequality as in the South (Doyle 1937). The position of the Northern laborer was never that of the "Doric knight" (Cash 1941, p. 40). The social system in the North did not provide the same support for sublimating economic interests so completely to the race issue. Politics in Northern states never focused as singularly on the race issue, allowing "all other considerations to be dissipated by the racist appeal of white supremacy floating out of the past on a cloud of inherited fears and misconceptions" (Ashmore 1982, p. 22; see also Key 1949).

The massive internal migration northward and the economic, political, and social advancement of the black population before and during the time of the Second Reconstruction created circumstances that made white supremacy an untenable and outmoded racial philosophy. Black enclaves in Northern cities produced a new generation of black leaders willing to directly challenge the system of white supremacy. The success of some of these challenges and the willingness of the government to hear demands for more during the Truman administration undermined the political consensus supporting the doctrine of social inequality. During the life span of most Boston residents affected by Judge Garrity's order, the legal supports for white supremacy and the doctrine of social inequality were removed. Discrimination in access to voting, public accommodations, housing, employment, and education was declared illegal. Enforcement of these rights was stringent enough that by the time of Judge Garrity's order most Boston residents lived in a world that was, in terms of racial domination, drastically different from the one they grew up in (Newman et al. 1978; Higginbotham 1978). Accordingly, strict apartheid was relaxed, making it easier to desegregate. Small amounts of desegregation in schools and in other realms were no longer endowed with the emotion and symbolism of miscegenation, foreign influence, and the end to a cherished way of life.

Some say that all that happened during the Second Reconstruction is that white supremacy lost "respectability" or that whites simply became "permissive" of interracial contact. It is clear that white supremacist thought has not perished. Many accounts of the Boston school desegregation controversy describe the threats, violence, and white supremacist sloganeering directed against blacks during this time (Hillson 1977; U.S. Commission on Civil Rights 1975; Richard, Knox, and Oliphant 1975; Hannon 1980). There still are segregationists who, in the words of Martin Luther King, desire "the total reversal of all reforms, with re-establishment of naked oppression and if need be a native form of fascism" (King 1967, p. 11).

But those who minimize the changes during the Second Reconstruction understate what has occurred. White supremacists, although still present, are now vastly outnumbered. They no longer represent the dominant position in American opinion, law, and governmental policy.

What needs to be explained is why public resistance to mandatory desegregation is so strong when public support for the doctrine of social inequality is so weak. Even though whites' attitudes on race have changed a great deal, there is still a long way to go. To understand why, the remainder of this chapter analyzes the racial fears that have survived the decline of white supremacy. The next chapter explores the doctrine of voluntary compliance and the concerns for justice and safety that justify antibusing actions among those who, otherwise, do not support the doctrine of social inequality.

Racial Fears during the Second Reconstruction

Fear of Racial Concentration

The second set of figures in row 4 of table 3.1 shows the percent who would object to sending their children to a school that was up to 50 percent black. As is apparent from these figures, the level of objection to desegregation is related to the level of black enrollment in the school. Thirty percent in the national sample say they would object to sending their children to a school where up to 50 percent of the children are black. In Boston the level of objection is even higher. In the Boston neighborhoods 48 percent say they would object to such an arrangement.[5]

White support for integration but uneasiness with high levels of black concentration is reflected in the next question as well. The fifth set of figures in table 3.1 shows responses to the question, "Speaking in general terms do you favor racial integration, separation of the races, or something in between?" This question is asked in wave 1 and wave 5 of the Boston survey. In each wave about 10 percent say they favor separation and about 50 percent say they favor something "in between." This question is not asked in the GSS survey, so parallel data are not shown. However, Schuman, Steeh, and Bobo (1983) study national trends for this question, and the results for Boston neighborhood residents in table 3.1 are close to what they report to be the national percentages during the middle 1970s.

The findings in table 3.1 are consistent with other analyses showing a positive statistical relationship between high black concentration in the local population and unwillingness of public authorities to implement desegregation (Dye 1968; Matthews and Prothro 1964; Stephen 1955; Pettigrew and Cramer 1959; Vanfossen 1968; Blalock 1957). Mumford reports that declines in white student enrollment in desegregated school districts increase with the level of black concentration (Mumford 1973). Clotfelter's aggregate analysis finds that white flight is more sensitive to changes in minority concentration than it is to desegregation per se (Clotfelter 1979). A study of school desegregation in 31 Georgia school districts concludes that "the single most important factor in predicting the level of federal coercion [necessary to eliminate dual schools] is the percentage of blacks in the community" (Rodgers and Bullock 1976, p. 65). Table 3.1 shows that fear of minority concentration is high in

---

5. The validity of the comparison between the two surveys on this question is threatened by differences in wording. In the Boston survey, respondents are asked if they would object to sending their children to a school that was 10 percent black, then 25 percent black, then 50 percent black. The GSS asks whether respondents would object to sending their children to a school with "a few" blacks and then 50 percent black. The "25 percent black" category, present in the Boston question but not in the GSS question, may partly explain why responses seem more opposed to integration in the Boston survey. Further experimental work along the lines reported by Schuman and Presser (1981) and Schuman, Steeh, and Bobo (1983) ought to be conducted on this matter.

Boston, in fact, it is higher in Boston than in similar American cities that are not faced with mandatory desegregation.

Is There a Specific Tipping Point?

Some authors have asked whether fear of racial concentration in the schools is a tipping-point phenomenon (e.g., Stinchcombe, McDill, and Walker 1969). Is there a particular percentage of black students below which white fears are not aroused but above which whites become greatly concerned about their children's schooling?

Studies arguing for a tipping point say it is in the 30 to 35 percent range.[6] Other studies, however, do not agree that there is a precisely defined tipping point. The importance of the 30 to 35 percent range is not so much that this is the threshold beyond which most whites cannot abide integration. Rather, this appears to be the range where whites expect their interests in quality education will not continue to be served and that the future of the school will only be one of deterioration and neglect.[7]

6. A study of enrollment stability in 100 desegregated Southern school systems found that over a two-year period districts with less than 35 percent black enrollments on average experienced no declines in white student enrollment. By contrast, districts above 35 percent black experienced losses, and their size increased with the percent black enrollment (Giles 1977). A survey of seven metropolitan school districts in Florida finds that whites are more likely to oppose local desegregation policy when their children are assigned to 30 percent or higher minority schools:

> When the assigned school was less than 30 percent black, the presence or absence of busing did not influence white opinions [for or against local desegregation policy]. However, when the assigned school was more than 30 percent black, whites whose children were bused were more likely to disapprove of the handling of desegregation than those not bused. Apparently, then, busing is a source of white parental disapproval not so much for its own sake but because it tends to place the white child in a more heavily black school. (Cataldo et al. 1978, p. 79)

7. The importance of the 30 to 35 percent range may indicate a racial encoding of expectations rather than a pure measure of tolerance for integration. Cataldo et al., for instance, support this interpretation when they find that the racial composition of a school before integration has a stronger impact on parental perceptions of educational quality than does the racial composition of the school after integration (1978, p. 60). Stinchcombe et al. (1969) suggest that racial encoding of expectations is the reason for the "tipping range" found in their study. My own

It is, in other words, unlikely that there is a tipping point, according to the usual definition of the term. There is not a specific percent beyond which whites will not tolerate integration. There is, rather, a widely held belief that schools beyond 30 to 35 percent black are going to be allowed to deteriorate physically and educationally and eventually become all black. Desegregation policies that specifically address fears about deterioration, lack of safety, and black domination will find concerns for a specific racial concentration in the 30 to 35 percent range to be less important.

My research on neighborhood change reveals a similar pattern. Comparative studies show that neighborhood tipping does not occur when a neighborhood passes a specific percent black. Rather, tipping occurs when whites believe that other whites will no longer seek housing in the area. Interestingly, this perception is nearly independent of one's level of racial prejudice and support for white supremacy (Taylor 1984c).

Racial Attitudes and Support for Alternatives to Judge Garrity's Plan

Judge Garrity's full plan (Phase I and Phase II) requires busing of both white and black students to achieve integration at all grade levels. The sixth set of figures in table 3.1 shows that the Boston neighborhood residents fluctuate between 86 and 91 percent opposition to this type of plan depending on the wave of the survey.[8] Another question in the survey that does not mention two-way busing but asks specifically about Judge Garrity's order finds about 85 percent opposition.

During the period of public reaction to the court order, a number of other proposals that would weaken various aspects of the Phase I and Phase II plans were put forward by community leaders. A number of these proposals are described, and the percent in favor of each proposal among those opposed to two-way busing is shown

---

analyses show that this is pointedly the case when neighborhood change and tipping processes occur in local housing markets (Taylor 1984a).

8. We should remind ourselves that it is busing for the purpose of school desegregation that is objected to, and not busing per se. Judge Garrity found that prior to his court order at least 30,000 pupils were transported daily for purposes of maintaining school segregation (Abrams 1975, p. 15).

Table 3.2   *Support for Alternatives to Judge Garrity's Plan*

	Percent in Favor among Opponents of Two-Way Busing
Open enrollment	Wave 1—82
Open magnet schools in black neighborhoods	Wave 3—58
Change school attendance boundaries, minimize busing	Wave 1—52 Wave 3—55 Wave 4—66
Bus older children only to balance high schools in the city	Wave 1—30
Busing black children to every white school in the city	Wave 1—26 Wave 4—25

Note: Question wordings: see Appendix 1, nos. 7–13.
   Data are combined from samples of white residents of six Boston neighborhoods.
   Data show responses among those personally opposed to busing at the time of the interview.

in table 3.2. The percentages are shown for those opposed to busing, because a number of those favoring two-way busing disapprove of plans requiring only a token amount of integration or a token amount of remedial state action as they do not think these proposals go far enough. Their responses to some of these questions are, therefore, ambiguous in meaning.

The responses in table 3.2 highlight tensions in public opinion that have plagued desegregation implementation all during the Second Reconstruction. The top row of table 3.2 shows that there is a high level of support for desegregation when the plan is completely voluntary. The "open enrollment" plan achieves 82 percent support among those who are opposed to the Phase I and Phase II plans implemented by Judge Garrity. As long as the remedy is phrased in terms of voluntary compliance, a high percent are willing to say it "ought to be done" to overcome the past harms of segregation.

The 18 percent of those opposed to two-way busing who also do not support voluntary compliance—i.e., do not support the open enrollment plan—may be the best estimate we have of the hard-core bedrock who support the doctrine of social inequality. They oppose any type of remedial action and may, in fact, believe that segregation is legal.

As table 3.2 shows, the rest of the community shows more or less support for a desegregation plan depending on the degree of minority concentration that is implied for their children, the extent to which the plan disrupts existing patterns of school attendance and zoning, and the extent to which participation in a desegregated setting is unavoidable and/or mandatory. The proposal for "magnet schools in black neighborhoods" receives 58 percent support among those opposed to two-way busing, a proposal to "change school boundaries and minimize busing" receives between half and two-thirds support depending on the survey wave, a proposal to "bus high school children only" receives 30 percent support, and a proposal to "bus black children to every white school in the city" receives about 25 percent support.

Racism and Opposition to Busing

The level of antibusing opinion is quite high in Boston and in every American community that has been surveyed (Useem 1980; Sears et al. 1979; Rubin 1972; McConahay 1982; Raffel 1977; Cataldo et al. 1978; Stinchcombe and Taylor 1980). As with the measures of fear of racial concentration, table 3.2 shows that the percent opposed to busing is higher in Boston than in other, comparable American cities. The national data show 80 percent opposition to busing in parallel neighborhoods.[9]

Table 3.3 shows the percent of Boston neighborhood residents who say they are opposed to two-way busing, classified by their opinions on each of the questions in table 3.1. Table 3.3 also shows a similar analysis of antibusing opinion and racial attitudes for white residents of central city neighborhoods in the Northeast and Midwest calculated from the GSS sample.[10]

The data in table 3.3 show that those who are more prejudiced

9. Further analysis, described in Chapter 5, shows that this difference is explained by the fact that Catholics in Boston are more opposed to busing and school integration than are Catholics in the GSS sample (see also Stinchcombe and Taylor 1980).

10. As before, the results from the two surveys are not strictly comparable because of differences in the definition of the sampling universe. The question about general preferences for integration, separation, or something in between was not asked in the GSS, so the parallel results are incomplete for this variable.

Table 3.3   *Racism, Fear of Minority Concentration, and Opposition to Busing*

	Boston Neighborhoods	New England/ Snowbelt Cities
	Percent Opposed to Two-Way Busing	
Whites have a right to segregated neighborhoods:		
Agree	98	85
Disagree	90	72
Object if black comes home to dinner:		
Object	99	84
Not object	89	77
Blacks should not push:		
Agree	97	86
Disagree	85	69
Object to school integration:		
10% black	100	89
10%–50% black	91	93
No objection	79	77
General preference:		
Wave 1:		
Separation	95	
In between	93	
Integration	75	
Wave 5:		
Separation	97	
In between	99	
Integration	79	

Note: Question wordings: see Appendix 1 for Boston survey, nos. 1–5; see Davis and Smith (1983) for GSS.

Boston data are combined from samples of white residents of six Boston neighborhoods. New England and Snowbelt city data are for white respondents in General Social Surveys conducted between 1973 and 1977.

and/or more fearful of minority concentration are more likely than those who are not to say they oppose two-way busing.[11] The relationship between prejudice and antibusing opinion is quite nearly the same in the Boston neighborhood sample as in the national sample. The principal difference between the two surveys is that the percent opposed to two-way busing is higher in Boston for those who are prejudiced (according to the survey measures) as well as for those who are not.

The data show a relationship between prejudice and antibusing attitudes. However, the data also show an extremely high level of opposition to busing even among those who are not prejudiced or racially intolerant. This group, in fact, is the key to understanding how a city reacts to a desegregation order. For Boston neighborhood residents who respond in the least prejudiced categories, the level of opposition to busing is always 75 percent or above. What does this mean for the size of the group who oppose the doctrine of social inequality but also oppose busing? The exact percentages fluctuate depending on which particular item is used; however, for most measures multiplying the approximately 80 percent who do not favor segregation by the 75 percent chance they will oppose busing gives about a 60 percent majority in Boston (and in the comparison cities) who oppose segregation but who also oppose busing.

These results are consistent with other research on this question. Using national data and a variety of survey measures, Kelley argues for a weak relationship between racism and antibusing attitudes and a high percent opposed to busing among those who are racially tolerant on other measures (Kelley 1974). A reanalysis of Kelley's data, with adjustment for "ceiling" effects caused by the high level of opposition to busing among all categories of respondents, finds the effect of prejudice to be consistently significant and supports the rest of the analysis (Erbe 1977).

There is a lengthy research tradition indicating a relationship between antiblack behavior and racial prejudice (Blalock 1957; Dye 1968; Harris 1968; Pettigrew and Cramer 1959; Vanfossen 1968). Cataldo, Giles, and Gatlin, in their survey study of Florida parents in school districts undergoing desegregation, support this conclusion:

11. Using simple random sampling formulas, the threshold for a statistically significant difference for the Boston neighborhood sample in table 3.3 is about 7 percent.

A little over 30 percent of [those who transferred their child to private school] also protested against school desegregation by signing petitions, attending meetings, writing to the school board, or engaging in demonstrations. . . . About 20 percent of [parents who did not transfer] engaged in similar behavior. An examination of these protesting parents shows them to be more racially prejudiced . . . and

Table 3.4   *Racism, Fear of Minority Concentration and School Desegregation Protest*

	Percent Willing to:		
	Defy Court Order (Wave 1) (1)	Boycott Public Schools (Wave 1) (2)	Boycott Public Schools (Wave 5) (3)
Whites have a right to segregated neighborhoods:			
Agree			58
Disagree			39
Object if black comes home to dinner:			
Object			59
Not object			37
Blacks should not push:			
Agree			51
Disagree			32
Object to school integration:			
10% black	67	62	
10%–50% black	55	42	
No objection	46	33	
General preference:			
Separation	64	63	55
In between	61	47	50
Integration	38	26	25

Note: Question wordings: see Appendix 1, nos. 1–4, 14–16.
  Data are combined from samples of white residents of six Boston neighborhoods.

more opposed to the principle of desegregation than nonprotesters. (1978, p. 50)

Table 3.4 shows the relationship between racism and/or fear of racial concentration and willingness to protest desegregation in Boston. Column 1 shows the percent in the wave 1 survey who support defiance of the court order. Column 2 shows the percent in the wave 1 survey who support the boycott of the public schools. The third column shows the percent in the wave 5 survey who support the boycott. (The wording for this question differs from the wording of the wave 1 question, making trend comparisons inadvisable.) Percentages are shown for instances where the measure of racism and/or fear of minority concentration and the measure of willingness to engage in antibusing actions are asked in the same survey wave.[12]

Table 3.4 shows that, for any of the measures considered, those who are racist and/or fearful of racial concentration are much more likely than those who are not to favor taking action against desegregation. The zero-order relationships shown in table 3.4 are all substantively large and statistically significant by any commonly accepted criterion. In this table, similar to the previous one, we also note the high willingness to protest busing among those who are opposed to segregation on the racism/prejudice measures.

Summary: Racism and Desegregation Protest

White resistance to desegregation was once predicated on defending apartheid, securing white womanhood, avoiding any appearance of social equality with blacks, and attacking "creeping communism." But the evidence shows that whites have, for the most part, aban-

---

12. Despite the change in some question wordings and the fact that not all questions are asked on all waves of the survey, it is possible to perform limited panel analyses to see if the patterns in the data are consistent with simple alternative hypotheses about the causal order between racism and willingness to protest busing. The data show little evidence that the causal order is other than in the direction represented in table 3.4. No panel procedure, of course, can definitively show the causal order between variables (Duncan 1969, 1972, 1975). It is always necessary to rely on substantive knowledge and theoretical reasoning as the basis for this conclusion.

doned these attachments and that opposition to school desegregation cannot be explained by the fear that these perquisites of domination will be lost. Desegregation protest in Boston cannot be explained by diffusion of white supremacist attitudes or support for the doctrine of social inequality. Boston residents are, if anything, more opposed to white supremacist beliefs than the residents of other, comparable American cities. This is one reason why I believe that unqualified use of the term "racism" to describe antibusing protest is inaccurate, if we are to keep a consistent definition of the term. It is better, I believe, to describe exactly how, when, and which racial attitudes come into play as causes of desegregation protest and to acknowledge that few Americans today favor the strict separation of the races that was prevalent even a generation ago.

Even though there has been a decline in white supremacist attitudes, white Americans remain fearful of minority concentration.[13] The limited evidence available in table 3.1 suggests that fear of minority concentration may be exacerbated by imminent plans for desegregation. On questions about fear of racial concentration and opposition to busing, Boston neighborhood residents are less tolerant than white residents of cities that are not faced with a desegregation order.[14]

The persistence of fear of minority concentration as a cause of protest points to a significant policy concern. School districts contemplating desegregation ought to forthrightly address white fears of high minority concentration. Adequately informing people of the exact racial concentration in the school district is one important

13. The pattern of low support for white supremacist thought but high fear of racial concentration does not conform to any of the typologies that have been suggested for classifying public attitudes on racial prejudice and tolerance for integration. Boston residents, compared to the parallel GSS sample, are not systematically less tolerant on "general" or "applied" questions (Jackman 1978). They are not systematically different from the parallel sample on questions about "principle" versus "practice" versus "personal intention and behavior" (Schuman, Steeh, and Bobo 1983). The complexity of American racial opinions and the importance of understanding these opinions for bettering our quality of life requires that we construct such typologies. The findings in this chapter suggest, however, that work in this area is not complete.

14. The analysis in Chapter 4 shows that fear of minority concentration remains a consistently significant predictor of antibusing protest even after a number of other explanatory variables are controlled. This is not true for the other measures of racism considered here.

step, since the data indicate that most whites will otherwise over-estimate the percent of blacks in each school (Cataldo et al. 1978, pp. 61–62; Hollander and Scarpa 1972). Taking steps to undo the psychology of tipping by guaranteeing enrollment balances is also important.

Tables 3.3 and 3.4 show that, when desegregation occurs, those who are racially prejudiced and fearful of minority concentration are more likely than those who are not to oppose busing. One might count this as evidence of the effect of racism on antibusing protest. The more dramatic finding from these tables, however, may be that there is a very high level of opposition to busing even among those who do not believe in white supremacy and the legality of segrega-tion. Moreover, this group constitutes the majority of the population in Boston and in most other American cities.

Those who do not believe in white supremacy or the legality of segregation are, nevertheless, against busing because they tend to believe that compliance with desegregation ought to be voluntary, not mandatory as with a busing order. To build a constituency around this view, the antibusing leadership in a community plays on fears of declining safety, declining educational quality, and on fears of large minority concentration which did not dissipate during the Second Reconstruction. The result is a widespread view that busing is unfair and unsafe: an "injustice frame of reference" that provides a con-temporary moral basis for the doctrine voluntary compliance. It is the widespread opinion that busing is unjust and not the narrow sup-port for white supremacy that provides the potentially massive con-stituency for antibusing leadership in a community.[15] The dynamics of this phenomenon are more fully explored in the next chapter.

15. It may be the widespread view that busing is unsafe and unjust rather than individual reactions of racism and prejudice that explains the "white flight" phe-nomenon. The research design for the Boston survey is not appropriate for fully analyzing the white flight question. The limited evidence available from the survey suggests, however, that individual decisions to move away from the city during the data collection period are not related to the measures of racism or antibusing opin-ion analyzed in this chapter. If there is a white flight effect the data suggest it is one where the likelihood of moving from city neighborhoods is increased whether indi-viduals are personally prejudiced or not. For demographic analyses of the white flight question in Boston and in other cities, see Coleman et al. 1975; Rossell 1978; Pettigrew and Green 1976; Frey 1980; Pearce 1980.

4 | Willingness to Protest: A Question of Injustice

The Moral Basis for Voluntary Compliance

During times of antibusing conflict it is the racists—those who favor white supremacy and the doctrine of social inequality—who are most likely to be active in creating disorder. But with a declining proportion being willing to express such views, the success of antibusing leaders in creating widespread conflict depends on their ability to convert others to the cause as well. The Citizens' Councils, a confederation of white supremacist organizations founded in Mississippi in the 1950s, recognized this strategic situation. One of their leaders, cited in the epigram at the beginning of Part I of this book, noted that it was not necessary to appeal to the fanatics. The fanatics were already willing to protest desegregation. It was necessary to appeal to the moderate in order to expand the basis of community opposition to the courts. This chapter examines more fully the reasons why moderates support antibusing protest.

Most white Americans, not only those who are supremacists, oppose busing because they believe it is not a legally "just" policy:

> Among white parents in our sample, there was widespread rejection of the idea that the government has a legitimate role to play in desegregating the schools. . . . Over 80 percent of the whites agreed with the statement "The government has no right to tell you where to send your child to school." Over 60 percent felt that the Supreme Court overstepped its proper boundaries in making decisions about school integration. (Cataldo et al. 1978, p. 76)

To most Americans the acceptable boundaries for government action are the ones implied by the doctrine of voluntary compliance.
The government is believed to have the right to declare discrimination illegal, but not the right to make desegregation mandatory. The
doctrine of voluntary compliance was, after all, publicly articulated
and had been accepted by the Supreme Court as policy until five or
six years before Judge Garrity's order (see Chapter 1). When Hubert
Humphrey sought Senate support for the 1964 Civil Rights Act, he
assured his colleagues that the law could not be used to promote
busing for school desegregation. His rationale quoted the doctrine
of voluntary compliance and even some of the exact words used
by South Carolina Federal Circuit Judge John Parker to clarify its
meaning:

> While the Constitution prohibits segregation, it does not require inte-
> gration. The busing of children to achieve racial balance would be an
> act to effect the integration of schools. In fact, if the bill were to com-
> pel it, it would be a violation, because it would be handling the matter
> on a basis of race and we would be transporting children because of
> their race.

Most whites also believe that busing is socially harmful. They
believe it threatens the interests of their neighborhood and the interests of school-age children in the neighborhood.

The belief that mandatory busing is socially harmful and the belief that it is legally unjust together constitute an "injustice frame of
reference" (Gamson et al. 1982) capitalized on by antibusing forces
to mobilize moderates to protest against busing. The injustice frame
of reference is, in Myrdal's term, a "rationalization" for antibusing
behavior. It provides a justification, in contemporary language and
in terms of local issues, for the doctrine of voluntary compliance.
The evidence in this chapter shows that those who accept the injustice frame of reference are considerably more likely than those
who do not to favor protest.

The doctrine of voluntary compliance is, at present, ingrained
in most Americans' perceptions of the law. In almost every community there is an injustice frame that rationalizes, in contemporary
and local terms, opposition to busing and support for the view that
segregation is illegal but desegregation is not mandatory. The fact of

an injustice frame is widespread. However, local circumstances—history, leadership and past conflicts—affect the *particular* aspects of the injustice frame that receive greatest prominence in the public mind in any community. In the language of this chapter, local "cultural filters," arising from the past political experience of a city, affect the aspects of the court order that are most widely viewed as socially harmful and unjust. The cultural filters relevant for understanding the widespread opposition to busing in Boston are analyzed here.

Whether or not perceived injustice leads to active protest in a community depends, as well, on cultural filters and the actions of local leadership. If there is a past history of mobilization and community conflict based on issues similar to those in the antibusing injustice frame, then organized conflict over desegregation is more likely to occur. If local leaders, referred to in this chapter as "political entrepreneurs" (Frohlich et al. 1971), call attention to the injustice frame and in other ways educate the public about the historical precedents and current harms that justify protest against mandatory desegregation, then mobilization of injustice into protest is more likely.[1] The attention-calling actions of political entrepreneurs in Boston are analyzed, and some comparisons are made with the circumstances in other American cities.

Legitimacy, Injustice, and Obedience to Public Policy

Most of the time public officials implement public policies without extensive conflict or negative public reaction. Of course, one reason for this is that the public usually agrees with the laws being implemented. Widespread public opposition is not likely to occur unless the law is unpopular (Rodgers and Bullock 1972; Dolbeare and Hammond 1971; Johnson 1967).

Unpopularity of the law may be necessary, but it is not a sufficient condition for popular protest. Citizens usually allow themselves to be governed peaceably even when the policies implemented are distasteful or when incumbents are believed to be incompetent and even dishonest. As a number of authors have noted, the perception of oc-

---

1. A political entrepreneur is defined as an individual who helps coordinate attainment of public goods in exchange for personal access to the rewards of public office (Frohlich et al. 1971, p. 6).

casional lapses of quality in the benefits received from public policy or from particular incumbents does not usually cause political distrust and political conflict (Hirschman 1970; Gamson 1968).

Public willingness to tolerate occasional disappointments is explained by the perceived legitimacy of the decision-making system. Actions of authorities are viewed as legitimate when citizens believe authorities use their power to coordinate the provision of collective community benefits in a way that is fair and does not cause social harm. Fairness means that:

1. The rules by which policy is made are not biased against one's interests.
2. One's voice is adequately represented in the policy-making process.
3. The goals of the policy are consistent with one's own view of what is moral and acceptable.

The perception that a policy does not cause social harm is based on one's judgment that:

4. The policy does not produce egregiously harmful results for those affected. A policy viewed as fair may still be undesirable if implementation causes social harm.

When actions of public authorities are seen as fair and socially efficient, then authorities are viewed from what Gamson et al. call a "legitimacy frame of reference" (1982, p. 122). Whether or not public officials are viewed this way makes a great deal of difference for the ease of public policy implementation because, to paraphrase Gamson et al. and the many authors they cite, legitimacy motivates obedience. Someone who disagrees with a public policy but who believes that it is fair is much more likely than someone who does not to be obedient and, in the event of some public opposition, to support only those actions that are legal.

Why does legitimacy motivate obedience? Perhaps the primary reason is that even though a person may not favor a policy, that person does not question his or her interest in the policy-making process. He or she still expects positive benefits will someday flow from the ordinary operation of the decision-making process. In this limited sense, self-interest is part of the reason for the link between legitimacy and obedience.

The Injustice Frame of Reference

Disobedience to authority arises most often when the legitimacy frame of reference is abandoned and people adopt, instead, an injustice frame of reference. Opponents of a public policy view it from an injustice framework when they believe the policy is the result of an unfair decision-making process and/or that the effects of the policy are socially harmful.[2]

The injustice frame of reference implies much more than dissatisfaction with a particular policy and/or a particular incumbent. The injustice frame implies a perceived violation of "shared principles about what is fair . . . a violation of some moral code" (Gamson et al. 1982, pp. 14–15). The moral code is the expectation that public policies should be fair and socially efficient. The injustice frame asserts that the opposite is true.

When viewed from the injustice frame of reference, negative effects of public policy are not believed to be the result of a desultory lapse in the quality of the decision-making process. Rather:

> The injustice frame makes sense of the agent's behavior by showing that it is consistent with some objective that the authority system is actively seeking. (Gamson et al. 1982, p. 153)

Just as legitimacy motivates obedience, injustice motivates disobedience. For someone who adopts the injustice frame, participation in collective actions that are legal are expected to be ineffective or even counterproductive, because such actions do not impede the operations of authorities (Gamson et al. 1982, p. 14). Participation in illegal action becomes especially likely as individuals seek ways to impede the operation of the authority system and to reverse its policies. This is an important point for theorists of political action. It implies that the primary goal of those who adopt the injustice frame of reference is not a tangible good or a victory in a specific

---

2. A third potential cause of perceived injustice is also discussed by Gamson et al. (1982). An individual may believe policies to be unjust if the authorities who implement them are seen as incompetent. Measures of perceived incompetence and distrust in government correlate with protest willingness in the experimental study reported by Gamson et al. Interestingly, such measures do not correlate with antibusing protest and are, therefore, not discussed at length in this book.

political contest. Rather, it is to impede the operation of the authority system. The evidence supporting this interpretation of the goals of antibusing protest, and further elaboration of the theoretical importance of this point are contained in Chapter 8.

From Injustice to Protest

Gamson et al. argue that "questionable acts by authorities must be called to everyone's attention" by group activists before collective protests can emerge (1982, p. 187). When abuses of authority are publicly noted by individuals speaking to the group or speaking on behalf of the group two changes occur:

1. Group members focus on and articulate those particular abuses by authority as parts of the injustice frame of reference. Attention calling molds the content of the injustice frame adopted by group members.
2. Group members become conscious of the group as a potential actor against injustice. They become aware of the fact that other members of the group are also aware of the injustice frame. Attention calling heightens the sense of group cohesiveness and commitment to protest injustice.

Frohlich et al. analyze community mobilization for collective action and assign particular significance to community spokesmen and attention callers who act as "coordination mechanisms":

Coordination mechanisms, such as political leaders or parties, may play a role in determining the expectations the individual members of the group ultimately form of each other's probable behavior with respect to contributions toward the supply of collective goods. (1971 p. 21)

Community spokesmen and attention callers have a great influence on community mobilization because their actions coordinate the expectations neighborhood residents have of each others' opinions and each others' likely behavior. This makes it more likely that individuals will support an action:

> In deciding on his own contribution (if any), each individual must esti-
> mate what others will contribute, taking into account the fact that their
> opinions will be influenced, in turn, by estimates of the probable be-
> havior of a subgroup of which he is a member. . . . In order to make
> any decision at all, including the decision not to contribute, the indi-
> vidual must ultimately attach some probability estimates to the behav-
> ior of others, even if only tacitly or on the basis of simple rules of
> thumb. . . . When mechanisms [for the coordination of expectations]
> . . . exist, the number of members of the group who consider it worth-
> while to make a contribution toward the supply of the collective good
> will generally increase (Frohlich et al. 1971, pp. 22–25).

Coordination is a valuable commodity that is supplied to a community by its spokesmen and attention callers. Those who provide
this commodity in exchange for public office are referred to by
Frohlich et al. as "political entrepreneurs" (1971, p. 6).

Some form of coordination or political entrepreneurship is necessary for the development of an injustice frame of reference in a
group. The subjects in the social psychological experiment reported
by Gamson et al. do not include entrepreneurs concerned about
building political careers. In communities undergoing conflict, however, it is ordinarily the case that group spokesmen and attention
callers have the resources and ambitions of political entrepreneurs.
During the Boston school desegregation controversy, for instance,
almost all of the individuals in this role are also candidates for election, reelection or appointment to public office.

Cultural Filters for the Injustice Frame

Community spokesmen are not just catalysts who excite but
otherwise do not affect the process of community change. Their political interests and past experiences in community service affect
their judgment of what injustices are "appropriate" focal points for
public attention. The injustice frame of reference adopted by antibusing protesters in a city depends, in this way, on its history and
political culture prior to desegregation.

Segregationists once relied heavily on the argument that the Supreme Court's decision in *Brown v. Board of Education* was the
product of Communist infiltration into the highest levels of government. President Eisenhower lent credibility to this view when, in a

September 1956 press conference he responded to a question about the *Brown* decision by saying, "We must all . . . help to bring about a change in spirit so that extremists on both sides do not defeat what we know is a reasonable, logical conclusion to this whole affair." His comment equates blacks who were peacefully seeking their rights with whites who were, at the time, threatening violence. The popularity of the view that desegregation is unjust because of extremist influence prompted Gunnar Myrdal's observation that the South is the only place in the world where one can get a reputation for being a liberal simply by urging obedience to the law.

The pre–Civil War doctrine of nullification is another cultural filter that significantly affected the content of the injustice frame in the South. After the New Orleans school board was ordered to desegregate its schools in 1960, the Louisiana legislature passed a law "interposing" its authority between the federal courts and the people to "relieve any person from any obligation to obey the offending federal injunctions." The attorney for Orval Faubus, then governor of Arkansas, walked out of a 1959 federal injunction hearing claiming:

> The governor of the state of Arkansas cannot and will not concede that the United States in this court or anywhere else can question his discretion and judgment as chief executive of a sovereign state when he acts in the performance of his constitutional duties.

A variation on the nullification doctrine came from *U.S. News and World Report* publisher David Lawrence, who contended in 1959 that the Fourteenth Amendment was ratified by Southern legislatures acting under duress, and is therefore not part of the Constitution.

In Boston past struggles over local autonomy shaped and filtered the way the busing issue was interpreted. In 1967 and in 1971, prominent antibusing leader Louise Day Hicks campaigned for the mayoralty of Boston on a platform of "removing the politics from city administration," meaning that the city government had lost too much of its authority to the state legislature. But this platform was not new with Hicks. It had been embraced by community political leaders since the days of the transition from Yankee to immigrant authority (Handlin 1959; Friedman 1973).

Most grating to local leadership were the "Boston bills," passed by the state legislature to retain control over city revenues and administration. Henry Parkman, writing in 1932, notes that because of laws passed and amendments made to the state constitution:

> The State still retains control of many of the municipal activities of Boston. . . . The city . . . is forced to resort to the Legislature for the authority to borrow for many projects; . . . the Mayor is forced annually to present the Legislature a request for the authority to obtain sufficient revenue from taxation to carry out the activities of municipal departments; the School Committee must obtain from the legislature the necessary authority for funds for school building and administrative purposes; . . . the control and management of the police force is in the hands of a Commissioner appointed by the Governor; the Licensing Board is subject to gubernatorial appointment; and, on many boards and commissions, established from time to time, the State insists on representation. (P. 141)

A more recent analysis concludes that there were few changes in this pattern between 1930 and 1967 (Levy 1971). For example, it was not until 1962 that the power to appoint the chief of police was restored to the city.

The 1965 Massachusetts Racial Imbalance Act seemed, to many, to be a continuation of the tradition of the "Boston bills." Because of the way the RIA was written, and because of the demographic distribution of racial groups in the state, the impact of the law was concentrated on the city of Boston. The April 1965 statewide census—the basis for enforcement of the act—found 55 racially imbalanced schools in the state of Massachusetts. Of these, 45 were located in the city of Boston.

When Judge Garrity's decision was announced in June 1974, many of the community spokesmen and political entrepreneurs, who had previously campaigned on the issue of restoring autonomy to city government, became leaders of the antibusing movement as well. They called attention to the busing issue as another instance of the removal of local autonomy, naming the principal citywide antibusing organization "Restore Our Alienated Rights" (ROAR).

In Boston in the 1970s the injustice frame of reference was called to public attention by community actors whose political experience before the time of Judge Garrity's court order was focused on the need to restore alienated rights to the city. The injustice frame of reference adopted by the antibusing movement was therefore grounded heavily in this argument against Judge Garrity's exercise of authority.

The Injustice Frame and the Boston Conflict

Unfairness of the Court Order

Most neighborhood residents recognize that there are a number of racially imbalanced schools in Boston. However, they do not think the school board is responsible for the problem. Therefore, they do not think the court order is fair. This point of view is consistent, in fact, with the civil rights law applicable in the case against the Boston school board. To order desegregation, a court must find the school board or other state officials guilty of intentional, segregative actions. If school board actions are not found to be the cause of racial imbalance, then the court cannot order a remedy even if there are a number of segregated schools in the city.

Table 4.1 shows the level of awareness of racial imbalance in the public schools. Before Judge Garrity's decision (wave 2), about 75 percent of the Boston neighborhood residents say there are "many" or "some" racially imbalanced schools in the city. After Judge Garrity's decision (wave 3), the level of awareness increases to more than 80 percent. Table 4.1 also shows that those who oppose busing are as likely to recognize the existence of racially imbalanced

Table 4.1   *Awareness of Racial Imbalance in the Boston Public School System*

	Percent Saying There Are "Many" or "Some" Racially Imbalanced Schools	
	Wave 2	Wave 3
Opinion on busing blacks and whites to achieve racial balance:		
Opposed	76	80
Neutral, favor	75	86

Note: Question wordings: see Appendix 1, no. 19.
    Data are combined from samples of white residents of six Boston neighborhoods.

schools as those who favor busing. A parallel question, not presented here, shows that about 60 percent say the number of racially
imbalanced schools in Boston has increased since the middle 1960s.
This percentage is about the same for those opposed to and those in
favor of court-implemented busing.

Table 4.1 shows there is widespread awareness of the facts of
racial imbalance in the public schools. Moreover, those who favor
busing and those who oppose busing do not disagree about the facts.
There is, however, disagreement over the interpretation of the facts.

The lower part of table 4.2 shows that just after Judge Garrity's
decision (wave 3), about 70 percent of those opposed to busing say
the school board did not intentionally maintain a segregated school
system. Of those in favor of busing, only 24 percent maintain this
view. Part of the injustice frame of reference, and one reason for the
unfairness felt by those opposed to busing, is the belief that the

Table 4.2   *School Board Responsibility for Racial Imbalance*

	Wave 2 (Percent Saying Responsibility Is:)			Wave 3 (Percent Saying Responsibility Is:)		
	Full	Partial	None	Full	Partial	None
Opinion on busing:						
Opposed	6	37	47	8	47	39
Neutral, favor	16	64	9	19	63	12

	Percent Disagreeing with the Statement That the Boston School Board Intentionally Maintained a Segregated School System	
	Wave 3	Wave 5
Opinion on busing:		
Opposed	70	62
Neutral, favor	24	17

Note: Question wordings: see Appendix 1, nos. 5, 20–22.
    Data are combined from samples of white residents of six Boston
neighborhoods.

court is imposing a remedy for a harm the school board did not cause. This belief changes only slightly during the first year of desegregation. By the end of the first year of desegregation (wave 5), 62 percent of those opposed to busing still say the school board did not intentionally maintain a segregated school system, whereas among those in favor this view is shared by only 17 percent.

The top part of table 4.2 shows that those in favor of busing almost unanimously believe the school board is "completely" or "partially" responsible for the existence of racially imbalanced schools in Boston. Among opponents of busing, however, 47 percent say the school board is "not at all" responsible for the existence of racially imbalanced schools in the interview before Judge Garrity's decision, and 39 percent maintain this view after the court order.[3]

The argument by busing opponents that Judge Garrity's actions are unfair can be summarized as follows:

1. Most say the school board did not intend the harm that was done to blacks.
2. Some who say the school board did not intend the harm recognize the school board might be responsible for it anyway.
3. But about 40 to 50 percent say the school board neither intended nor is responsible for the harm found by Judge Garrity's court.
4. Therefore, in their minds, court-implemented desegregation is unfair.

Social Harm Caused by Busing

Ten days after the beginning of desegregation implementation, City Council member Louise Day Hicks, State Senator Bulger, and State Representative Flaherty issued what they called a Declaration

3. The remainder of those opposed to busing, with little exception, say the school board is "partially" responsible for racial imbalance. Those who assign partial responsibility to the school board may not realize they actually agree with Judge Garrity's finding. The law does not require a finding of complete school board responsibility to require desegregation implementation. The idea that the board is only "partially" responsible but must suffer the consequences of "full" desegregation may, however, add to the sense of injustice felt by those opposed to busing.

of Clarification to call attention to the harm caused by Judge Garrity's order:[4]

> There is resistance in South Boston because it is against our children's interest to send them to school in crime infested Roxbury. [The statement was accompanied by charts showing neighborhood crime statistics.] Routine, everyday violence ravages the black community [but is hidden from the public by a] conspiratorial press.

Boston neighborhood residents are greatly afraid of the negative effects of school desegregation suggested in the Declaration of Clarification. The data are shown in the top part of table 4.3. At the time of the Declaration (wave 4), 79 percent of those opposed to busing say that violence in the public schools is an "extremely serious" problem. A little more than half of those in favor of busing agree with this assessment. Other survey studies also find that fear for children's safety is widespread at the time of a desegregation order, and is one of the primary reasons for white fears of minority concentration (Cataldo et al. 1978, p.42; Rossell 1983, p. 16).

An evaluation of the experience of school districts undergoing desegregation finds that the problem of violence is actually less widespread than parental fears warrant. A study conducted by the United States Department of Justice suggests that school desegregation seldom produces increased school violence and that, contrary to expectations, the desegregation process can even lower the level of violence in a school system when it is specifically addressed as part of the plan (U.S. Department of Justice 1976; Orfield 1978, p. 127).

The Boston survey evidence shows that experience with desegregation may reduce fear of violence. After the end of the first year of busing (wave 5), belief that violence is an "extremely serious" problem falls from 79 percent to 68 percent of those opposed to busing. Endorsement of this view falls from more than half to 23 percent among those in favor of busing.

---

4. As an attention-calling tactic, the Declaration is similar to the Southern Manifesto, issued 12 March 1956, by 101 Congressmen from 11 states of the old Confederacy. The Manifesto was quoted in Chapter 1.

Table 4.3   *Social Harms Believed to Accompany Desegregation*

	Percent Saying Violence in the Schools Will Be an Extremely Serious Problem	
	Wave 4	Wave 5
Opinion on busing:		
Opposed	79	68
Neutral, favor	58	23

	Opinion on Whether Integration Causes a Decline in White Students' Test Scores			
	(Wave 2 Percentage)		(Wave 5 Percentage)	
	True	False	True	False
Opinion on busing:				
Opposed	33	33	58	24
Neutral, favor	18	58	20	69

Note: Question wordings: see Appendix 1, nos. 5, 23–26.
  Data are combined from samples of white residents of six Boston neighborhoods.

A second injury, not mentioned in the Declaration of Clarification, is the belief that desegregation causes a deterioration in educational quality. Before the first year of implementation (wave 3), about 30 percent of those opposed to busing say Judge Garrity is "not at all" concerned about how Phase I desegregation will affect the education of school children. Virtually none of those in favor of busing share this view.

The impact of Judge Garrity's order on student achievement became a divisive issue during the time of the desegregation controversy. The second part of table 4.3 shows that before Judge Garrity's order (wave 2), 33 percent of those opposed to busing believe that "white student test scores often decrease when they attend desegregated schools." Only 18 percent of those in favor of busing share this view. As desegregation proceeds (wave 5), table 4.3 shows that those who favor busing become more certain the proposition is false and those opposed to busing become more certain the proposition is true.[5]

The facts of the matter tend to support those who favor desegregation. The most careful and extensive review of the effect of desegregation on student achievement (Crain and Mahard 1978; Mahard and Crain 1983) finds:[6]

1. Desegregation tends to improve minority academic achievement and does not harm white achievement.
2. The greatest gains in achievement occur when students are first desegregated in the early elementary grades.
3. Studies with stronger methodologies show greater achievement gains with desegregation than studies with weaker methodologies.

However, the facts do not always speak for themselves. Both contesting groups—i.e., those opposed to busing and those in favor—had community spokesmen and academic experts supporting and otherwise calling attention to their views on the test score debate. The data in table 4.3 suggest that the loyalists of each group became more firmly committed to the views espoused by the group's experts.

"Alienation" of Parents' Rights

During the early stages of the controversy, busing opponents attempted several times to enact laws restoring to parents the right to accept or reject school assignments for their children. Sometimes these laws were even passed, in spite of the fact that the United States Supreme Court had in numerous instances declared such laws to be unconstitutional. For instance, the year before Judge Garrity's

5. The percent in Boston saying desegregation causes declining test scores is about the same as found in studies of other communities. A survey done in Florida metropolitan areas a few years after desegregation asked respondents to agree or disagree with the statement, "White students' test scores have fallen sharply in integrated schools." Seventy-two percent of those who avoided sending their children to desegregated schools and 64 percent of those who eventually complied with the court order agreed (Cataldo et al. 1978, p. 65).

6. For other, sometimes contrasting views on the effect of desegregation on student achievement, see Armor (1972), Pettigrew et al. (1973), St. John (1975), Weinberg (1968, 1975).

decision, representatives from Boston neighborhoods were able to obtain passage of a state law requiring parental consent before a child could be bused past the nearest school. This law would have made enforcement of the Massachusetts Racial Imbalance Act (RIA) all but impossible. For this reason, in November 1973, Massachusetts Governor Francis Sargent vetoed the legislation. But at the time of Governor Sargent's veto, State Representative Raymond Flynn of South Boston (now the mayor of Boston), State Representative Flaherty, and Mrs. Hicks called attention to this action and publicly vowed to seek other legislation to guarantee "the custodial rights of parents over their children" (*Boston Globe* 11 November 1973).

The belief that court-implemented busing illegitimately takes away parental rights to control their children's education is accepted by nearly 100 percent of those opposed to busing and, remarkably, by more than half of those who say they favor court-implemented busing to achieve racial balance. The data are in the top part of table 4.4. The lower part of table 4.4 shows a similar pattern for a related question—whether children should always go to school in their own neighborhood and whether busing, by implication, violates this principle. For this question as well, nearly 90 percent of those opposed to busing and between one-third and one-half of those in favor of busing agree that Judge Garrity's policy alienates parental rights.[7]

The time trends in table 4.4 show that beliefs about parental rights over educational choice and the desirability of neighborhood schooling were well established in public opinion before the time of Judge Garrity's order. The cultural context for this aspect of the injustice frame was, of course, established in Boston politics many years before busing became an issue. After Judge Garrity's order there is some tendency for those in favor of busing to fall away from the view that the policy violates parental rights. However, even after the first year of implementation (wave 5), more than half of this group believe busing alienates parental rights of control, and 32 percent say children should always go to neighborhood schools.

Parental rights to control public education were never, in fact,

7. In their survey of residents of Florida metropolitan school districts, Cataldo et al. (1978, p. 76) report that over 80 percent of white parents agree with the statement, "The government has no right to tell you where to send your child to school."

Table 4.4   *Alienation of Parents' Rights to Control Their Children's Education*

	Percent Saying the Amount of Influence by Parents on Children's School Choice Compared to the Amount Deserved Is:					
	Wave 3			Wave 5		
	Much Less	Less	Right, More	Much Less	Less	Right, More
Opinion on busing:						
Opposed	54	33	12	70	24	5
Neutral, favor	23	42	30	18	35	47

	Percent Agreeing with Statement That Children Should Always Go to Neighborhood Schools				
	Wave 1	Wave 3		Wave 5	
	Agree	Strongly Agree	Agree	Strongly Agree	Agree
Opinion on busing:					
Opposed	89	70	22	65	25
Neutral, favor	43	9	28	6	26

Note: Question wordings: see Appendix 1, nos. 5, 27–31.
   Data are combined from samples of white residents of six Boston neighborhoods.

recognized by the system of authority before or after Judge Garrity's order. Massachusetts law always maintained the state's primary interest in educational decision making. In the years before court-implemented busing, however, the willingness of authorities to bend policies to accommodate public opposition to desegregation created the impression that such parental rights might, in fact, exist. In Max Weber's terminology, parental power over school policy was a right in usage if not a right in law (1967). Parents had this right in usage because for years school board members and other neighborhood representatives were almost always able to preempt the exercise of state authority in matters of public school choice by using tactics of litigation and delay to respond to proposals for desegregation (Levy 1971).

In 1972, for instance, federal funds for education were withheld by HEW because of the unwillingness of the Boston school board to desegregate. The school board filed litigation, and the funds were restored by the state supreme court with no change in the status of the public schools. In 1973 the state board of education announced a plan for implementing the RIA that significantly affected only one-third of the racially imbalanced schools in the city. Boston school board intransigence forestalled further attempts to desegregate the public schools at that time.

Before Judge Garrity's order those opposed to busing had many reasons to believe the system of authority recognized parents' rights to control public school choices. The uncompromising enforcement of Judge Garrity's decree, however, signaled a change. If we accept the usual dictionary definition of "alienation" as "taking away something that once belonged to someone," then parents' rights (rights in usage if not rights in law) were, in fact, alienated by the court order.

Public opinion regarding the unfairness of Judge Garrity's order changed greatly during the span of time covered by the panel survey analyzed in this book. Table 4.5 shows that before Judge Garrity's order (wave 1), about half of those opposed to busing say the "people in the neighborhood" and "they themselves" (i.e., the respondent) have less influence than they are entitled to when public officials make decisions about "busing school children to achieve racial balance." By the end of the first year of desegregation implementation (wave 5), 75 to 80 percent of those opposed to busing share this view. Those in favor of busing are more likely to feel represented in the decision-making process. Nevertheless, even in this group about 40 percent say the system does not legitimately represent their interests. By the end of the first year of desegregation implementation, 57 percent say their neighbors' interests are not fairly taken into consideration by public officials who enforce busing.[8]

8. Cataldo et al. astutely observe that delay by school officials in implementing desegregation is often the reason there is little time for parental participation:

Parents may not even know what schools their children have been assigned to attend until the school year is about to begin. . . . Little wonder that parents resented the subject role to which they had been relegated and disapproved of the handling of desegregation locally (1978, p. 101).

In the eyes of busing opponents, the system of authority alienated parents' rights to have their preferences guide school policy
and to choose their children's schools. Neighborhood residents may
have felt the loss of a third right as well—the right of the majority to
determine public policy.

Just before (wave 2) and just after (wave 3) the court order,
neighborhood residents were asked whether courts "have the right to
make decisions many people disagree with." In each wave 60 per-

Table 4.5   *Alienation of Citizens' Rights to Influence
Public Policy*

	Percent Saying the Amount of Influence of People in the Neighborhood on Decisions Compared to the Amount Deserved Is:					
	Wave 1			Wave 5		
	Much Less	Less	Right, More	Much Less	Less	Right, More
Opinion on busing:						
Opposed	19	33	42	44	35	18
Neutral, favor	8	30	54	14	43	34

	Percent Saying the Amount of Their Own Influence on Decisions Compared to the Amount Deserved Is:					
	Wave 3			Wave 5		
	Much Less	Less	Right, More	Much Less	Less	Right, More
Opinion on busing:						
Opposed	23	30	45	40	32	26
Neutral, favor	15	31	48	14	23	54

Note: Question wordings: see Appendix 1, nos. 5, 32–33.
    Data are combined from samples of white residents of six Boston
neighborhoods.

cent of those opposed to busing say the courts do not have this right.[9] Just after the court order (wave 3), respondents were asked whether they agree or disagree with the statement that "no amount of public opposition can justify delay" in implementing desegregation. Sixty-eight percent of those opposed to busing disagree with this statement, endorsing instead a principle of majority rule. Only 7 percent of those in favor of busing take this view.

The Impact of Community Leadership

In their comparative analysis of eight Northern cities, Crain et al. argue that public statements by school board members and the civic elite guide public opinion on desegregation (1968). Cataldo et al. report that once appropriate steps are taken to control for the tendency of respondents to "project" their views, "school officials do not exercise any genuine causal impact on parental support" (1978, p. 90). Their survey measures are retrospective (the study was conducted after, not during, the period of implementation) and, compared to the Boston data, somewhat general. Perhaps this is why the findings in this chapter support the findings of Crain et al. and not the findings from the Florida survey.

Louise Day Hicks and John Kerrigan are two antibusing leaders for whom there is adequate survey data to explore the effect of attention-calling on public perceptions of injustice. Both are successful political entrepreneurs who were extensively involved with the antibusing movement.

Louise Day Hicks was chairman of the Boston school board when the RIA was passed, a member of the city council during the time of Judge Garrity's order, and a candidate for city mayor in 1967 and 1971. She was a founder of ROAR. (It is said she gave the organization its name.) Her public position made it possible for her to coordinate the use of neighborhood precinct organization and city council facilities by the antibusing movement.

According to the neighborhood survey, her views on busing are clearly perceived in the community. Before the court order (wave 1),

9. Only 15 to 20 percent of those in favor of busing say courts do not have the right to go against the public will.

83 percent say she is opposed to busing. By the end of the first year of implementation (wave 5), 94 percent correctly perceive her views.

John Kerrigan is an equally successful political entrepreneur and antibusing leader, although he is not as well-known outside Boston as Mrs. Hicks. During the early years of community reaction against the RIA, he was a member of the school board and nominal head of the Save Boston Committee—the nucleus of ROAR. He was school board chairman from the time Mrs. Hicks was elected to the city council until the end of Phase I. After the first year of implementation he was elected to the city council. As school board chairman it was his job to publicly explain the procedure and rationale for the legal tactics used to forestall desegregation.

During the time of the panel survey analyzed here, Mr. Kerrigan's views on busing are fairly accurately perceived by the community as well. Just after Judge Garrity's court order (wave 3), 67 percent correctly say he is opposed to busing.

In the summer before the second year of desegregation (wave 5), neighborhood residents were asked about the actions taken by community political leaders in the past and about the actions these leaders could be expected to take in the future. About two-thirds (66 percent) of the neighborhood residents say Mrs. Hicks "strongly encourages" public defiance of Phase II implementation and about half (48 percent) say the same for Mr. Kerrigan.

The survey data show that attention-calling activities significantly affect the diffusion of the injustice frame and the perception of cohesive community opposition to the court order. Neighborhood residents who perceive strong, consistent opposition to authority by community leaders are more likely than those who do not to adopt the injustice frame and to believe there is widespread community support for unauthorized actions to impede desegregation.

The top half of table 4.6 shows that opponents of busing who say Mrs. Hicks strongly encourages defiance are more likely than those whose attention is less focused on her actions to say the court order is inefficient because of violence and that citizens' rights are alienated by Judge Garrity's actions. The bottom half of table 4.6 shows the same effects of Mr. Kerrigan's actions on the beliefs of busing opponents.

Is the pattern in table 4.6 due to some uncontrolled variable? For instance, the earlier part of this chapter shows that those op-

Table 4.6   *Attention-calling and Belief in the Social Harm and Injustice of Busing*

	Percent in Wave 5 Saying:				
	Violence Will Be Serious Next Year	Children Should Go to Neigh-borhood School	Parents Have Much Too Little Influence	Respon-dent Has Much Too Little Influence	Neigh-bors Have Much Too Little In-fluence
Mrs. Hicks' message:					
Strong defiance	73	70	76	49	49
More conciliatory	54	57	66	28	40
Mr. Kerrigan's message:					
Strong defiance	71	66	79	52	54
More conciliatory	63	66	68	31	37

Note: Question wordings: see Appendix 1, nos. 34, 24, 31, 28, 33.

Data are combined from samples of white residents of six Boston neighborhoods.

Data show responses of those personally opposed to busing at the time of the interview.

Patterns shown are significant (.05) when racial prejudice/fear and strength of antibusing opinion are controlled.

posed to busing are more likely to adopt the injustice frame. It may seem plausible to argue that those opposed to busing are more likely to say community leaders strongly encourage defiance because busing opponents selectively perceive the actions of community leaders or desire to believe the actions of community leaders are consistent with their own beliefs. The mistaken belief that others agree with one's own opinion is also referred to in the survey literature as projection or the "looking glass effect" (Fields and Schuman 1976).

Controlling for respondents' opinions on busing is one method for controlling the projection or "looking glass" effect. The pattern in table 4.6 cannot be due to the tendency of those who are more strongly opposed to Judge Garrity's policy to adopt the injustice frame and also to believe community leaders support defiance. The reason is that the group analyzed in table 4.6 is homogeneous with respect to busing opinions. Therefore variation in busing opinions cannot be the explanation of the findings.[10] This is the method used by Cataldo et al. to control for projection effects in their analysis as well (1978, pp. 90–91).

In addition to the survey findings, there is ample historical evidence to support the inference of a causal connection between leadership action and public response. Newspaper records and judgments by other analysts indicate that Mrs. Hicks and Mr. Kerrigan intended to affect community opinion in the way shown (e.g., Richard, Knox, and Oliphant 1975). Table 4.6 and the other analytic tables in this book can be thought of as tools for examining the consistency between survey data and predictions based on historical and theoretical analyses in each chapter. The weight of the evidence, in this case, indicates that attention-calling by political entrepreneurs significantly affects diffusion of the injustice frame.

Attention-calling also affects the perception of cohesive community opposition to school desegregation. In the summer before the second year of desegregation, neighborhood residents were asked whether the level of community participation in the public school boycott will increase, decrease, or stay the same when Phase II begins. Survey respondents were also asked what percent of parents in the neighborhood will participate in the boycott during Phase II. Table 4.7 shows that those who say Mrs. Hicks and/or Mr. Kerrigan are strongly encouraging defiance are more likely to say the boycott will increase and that a high percent of parents in the neighborhood will participate.

Attention-calling by political entrepreneurs affects public adoption of the injustice frame and public perceptions of neighborhood support for protest actions. The impact of attention-calling by political entrepreneurs is, however, limited in scope. The statement from ROAR's Declaration of Clarification cited earlier in this chapter emphasizes alienation of parents' and neighbors' rights as the

---

10. Further steps were also taken to examine the validity of the conclusions. In preparing tables 4.6, 4.7, 4.9, 4.10, and 4.11, statistical relationships were tested using more detailed controls for the strength of antibusing opinions and racial prejudice. Results are shown in these tables when the pattern of findings shown is statistically significant (.05) using these more detailed controls as well. In addition, there are a few instances where the data collection design permits estimation repeated-measure panel models for testing simple alternative hypotheses about the causal direction between the variables involved. Tabular analyses are presented when the conclusions hold up under more elaborate analytic techniques as well.

Table 4.7   *Attention-calling and Perception of Cohesive Community Opposition to Busing*

	Percent in Wave 5 Saying:	
	Boycott Participation Will Increase Next Year	More Than 45 Percent Will Boycott Next Year
Mrs. Hicks' message:		
Strong defiance	58	38
More conciliatory	44	31
Mr. Kerrigan's message:		
Strong defiance	56	40
More conciliatory	51	29

Note: Question wordings: see Appendix 1, nos. 34, 54–55.
    Data are combined from samples of white residents of six Boston neighborhoods.
    Data show responses of those personally opposed to busing at the time of the interview.
    Patterns shown are significant (.05) when racial prejudice/fear and strength of antibusing opinion are controlled.

principal injustice of Judge Garrity's order and school violence as the primary inefficiency of desegregation implementation. As table 4.6 shows, public opinion on these issues is influenced by attention calling on the part of Mrs. Hicks and Mr. Kerrigan. Statistical findings not presented here show that other aspects of the injustice frame, such as educational quality or school board culpability are not affected by the attention-calling activities of antibusing leaders. The impact of attention-calling is limited to the issues most directly related to the message of community leaders.

Finding an issue-specific effect of attention-calling helps eliminate another challenge to the validity of the conclusions drawn from tables 4.6 and 4.7. It may seem reasonable to say that the causal direction between the variables works in the other direction: those who adopt the injustice frame are more likely to perceive strong opposition among community leaders and among other residents of the neighborhood. If the causal connection between the variables worked primarily in this direction, however, there would be no reason to find the issue-specific effect noted in connection with tables 4.6 and 4.7.

Table 4.8   *Support for Protest against Desegregation*

	Wave 1	Wave 2	Wave 3	Wave 4	Wave 5
Percent willing to support school boycott	43		60		
Percent willing to support boycott (variant)					44
Percent willing to support school board defiance	57	52	59		
Percent saying the most important thing for neighbors to do is to defy, resist, or evade the court order			79		

Note: Question wordings: see Appendix 1, nos. 14–17.
    Data are combined from samples of white residents of six Boston neighborhoods.
    Data show responses of those personally opposed to busing at the time of the interview.

Injustice and Protest

Those who adopt the injustice frame question their interest in "business as usual." They do not expect positive benefits to flow to them from the ordinary working of the authority system. In this situation unauthorized actions against authority may hold the promise of positive results that cannot be obtained by other means.[11]

About half of the Boston neighborhood residents opposed to busing are willing to engage in illegal protests against school desegregation. Table 4.8 shows that before the court order (wave 1) just over 40 percent of those opposed to busing say they would support a school boycott. By the time of the court order (wave 3), the level of support for boycotts among busing opponents rises to 60 percent. After the first year (wave 5), it appears that the level of support for

    11. Willingness to challenge authority is operationally defined here as willingness to engage in illegal actions. Other attempts to operationally define willingness to challenge authority that lead to a comparable conclusion are reported by Barnes and Kaase (1979), Muller (1979), and Sniderman (1981).

the boycott declines to near 40 percent again, but the wave 5 measure is substantially different in wording from the wave 1 and wave 3 measures, so this conclusion may not be warranted. Table 4.8 also shows that between 50 and 60 percent of those opposed to busing say they support school committee defiance of the court order and that almost 80 percent say the most important thing for their neighbors to do when the first year of implementation begins is to resist or evade the court order.

To what extent is mobilization related to the injustice frame? The next three tables examine the relationship between willingness to protest and people's views on the unfairness, social harm, and alienation of rights caused by court-implemented desegregation.

Table 4.9 shows that believing the court order unfairly assigns fault for school imbalance is related to willingness to protest in the early stages of the controversy (wave 3) but not later (wave 5).

Table 4.10 shows that believing desegregation is socially harmful because of its negative effect on educational quality and the threat of violence is related to willingness to protest in both the earlier and the later stages of the conflict.

Table 4.11 shows that believing the court order takes away (alienates) parental and community rights to control school policies

Table 4.9   *Unfairness and Protest*

| | Percent in Favor of: | | | |
	Defiance Wave 3	Boycott Wave 3	Resistance Wave 3	Boycott Wave 5
Opinion on the statement that the school board intentionally segregated:				
Disagree	64	64	86	47
Agree	47	51	60	44

Note: Question wordings: see Appendix 1, nos. 21, 22, 14–17.

Data are combined from samples of white residents of six Boston neighborhoods.

Data show responses of those personally opposed to busing at the time of the interview.

Patterns shown are significant (.05) when racial prejudice/fear and strength of antibusing opinion are controlled.

Table 4.10   *Social Harm and Protest*

	Percent in Favor of:			
	Defiance Wave 3	Boycott Wave 3	Resistance Wave 3	Boycott Wave 5

Opinion on whether white
  students' test scores
  decline with deseg-
  regation:				

True	62	65	86	51
False	55	55	71	39

Opinion on how much of
  a problem violence in
  the schools will be:				

Very Serious				50
Less Serious				35

Note: Question wordings: see Appendix 1, nos. 24, 25, 14–17.

   Data are combined from samples of white residents of six Boston neighborhoods.

   Data show responses of those personally opposed to busing at the time of the interview.

   Patterns shown are significant (.05) when racial prejudice/fear and strength of antibusing opinion are controlled.

is strongly related to willingness to protest at both early and late stages in the conflict.

   Tables 4.9, 4.10, and 4.11 show that the willingness of busing opponents to protest policies they reject is strongly related to whether or not they consider those policies to be unjust. These tables also suggest that as a conflict over public policy implementation evolves, different issues become salient in mobilizing opposition. Concern for test scores and concern for alienation of rights by the court's action are important predictors of willingness to protest at all stages in the conflict (table 4.11). These concerns, however, become more widely held as the conflict evolves (tables 4.3 and 4.4). The increased concern for alienation of parents' rights is related to the attention-calling actions of political entrepreneurs who are opposed to busing (table 4.6). In the early stages, concern for unfairness strongly motivates opposition, but the salience of this issue may give way as other, more immediate perceived harms become the focus for conflict (table 4.9).

Racism, Perceived Injustice, and the Rationalization of Protest

So far Chapter 3 and the analysis here have treated racism and perceived injustice as two distinct patterns of belief that rationalize, in contemporary and personal terms, the doctrine of voluntary compliance and antibusing protest. Chapter 3 finds that racism is correlated with opposition to busing but points to the necessity for additional explanatory concepts because of (1) the trend away from white supremacist belief in the American public; and (2) the high level of opposition to busing among those who, by the usual defini-

Table 4.11   *Alienation of Rights and Protest*

	Percent in Favor of:			
	Defiance Wave 3	Boycott Wave 3	Resistance Wave 3	Boycott Wave 5
Opinion on whether children should always attend neighborhood schools:				
Strong agree	67	64	86	52
Agree	48	59	68	27
Disagree	22	33	48	34
Opinion on amount of influence of parents on school policy compared to amount deserved:				
Much Less	65	65	89	47
Less	52	59	70	40
Right, more	51	47	62	33

Note: Question wordings: see Appendix 1, nos. 27, 28, 30, 31, 14–17.
    Data are combined from samples of white residents of six Boston neighborhoods.
    Data show responses of those personally opposed to busing at the time of the interview.
    Patterns shown are significant (.05) when racial prejudice/fear and strength of antibusing opinion are controlled.

tion, would not be considered racist. The analysis in this chapter finds that the injustice frame of reference also correlates with anti-busing protest and is widespread, adding greatly to our ability to explain the high level of opposition to busing.[12]

The next few pages show that the injustice frame takes on another dimension of importance as well: belief in white supremacy does not, in general, lead to support for antibusing protest unless it is accompanied by a perception of injustice and social harm. The injustice frame, in other words, mediates or "explains" (in the statistical sense) the relationship between most of the white supremacy measures and support for antibusing protest shown in table 3.4. One way to illustrate this finding is to begin with the relationship between racism and protest shown in table 3.4, and then show what the pattern of percentages in that table is when the measures of injustice are controlled. This technique is known as "standardization" (Rosenberg 1962; Davis 1984) or "regression-adjustment" (Taylor 1984b; Kmenta 1971).[13] If, in the standardized table, the effects of racism become insignificant, then the impact of the injustice frame as a mediating variable is confirmed.

Table 4.12 shows the standardized relationship between each measure of prejudice and willingness to protest.[14] The first column shows the percent who say they would defy the court order if they

12. It is not possible to comment on trends in the perception of injustice and social harm caused by mandatory desegregation since the appropriate questions are rarely asked in surveys. Adding such measures to the data base for understanding American race relations is a high priority.

13. The exact procedure for regression-adjustment used here is described in a previous publication (Taylor 1984b). In brief, the method uses a weighted-regression technique to calculate partial slopes relating prejudice to willingness to protest, controlling for perceived injustice. The percentages in the table are then recalculated using the partial slopes to determine how much the adjusted percent willing to engage in protest within each category of prejudice deviates from the overall percent willing to protest.

14. The wave 1 injustice measures are used as control variables when calculating regression-adjusted percentages for the wave 1 dependent variables, except for cases (test scores, number of imbalanced schools, school board responsibility for imbalance court's right to go against popular opinion) where only wave 2 measures are available. The wave 5 injustice measures are used when calculating regression-adjusted percentages for the wave 5 dependent variable except for two cases (Garrity's right to go against popular opinion, public opposition does not justify delay in implementation) where only wave 3 measures are available.

Table 4.12   *Racism, Fear of Minority Concentration and Protest, Controlling for Injustice Frame Measures*

	Percent Willing to:		
	Defy Court Order Wave 1	Boycott Public Schools Wave 1	Boycott Public Schools Wave 5
Whites have a right to segregated neighborhoods:			
Agree			48
Disagree			39
Object if black comes home to dinner:			
Object			53
Not object			39
Blacks should not push:			
Agree			46
Disagree			38
Object to school:			
10% black	60	57*	
10%–50% black	52	42*	
No objection	49	31*	
General preference:			
Separation	60*	59*	53*
In between	59*	46*	47*
Integration	41*	28*	29*

Note: Question wordings: see Appendix 1, nos. 1–5, 14–17.

Data are combined from samples of white residents of six Boston neighborhoods.

Data shown are percentages standardized for perceived injustice (see text and notes for exact measures used).

Asterisk (*) denotes significant partial effects (.05 level) of prejudice/fear.

were on the school board. Unlike table 3.4, however, the percentages now show how much difference there is between those who are
prejudiced and those who are not after taking account of the tendency of those who are more prejudiced to be more likely than
others to view the issues in terms of the injustice frame of reference.
The pattern reflects what methodologists call the "partial correlation" or "partial percentage difference" between prejudice and willingness to protest (Davis 1984; Taylor 1984b). The asterisks in the
table show instances where the relationship remains significant (at
the .05 level).

The first three racial attitude questions analyzed in table 4.12
ask whether or not one agrees with the statement "blacks shouldn't
push where they are not wanted," whether or not one agrees with the
statement "whites have a right to live in segregated neighborhoods,"
and whether one would object if a family member brought a black
friend home to dinner. Table 3.4 in the previous chapter shows a
strong relationship between each of these measures and willingness
to protest. Table 4.12 shows, however, that for these measures the
relationship between racism and protest is explained by the injustice
frame variables. Each measure shows no significant "partial" relationship to willingness to protest.

The fourth set of figures shows that those who fear even a small
level of minority concentration—i.e., 10 percent—are much more
likely than others to favor a public school boycott. The asterisks in
table 4.12 show that the effect of fear of minority concentration on
willingness to protest is significant even after the injustice frame
measures are controlled. The results are not completely consistent,
however. Those who fear even low concentrations are only a little
more likely than others to favor defiance of the court in other ways.

The fifth set of figures in table 4.12 shows that those who say
they prefer "separation" or "something in between" are significantly
more likely than those who say they prefer "integration" to support
the school boycott and other acts of defiance.[15] The pattern remains

15. Schuman et al. (1983) report a number of instances where questions
about preference for integration, separation, or something in between show different trends and correlations than questions more directly asking about white supremacy and racist opinions. The findings in this chapter reinforce their call for
new, differentiated approaches to studying the social and political significance of
racial attitudes.

highly significant even after the injustice measures are controlled.[16]

What is the significance of the mediating role of perceived injustice? One interpretation of the findings in table 4.12 is that, at least for the top three measures, the injustice frame is a rationalization of racial prejudice. Those who are prejudiced are more likely than others to view mandatory busing in the light of the injustice frame because this point of view allows them to challenge busing in terms of issues that mention fairness and safety but not, at least explicitly, race. This might, for instance, be the correct interpretation of the finding in table 3.2 of more support for desegregation plans that minimize challenges to parental control and make exposure to minority concentration and inner city school conditions voluntary for whites. If Judge Garrity's plan was designed to preserve parental control over school choice and voluntary participation, there would be little change in the pattern of segregation that was established before the time of his ruling. Plans that do not challenge the parent's right to control educational choice also, as a practical matter, minimize the amount of desegregation that is achieved. Proposals that prevent racial integration in the name of minimizing risks to safety and educational quality also minimize a fortiori the amount of desegregation that is achieved at all. This argument is consistent with the view that whites' objections to busing primarily indicate "symbolic racism" (Sears et al. 1979; Sears et al. 1980; McConahay and Hough 1976; McConahay 1982; Kinder and Sears 1981).[17]

16. The last two prejudice measures remain significant predictors of willingness to protest even after controlling (1) strength of antibusing opinion (as a check for convergent/discriminant validity, see note to table 4.6), and (2) religion (see Chapter 5).

17. Other considerations suggest that symbolic racism, however, is not the full explanation of the findings. Some of the prejudice measures—i.e., those in the bottom two rows of table 4.12—remain as significant predictors of willingness to protest even after the "symbolic" arguments are controlled. This suggests that symbolic racism is, at best, a partial explanation. An even broader question has to do with the interpretation of the injustice frame measures. Part of the reason perceived injustice motivates protest is that people believe their interests will no longer be served by the system. The social harm measures suggest specific interests that people may believe are threatened by a busing order. The injustice frame measures, in other words, may partly reflect self-interests in maintaining the status quo. To the extent that this is true, the self-interest effects on willingness to protest also contradict·the symbolic racism model. The purpose of this note is not to challenge the

The findings on the injustice frame show the important mediating role of "rationalizing" perceptions. Table 4.12 shows that, as far as understanding willingness to protest, it is more important to know people's views on the injustice frame than it is to know the distribution of public opinion on most matters of racial tolerance. Supremacists who do not believe the court order is unjust and socially harmful are not likely to join antibusing protests. On the other hand, those who reject white supremacy but who view the issues in terms of the injustice frame are likely to protest desegregation. One caveat that must be added here and to the next few paragraphs is that the statements about the impact of racism do not apply for fears about minority concentration. Concerns about this issue, which apparently become more salient during desegregation, strongly and directly affect willingness to protest, whatever one's views on the injustice frame. The significance of this finding and the steps that might be taken to deal with this fear during a time of school desegregation are discussed in Chapter 3.

This is not to discount the importance of racism for understanding the history of the conflict, the contemporary issues, or the interests at stake (Rubin 1972, 1976). Racist beliefs are discomforting and socially objectionable. But those who hold racist beliefs are not subject to legal action unless they act to impede the law. To understand public willingness to take actions against school desegregation, the analysis in this chapter shows that, for the most part, it is the perception of injustice that is critical. Whites who believe busing is unfair, unjust, and socially harmful are more likely to contribute to protest whether they favor white supremacy or not.

This insight about the impact of the injustice frame also helps to understand the ways that community leadership and mass media contribute to antibusing mobilization. The kinds of actions and statements that do the most to inflame antibusing conflict are those that contribute to the perception of threat and injustice and to the belief that threat and injustice are acceptable reasons for protest.

This chapter, and the previous one, have shown that without the widespread perception of injustice there would not be antibusing mobilization. Results I have seen from surveys in other cities sug-

---

findings of symbolic racism research so much as it is to add to its discussion of ways to define and measure self-interest.

gest, however, that widespread perception of injustice is not, in itself, enough to cause antibusing protest. For school desegregation conflict to occur, a widespread feeling of injustice must be present *along with* political circumstances, political actors, and political perceptions that enhance the likelihood of mobilization. These are the topics studied in Part II of this book.

Part Two
Political Process and Desegregation Protest

While I entertained doubt as to the perfectability of man, I have come to believe that most of us are better than we usually have a chance to be.

Harry Ashmore, Editor
The Arkansas Gazette

5 | Religion, Politics, and the Boston Conflict

The Church and Civil Rights Politics

There is a tradition of organized religious involvement in American racial politics. In the decade prior to Judge Garrity's order in Boston, black and white churches played a key role, providing an emotional, financial, and organizational base for the civil rights movement (Oberschall 1973; McAdam 1982). John Lewis, president of the Student Nonviolent Coordinating Committee, observed:

> Many Negroes . . . were involved in the movement out of a strong moral, religious feeling, conviction. Sharecroppers, poor people, would come to the mass meetings because they were in the church. People saw the mass meetings as an extension of the Sunday services. (Quoted in Watters 1971, p. 24)

Martin Luther King wrote of the religious basis for individual involvement in the movement:

> The invitational periods at the mass meetings, when we asked for volunteers, were much like those invitational periods that occur every Sunday morning in Negro churches, when the pastor projects the call to those present to join the church. By twenties, thirties and forties people came forward to join our army. (King 1963, p. 59)

Many authors have noted, favorably, that the segregation of religion in America provides blacks with an independent base for community organizing (Matthews and Prothro 1966; Mays and Nicholson

1969; Washington 1964). But religious segregation also means that whites may capitalize on church organization to oppose black interests. At the time of the Boston conflict there were few documented instances of church resources providing support for opponents of desegregation and little appreciation of the impact church resources could have if they were directed against the civil rights movement. However, the evidence in this chapter shows that, in spite of the intentions of Cardinal Medeiros and other Catholic leaders, some of the church's organizational resources—networks of membership, communication, and leadership—played a significant role in stimulating antibusing protest and amplifying perceptions of the extensiveness of opposition to the court order.

The Yankee-immigrant conflict over city government autonomy (see Chapter 4) was always, for demographic reasons, a struggle along religious and ethnic lines. Boston is one of the most predominantly Catholic cities in the United States: current estimates place the Catholic population at 70 percent. Outside the city, the Catholic population in Massachusetts is much closer to the national average: about 25 percent (Hannon 1980). In addition, for many years before the school desegregation conflict, the political leadership of the city was concentrated in the hands of Catholics. At the time of Judge Garrity's order, for instance, the mayor and all the members of the city council were Catholic.

This chapter shows how some of the organizational resources of the Catholic church were co-opted into the struggle between ethnic and religious groups over administration of local school policy. The point of the chapter is not to argue that the conflict was "religious" instead of "ethnic." Rather, the purpose of the chapter is to analyze co-optation of church resources. What dynamics of church politics and what strains between the church and its constituency led to this outcome? What was the impact of these resources on the dynamics of desegregation protest?

As with all other chapters in this book, the argument here relies in part on tabulations from the survey and in part on other sources of historical and contextual information. The analysis of changes in church policy makes use of church records and statements in the public media, using survey evidence to document the pressure of lay opinion on church guidelines for desegregation. As explained more fully in the section on methodology in Chapter 1, church records and statements in the media also provide evidence of the intentions and actions of church leadership. This information, taken along with the results of the survey, together show how the actions of leadership as well as other church resources affect the community's response to busing.

Church Involvement and Social Movement Success: Theory

What is it about church involvement that makes it a significant factor in the success of social movements? The church is usually one of the most stable, best-endowed organizations in the community. As an "indigenous community organization," the church is "an important source of resources that, when mobilized for political purposes, has been proven capable of generating organized insurgency" (McAdam 1982, p. 32).

What church resources figure in the success of a social movement? The church usually comprises one of the most strongly established networks of leadership, communication, and social participation in a community. Studies consistently show that movement participants are very likely to be recruited along established lines of social and organizational interaction (Gerlach and Hine 1970; Pinard 1971; Oberschall 1973; Snow, Zurcher, and Ekland-Olson 1980). Interpersonal links among organizational members provide a ready-made network for the flow of information, making it easier to develop a collective definition of political issues, a favorable assessment of the size of one's constituency, and a favorable feeling about one's chance for success. In McAdam's words:

> One of the central problems of insurgency . . . is whether favorable shifts in political opportunities will be defined as such by a large enough group of people to facilitate collective protest. . . . Existent organizations . . . figure prominently in the development of this insurgent consciousness. . . . In the absence of strong interpersonal links to others, people are likely to feel powerless to change conditions even if they perceive present conditions as favorable to such efforts. . . . One effect of existent organizations is to render this process of "cognitive liberation" more likely. (1982, pp. 48–50)

Church leaders are already established as effective "attention-callers" (see Chapter 4 for a definition of this term) in the community and are already experienced in some of the organizational skills nec-

essary for successful collective political action. When church resources become associated with a political movement, interpersonal
and emotional rewards arising from church participation become
linked with movement participation as well. A sense of common
purpose between the church and the movement develops, giving
movement goals a justification in religious terms and making movement participation seem to be a logical extension of religious belief.

Not only do studies of collective action suggest that participation
of community institutions make social movements more powerful,
without some kind of organizational involvement, movement success
appears to be less likely. A lack of leadership, communication networks and coordinated membership is often enough to keep potentially contentious group mobilization at bay (Tilly 1978; Gamson
1975).

This chapter reviews the evidence showing organized religious
involvement in the Boston antibusing movement and examines survey evidence to shed light on ways this involvement affected the
development of the conflict.

Early Church Support for Desegregation in Boston

In the very early stages of the school desegregation conflict—i.e.,
in the 1960s—the Catholic church in Boston was part of the ecumeni-
cal coalition of American churches supporting the civil rights movement. In April 1965, in response to black school boycotts and other
actions, an advisory committee to the Massachusetts Commissioner
of Education which included Richard Cardinal Cushing, the Roman
Catholic archbishop of Boston published a census of racially imbalanced schools in the state. In response to the advisory committee
report (and other actions as well), the Massachusetts legislature enacted the Racial Imbalance Act (RIA) in August 1965.

The RIA was the most stringent school integration law of any
state in the nation. It required local school committees to take affirmative action to eliminate racial imbalance, using such techniques as
redistricting, pupil reassignment, strategic placement of new schools
and busing. Strong sanctions were available for use against local
school committees, for instance, the state commissioner of education
could refuse to certify all state school aid for that system. When the
report was accepted by the governor, the archbishop and 300 other
clergymen from all denominations joined in a march on the state

house to show their support for its recommendations (*Boston Globe*, 22 June 1965).

In 1972 Humberto Medeiros (Cushing's successor as Boston archbishop in March 1973) published a pastoral letter on race relations that was the most important statement by the American Catholic church on civil rights issued during this period (Hannon 1980). The letter, titled *Man's Cities and God's Poor,* was a plea for social justice and racial equality that strongly supported the transportation of pupils to achieve that end (U.S. Commission on Civil Rights 1975, p. 476).

In February 1974 (four months before Judge Garrity's decision but after enforcement of the RIA had begun), the Boston Catholic church took steps to assure compliance with its pastoral letter. The Archdiocesan Board of Education, with Cardinal Medeiros as president, announced its decision to restrict transfers from public to Catholic schools. Guidelines were announced to regulate the conditions under which a transfer could be accepted. By these guidelines, applications could not be accepted unless:

1. The acceptance improves racial balance.
2. The application is due to change of address of the family.
3. The family already has other children in the school.
4. The number accepted in a school conforms with the average number in previous years.
5. The acceptance policy is consistent with principles of social justice as enunciated by official teachings of the Church.

Subsequent Catholic Opposition to Busing

The early attempts at moral leadership by Cardinal Medeiros and the Catholic church hierarchy did not prevail. Antibusing leaders found a receptive home for their rhetoric in the Catholic doctrine of "parent's control over children's education"—at least as this doctrine was interpreted by the average parishioner. The strength and intensity of community opposition to busing brought the laity into conflict with church leadership over the issue of school transfers as well as other types of symbolic support for Judge Garrity's order. The imprudence of extended confrontation between the church and the laity, and the slackness of bureaucratic control between the upper and lower levels of the church hierarchy, led to changes in church policy and practice in a direction more supportive of the antibusing movement.

Cultural Filters and the Catholic Experience

Catholic tradition emphasizes the parent's right to decide on the appropriate type of education for children and minimizes (to the point of understating) the state's interest and authority in such matters. The church's position on parents' rights was established well before desegregation became an issue and had divided Catholics from the state government for more than a century before Judge Garrity's order (see Ravitch 1974). The tradition of support for, and conflict over, parochial education is, in other words, a cultural filter for the desegregation issue for Catholics.

The church emphasizes the parent's right and responsibility for controlling educational choice because the church wants to encourage enrollment in parochial schools. To many Catholics, however, the principle of a parent's right to control the child's education appears to be recognized in American law since our society freely accommodates public, private, and parochial educational choices. Catholics using the public schools may think they have the legal right to control their children's schooling because of the existence of parochial schools, because the church supports parents using these schools, and because there have been few challenges to the myth that the right to parental control of education is the legal basis for the existence of these schools. To borrow, once again, Max Weber's terminology, the experience of Catholic parents makes them more likely to believe they have a right in usage, if not a right in law, to control educational choices for their children.

Catholic belief in the natural right of parents to control educational choice was explicitly raised at almost every stage of the antibusing conflict in Boston. In November 1973, Governor Francis Sargent successfully vetoed legislation requiring parental consent before a child could be bused beyond the nearest school. State Representative Raymond Flynn of South Boston (now mayor of Boston) vowed to introduce other legislation to guarantee "the custodial rights of parents over their children" (*Boston Globe*, 11 November 1974). In the courtroom Federal Judge Arthur Garrity and State Representative Flynn recorded the following exchange:

"Parents," said Garrity, "do not have the right to keep their children out of school. Parent's rights are limited. The state has the responsibility for their education and welfare. . . ."

Rising from his seat among the spectators, Flynn said that he had been brought up and schooled under the philosophy of St. Thomas. He said he was taught that parents have a natural right which takes precedence over the state's rights. (*Boston Globe,* 11 November 1974)

During protests which marked the opening of schools in September 1974, parents carried placards that read, "God gave them to us, Judge Garrity is taking them away" (*Boston Globe,* 9 September 1974).

Lay Opposition to Busing

The survey shows approximately 90 percent opposition to busing among Boston Catholics. This is significantly higher than the 75 to 80 percent opposition to busing among non-Catholics in Boston and significantly higher than the 80 percent opposition to busing among both Catholics and non-Catholics in comparable American cities of the Northeast and Midwest. The Boston survey data are shown in table 5.1. The data for other cities are from the General Social Survey (GSS).

The correlation between religion and opposition to busing in Boston is not characteristic of the pattern in other American cities. The exceptionally high level of opposition to busing among Catholics is probably due to the "targeting" of the busing issue on the

Table 5.1   *Religion and Anti-Busing Opinion*

	Percent Opposed to Busing				
	Wave 1	Wave 2	Wave 3	Wave 4	Wave 5
Catholic	88	93	91	89	94
Non-Catholic	76	76	78	76	79

Note: Question wording: see Appendix 1, no. 5.
   Data are combined from samples of white residents of six Boston neighborhoods.

Catholic population in Massachusetts, the willingness of Boston church officials to contribute to nonviolent mobilization, and the resonance between Catholic doctrine on parental control and the mass appeal of the antibusing movement to "restore alienated rights."

The conflict between the laity and church leadership focused on the guidelines governing transfers to the Catholic schools which were announced in February 1974. During the years preceding Judge Garrity's order, desegregation in the South was frequently a catalyst for the growth of religious denominational schools (Nevin and Bills 1976). The growth of private schools in the South was particularly pronounced among the more fundamentalist Protestant sects, many of whom were already leaning toward the establishment of their own schools because of the Supreme Court's decision removing religious observances and instruction from the public schools (Cataldo et al. 1978, p. 37). The February 1974 guidelines were devised to keep this from happening in Boston. Nonetheless, the demand for alternative, parochial schooling was very high.

Approximately two-thirds of the Catholics in Boston neighborhoods advocate an abandonment of all restrictions on transfers and admission to parochial schools. This result is shown in the bottom row of table 5.2. The demand for removal of barriers to transfer and admission is also quite high among non-Catholics—i.e., about 61 percent.

Table 5.2 shows that Catholic demand for open access to parochial schools is greater among those who are opposed to the court order. Even so, 44 percent of Catholics personally in favor of the court order still think the cardinal should open access to parochial schools. Among those in favor of busing, more than half think Catholic schools should be available to all. Among those with children already in Catholic schools (who, by the new guidelines, enjoy unhindered access for themselves), fully 64 percent still favor open access for everyone else. Finally, support for open transfer is not related to the measures most often used by survey researchers to study racial fear and racial prejudice (see Chapter 2). For example, those in favor of separation of the races are about as likely to favor open admission as those who favor integration. Those who would object if a family member brought a black friend home for dinner are about as likely to favor open admission as those who would not object.

Lay Confrontation with Church Policies

Catholic demands for open access to parochial schools eventually brought the laity into direct confrontation with church leadership. In October 1974, Catholic groups in South Boston and Hyde Park pledged to boycott church fundraising for the United Way because of the Cardinal's enforcement of the new transfer guidelines (*Boston Globe*, 9 October 1974 and 16 October 1974).

Table 5.2   *The Demand Open Transfer to Parochial Schools*

	Percent Favoring No Restrictions Wave 5
Personal opinion on Judge Garrity's decision:	
Favor	44
Oppose	74
Personal opinion on busing for desegregation:	
Favor	53
Oppose	68
Personal preference for integration, separation, or something in between:	
Integregation	66
Between	69
Separation	64
Objection to black at home for dinner	
No objection	67
Objection	72
Family status, access to parochial schools	
No children	39
Preschool only	62
Public school only	71
Any parochial school	64
Total for all Catholics	67

Note: Question wordings: see Appendix 1, nos. 2, 4, 5, 6, 36.

Data are combined from samples of white residents of six Boston neighborhoods.

Data show percentages among Catholic neighborhood residents.

Two months later, an attempt by Cardinal Medeiros to take the message of the pastoral letter to the neighborhoods resulted in a heated confrontation and a diplomatic retreat:

> In December 1975 Cardinal Medeiros went to South Boston for a church service. He criticized the people of South Boston for their intransigent opposition to desegregation. Citing the low percentage of Catholics in attendance at Sunday masses, he attributed their hard-heartedness to a lack of faith and Christian committment.
>
> South Boston was less chastened than outraged. Protests were immediately forthcoming, often with the support of clergy. Within a few days Cardinal Medeiros attributed his remarks to tiredness and the stress he had experienced as a major figure in the desegregation controversy. He retracted his remarks about the people of South Boston and apologized for casting aspersions on their morality and spirituality, in a letter read at Sunday masses in South Boston's churches (Hannon 1980, p. 109).

As the cardinal's actions during this incident suggest, it is usually imprudent for church leadership to remain in confrontation with its laity.[1]

Conflict within the Church Hierarchy

As the conflict between the church and its parishioners became more pronounced, strains within the church hierarchy became more pronounced, which led to inconsistency (and even a reversal in some instances) in the church's position regarding Judge Garrity's order.

At the time of the court order, Cardinal Medeiros was new to his position and new to Boston. He did not come to Boston until 1970 and did not become cardinal until 1973. Besides being new, he was perceived to be an outsider ethnically. He was the first bishop of Boston in more than 125 years who was not Irish-American.

Unfamiliarity with desegregation, particularly at the lower levels of the church hierarchy, also contributed to organizational strain. In its day to day operations, the Catholic church in Boston had little

---

1. An analysis of the imprudence of conflict between church leadership and laity over matters of family planning is reported by Greeley, MacCready, and McCourt (1976).

contact with black Americans. In Boston, as in most American cities, there are few black Catholics, and residential segregation tends to restrict them to a few inner-city parishes. For most priests and lay Catholics, the appearance of a single black person in their church on Sunday would be a rare experience. Less than 1 percent of the priests in the archdiocese were black. The vast majority of priests were from Irish, urban, working-class families and neighborhoods (Hannon 1980).

A survey of priests in Boston parishes after the second year of desegregation implementation found:

> Priests in minority parishes are much more likely than others to support the court order. Those in white parishes who had previously lived and worked in a minority parish were more active than those who had not in defusing potentially violent situations and in trying to allay the busing-related fears of their white parishoners (Hannon 1980).

But the lower echelons of the church hierarchy had virtually no contact with the blacks in Boston. Few priests or parishes, therefore, experienced these benefits of integration.

The lack of involvement with integration and the lack of sympathy for the message of the cardinal's pastoral letter within the hierarchy created an organizational dilemma for the church. Church leaders could not realistically hope to ensure a consistent probusing message in communications between church officials and parishioners. Some church spokesmen took it upon themselves to publicly differ with the cardinal's views in his pastoral letter. In some cases church officials even became spokesmen for the antibusing cause, calling attention to the injustice of the court order and suggesting ways to oppose the order while staying within the general boundary of nonviolent resistance.

In March 1974, the cardinal convened a seminar for priests "to explain to them and to offer to them theological perceptions on the moral correctness of integration." The testimony at this seminar of Bishop Lawrence Riley, auxiliary bishop of the Boston region of the archdiocese, however, differed greatly from that of the cardinal:

> Please God . . . public officials, education experts, and our citizens must strive without ceasing to devise some plan for integration that need not resort to mandatory transportation of students.

In August 1974, just before the beginning of Phase I, the clergy of South Boston gathered to make a televised statement on the busing issue. They neither supported nor did they overtly oppose the school boycott. They suggested instead that an individual's conscience should be his or her guide:

> We believe that the people of the South of Boston are well aware of their obligations to promote equality of opportunity and of education for all. We know that the vast majority of the people in our community are fairminded. . . . We do not question the motives of those in our community who have taken positions on either side of this issue. Rather we presume their good faith and lack of prejudice.

As public reaction to Judge Garrity's order became more negative, statements by church officials increasingly called attention to the rationale and method for nonviolent protest. A November 18 editorial in the citywide Catholic newspaper, the *Pilot*, criticized violent protest but not protest per se. One Catholic pastor explained the rationale for nonviolent opposition in terms reminiscent of the argument for civil disobedience during the Montgomery bus boycott:

> The antibusing forces have a good slogan, Restore Our Alienated Rights (ROAR). The coincidence of their fight with the bicentennial of the American Revolution can be a weapon in the fight. . . . They are fighting against one specific immoral infringement of their rights and nothing else. It is vital that nothing distract the antibusing movement from its simple objective and that its members avoid all action that can be interpreted, or distorted so as to obscure their real cause or impede its attainment. (Fr. J. McMahon, Pastor of St. Mary's Church in Quincy, quoted in the *South Boston Tribune*, 20 February 1975)

On November 25, the *Pilot* made a distinction between its support for integration and its opposition to the means for attaining it in Boston. Without explicitly mentioning it, the church lent its approval to the doctrine of voluntary compliance that had followed in the wake of desegregation protest in every city from Dallas to Wilmington.

Private conversations between church officials, priests, and the laity are, of course, not available for historical analysis. Hannon's personal interviews, however, suggest that parish priests tacitly supported public statements favoring the doctrine of voluntary compliance and nonviolent resistance:

> The priests of South and East Boston tended to avoid the issue of desegregation when speaking to parish groups and writing in parish bulletins or newsletters. For some, reasons for this included their own belief that busing should be resisted, in a non-violent fashion, but that it was unwise for a priest to publicly say so. Others who were more supportive of busing refrained from expressing their views because they believed they would not change anyone's mind and would only antagonize and alienate the parishioners. (Hannon 1980)

In sum, the threat of extended conflict with parishioners and the inability to ensure consistent support for the court order in the hierarchy forced church leadership to change its position on the busing controversy. A person's decision to protest the court order and boycott the public schools came to be defined as a matter of individual conscience and choice. Church opposition to public protest came to be focused specifically on condemning violence and not on other forms of civil disobedience.

Ultimately, the church weakened its position on school transfers as well. During the first year of desegregation, only three Catholic schools were found to have violated the cardinal's February 1974 guidelines (described at the beginning of this chapter). No official action was taken by the church hierarchy with regard to these schools. In January 1975 the Archdiocese Board of Education re-revised the guidelines. The new rules were interpreted by many, including the media, as weakening of the policy. There were many more transfers into Catholic schools in 1975 than in 1974, and many more schools (22) were identified as policy violators by the Archdiocesan Board of Education (Hannon 1980, pp. 61–62).

Church Involvement and Antibusing Mobilization

Survey measures are not available to determine the impact of particular contributions of the resources of the Catholic church to antibusing mobilization. Respondents were not asked whether they were influenced by the parish priests' arguments for voluntary compliance with the court order, whether they read the justifications for civil disobedience published in church newsletters, whether they discussed the church's doctrine of parental authority, whether the matter of antibusing protest arose in discussions with their neighbors at church meetings, or the strength of their identification as Catholics. The next several tables suggest, however, that Boston neighborhood residents were affected by these factors.

Religion and the Perception of Widespread Opposition to Busing

Catholics are somewhat more likely than non-Catholics to believe there is widespread community opposition to Judge Garrity's order. The data are shown in table 5.3. The first set of figures shows that just after Judge Garrity's decision (wave 3) Catholics opposed to busing believe that, on average, about 14 percent of their neighbors are in favor of the court. Table 5.3 controls for the possibility that the religious difference arises because of the greater tendency of

Table 5.3   *Religion and the Perception of Public Opinion against the Court*

	Average Perceived Percentage of Neighbors Agreeing with Judge Garrity's Decision				
	Wave 3				
Catholics	14%				
Non-Catholics	19%				

	Percent Saying Other Parents in the Neighborhood Are "Very Strongly Opposed" to Busing				
	Wave 1	Wave 2	Wave 3	Wave 4	Wave 5
Catholics	83	91	86		85
Non-Catholics	71	84	83		84

Note: Question wordings: see Appendix 1, nos. 48, 49.

Data are combined from samples of white residents of six Boston neighborhoods.

Data show responses of those personally opposed to busing at the time of the interview.

Patterns shown are significant (.05) when racial prejudice/fear and strength of antibusing opinion are controlled.

those who are opposed to busing to project their views onto their neighbors by showing the perception of public opinion among Catholics and non-Catholics who are personally opposed to busing.[2] For non-Catholics the perceived level of support for the court order in the community is higher, about 19 percent. (These figures are average scores on a question asking the percent of the neighbors one believes are in agreement with the court; the difference in averages is significant at the .05 level according to a t-test.) The second set of figures in table 5.3 shows that in the period before the court order (waves 1 and 2) Catholics are more likely than non-Catholics to perceive their neighbors as "very strongly opposed" to busing as a means for desegregation. The religious difference on this question, however, disappears after the court order (waves 3 and 5) as the proportion of non-Catholics who view their neighbors as "very strongly opposed" to busing rises.

The link between perceived community opposition and willingness to protest is explored in Chapter 7. There is a strong relationship between these factors. Those influences that increase the perception of cohesive community opposition add to the climate of opinion supportive of antibusing mobilization and also increase the likelihood an individual will join in protest.

Not only do Catholics believe that public opinion is more strongly aligned against the court than do non-Catholics (at least during the early stage of community reaction), they are somewhat more likely to believe that the level of public participation in protest action is higher. The data are in table 5.4. Once again, to control for "projection" effects, data are shown for individuals opposed to busing. Catholics, compared to non-Catholics, see a greater willingness among parents in their neighborhood to participate in antibusing actions:

1. Catholics are more likely than non-Catholics to say people in the neighborhood will take action against the court order (wave 3).

2. In addition to controlling for antibusing opinions, the analyses in tables 5.3, 5.4, 5.5, and 5.8 were also performed controlling for more detailed measures of the intensity of antibusing opinion, racial prejudice, and when possible using repeated-measures panel analysis techniques. Nothing from the more detailed analyses challenges the discriminant validity and causal ordering suggested by the findings as they are presented in the tables here.

Table 5.4   *Religion and Perceived Public Protest against the Court*

	Wave 3	Wave 4	Wave 5
Percent saying the neighbors will "resist," "defy," "openly oppose" or "avoid" Phase I:			
Catholic	68		
Non-Catholic	62		
Percent saying the neighbors did "defy," "demonstrate against," "avoid," "interfere with," or "work to oppose" Phase I:			
Catholic		83	
Non-Catholic		74	
Percent saying the neighbors will "avoid," "demonstrate against," "openly oppose," or "make problems to hinder" Phase II:			
Catholic			80
Non-Catholic			70
Average perceived percentage boycotting public schools in early fall, 1974:			
Catholic		20%	
Non-Catholic		15%	
Percent saying boycott level has been "increasing" or "the same":			
Catholic		68	
Non-Catholic		61	
Percent saying the boycott will "increase" or "stay the same":			
Catholic		87	
Non-Catholic		82	
Average perceived percentage boycotting public schools in 1974/75:			
Catholic			35%
Non-Catholic			27%

Note: Question wordings: see Appendix 1, nos. 50–57.

Data are combined from samples of white residents of six Boston neighborhoods.

Data show responses of those personally opposed to busing at the time of the interview.

Patterns shown are significant (.05) when racial prejudice/fear and strength of antibusing opinion are controlled.

2. Catholics are more likely to believe their neighbors actually are taking actions against busing (wave 4).
3. Catholics are more likely to expect their neighbors to continue protesting the court order during Phase II (wave 5).

On the particular question of parental support for the public school boycott, Catholics are also more likely than non-Catholics to see greater support:

4. Catholics say a higher percent are boycotting the public schools than do non-Catholics (wave 4).
5. Catholics are more likely to believe the boycott is increasing (wave 4) and will continue to do so (wave 4).
6. And, finally, after the first year, Catholics believe a higher percent of parents participated in the school boycott than do non-Catholics (wave 5).

The findings in table 5.4 are weak but consistent. Four percentage differences are individually significant using the 7–8 percent criterion (7%, 9%, 10%, and 18%), one comparison is a difference of means more than twice its standard error (and therefore individually significant), and two percentage differences are in the hypothesized direction (5%, 6%), although they are not individually significant. When these results are considered together, the pattern should be considered to be significant. As explained in the discussion of statistical inference in Chapter 1, there is no simple formula for reworking the results in a complex percentage table to determine what the significance levels would be in a multiple indicator framework. By the rule of thumb suggested in Chapter 1, however, there is little question about the overall inference to be made: most of the comparisons are individually significant and the rest are in the "right" direction.

To what extent can we argue that Catholic perception of cohesive community opposition to Judge Garrity's order is due specifically to the involvement of church resources in the conflict? The evidence on this point is indirect but very persuasive. The literature explaining how people perceive the opinions and actions of those in the community around them is just beginning to develop (Taylor 1982; Salmon and Kline 1984; Glynn and McLeod 1984). Even at this early stage, however, there is agreement that perceptions of the content of public opinion are shaped by:

1. the content of communication networks of which an individual is a member;
2. the content of visual stimuli—including media, posters and other types of messages—to which the individual is exposed; and
3. the perceived opinions of "influentials" (Katz and Lazarsfeld 1955), "political entrepreneurs" (Frohlich et al. 1971), or "opinion leaders" whose views are taken as representative of blocs of individuals in the community.

Leadership, communication networks, and membership interaction are not only crucial for the success of social movements, they are also the social factors that most strongly influence people's perceptions of the opinions and actions of the community around them. Tables 5.3 and 5.4 suggest that Catholic church resources influenced peoples' perceptions of the cohesiveness of community resistance to the court order. The analysis in Chapter 7 shows that perception of widespread community opposition significantly increases the likelihood that someone will protest.

Religion and Support for Parents' Protests

Catholics appear to be more likely than non-Catholics to favor the public school boycott and neighborhood resistance to the court order. The data are in table 5.5. The first two sets of figures show that Catholics are more likely than non-Catholics to say parents should boycott the public schools and that the most important thing for parents in the neighborhood is to "resist," "defy," or "evade" Judge Garrity's recently announced decision.[3]

The Catholic versus non-Catholic difference is not consistent, however, for all measures of protest used in this book, and the data

---

3. As with previous tables, the figures are shown for Catholics personally opposed to busing at the time of the interview. In addition to the usual controls for intensity of antibusing opinion and racial attitudes, the relationships in table 5.5 were also tested controlling for the impact of perceived strength of community opposition on willingness to protest (see Chapter 6).

are too sparse to make a firm determination of the precise reason for the pattern. The third set of figures in table 5.5 shows that Catholics and non-Catholics are about equally likely to say they would support a school boycott if they were on the school board. The absence of a significant religious difference here may have to do with the variant wording of the question (compared with the other boycott question). Or the explanation may be that the third set of figures measures survey responses late in the conflict (wave 5) and that by this time the religious differences in mobilization began to even out, as suggested by the diminishing religious differences in perception of the extent of community antibusing mobilization in table 5.3.

Table 5.5   *Religion and Antibusing Protest*

	Wave 1	Wave 2	Wave 3	Wave 4	Wave 5
Percent supporting public school boycott by parents:					
Catholic	46		63		
Non-Catholics	26		48		
Percent saying people in neighborhood should "resist," "evade," or "work to reverse" the court order:					
Catholic			81		
Non-Catholic			70		
Percent supporting public school boycott (variant wording):					
Catholic					45
Non-Catholic					42
Percent supporting school committee defiance:					
Catholic	57		59		
Non-Catholic	57		58		

Note: Question wordings: see Appendix 1, nos. 14–17.
    Data are combined from samples of white residents of six Boston neighborhoods.
    Data show responses of those personally opposed to busing at the time of the interview.
    Patterns shown in the top two rows are significant (.05) when racial prejudice/fear and strength of antibusing opinion are controlled.

The fourth set of figures shows that Catholics are no more likely than non-Catholics to say they would favor defiance of the court order if they were members of the school committee. The absence of a relationship here cannot be explained by the tendency for religious differences to diminish as the controversy continues—the fourth set of figures are wave 1 and wave 3 measures. The explanation has to be in terms of the content of the questions. The first two sets of questions may dramatize the conflict between the rights of "the people"—i.e., parents or neighbors—and the courts in a way that the fourth set of questions does not. As explained earlier in this chapter, the doctrine of parent's control over education is one of the cultural filters strengthening Catholic antibusing protest. It may be that the first two sets of questions, which ask about parent's boycotts and resistance by "people in the neighborhood," tap an extra reservoir of hostility to busing among Catholics that questions about "school committee defiance" miss.[4]

The impact of participation in the Catholic network of leadership, communication, and membership on willingness to protest was significant. It increased the general perception of widespread community opposition and appears to have increased support for certain types of protests, at least during early stages of the conflict.

The Impact of the Cardinal's Leadership

The United States Commission on Civil Rights, in its analysis of the first year of the Boston school desegregation controversy, concluded:

> The leadership of the various groups which comprise the religious community of Boston was not as effective as it could have been in identifying and supporting moral issues confronting Boston during Phase I school desegregation. (1975)

The commission did not single out Cardinal Medeiros for criticism. The evidence suggests, however, that in spite of his initial efforts to support desegregation and the court order, his newness to the Boston church and the permeability of the church hierarchy to needs and

---

4. It was found in the previous chapter that the impact of antibusing leadership is significant but apparently limited to issues specifically voiced by leaders. In this chapter a focused impact is suggested as well.

demands of the lay public limited his effectiveness in this role. This chapter now explores the cardinal's effectiveness as a leader of public opinion and public reaction to the court order.

The Cardinal as Opinion Leader

An evaluation of the cardinal's effectiveness as a leader of public opinion begins with a consideration of the resources available to him:

1. The degree to which church laity respect him and his office. If there is little respect for the cardinal, then it is unlikely he can influence public acceptance of desegregation implementation.
2. The extent to which he can counter public disagreement with his position by the force of his appeals and by his personal example.

The kinds of resources available to the cardinal in his interactions with lay Catholics in the city are, in other words, similar to those of other types of incumbents who seek to influence public support for their policies (see Neustadt 1960).

Just after the beginning of the Phase I implementation, the wave 4 survey asks Boston neighborhood residents how much respect they have for the statements and policies "about the quality of education" of a number of figures active in the controversy, including Cardinal Medeiros. Among Catholics, 49 percent of Catholics say they have "a great deal" or "some" respect for the statements and policies of the cardinal. Among non-Catholics, the level of respect is about the same—i.e., 50 percent. The level of respect for the cardinal is about as high as for other public officials who are seen as being in favor of busing: Massachusetts Governor Francis Sargent, 48 percent; Boston Mayor Kevin White, 48 percent; and U.S. Senator Edward Kennedy, 47 percent.

What can the level of respect for the cardinal tell us about his power to lead public opinion? Table 5.6 shows the percentages for a threefold classification of Boston Catholics into:

1. Those who oppose busing and have "hardly any" or "no" respect for the Cardinal (49 percent).

Table 5.6   *Catholic Opinion on Busing and Respect for the Cardinal's Leadership*

Opinion on Busing Wave 4	Level of Respect for the Cardinal's Leadership Wave 4	Percent of Catholic Neighborhood Residents
Opposed	Hardly any, none	49
Opposed	Some, a great deal	41
Neutral, favor	All levels	10
		100

Note: Question wordings: see Appendix 1, no. 5, 37.
     Data are combined from samples of white residents of six Boston neighborhoods.
     Data show responses for Catholic neighborhood residents.

2. Those who oppose busing but have "some" or "a great deal" of respect for the Cardinal (41 percent).
3. Those who favor busing (10 percent).

The second and third groups comprise what might be called the constituency for the cardinal's probusing views among Boston Catholics. It is reasonable to say that Catholics who favor busing— group 3—will respond favorably to the cardinal's support for that policy. In this group, 83 percent have "a great deal" or "some" respect for the cardinal's statements and policies. It is also fair to say that those who oppose busing but who respect the cardinal—group 2—ought to be extremely susceptible to influence by his moral leadership.

One immediate observation is that the cardinal's ability to provide aggressive moral leadership is compromised by the extent of division of Catholic opinion over his views. The 51 percent constituency for the probusing position in the pastoral letter is, from the cardinal's point of view, too small. To risk the divisions in the neighborhoods and in the church that could result from stringently enforcing the February 1974 guidelines on school transfer or other policies urging strict compliance with the court order would be organizationally unwise. With the level of potential support this low, the cardinal must consider the possibility that confrontations between the laity and the church hierarchy over his pronouncements or over restrictive transfer policies could become more frequent, involve growing numbers of people, and produce growing losses for his organization. It is thus with a bit of hesitancy that the cardinal sought to explain his views to the Catholic laity and overcome their disagreement with the court order.

Effectiveness in Countering Public Disagreement

The cardinal's position was effectively publicized. Table 5.7 shows, at several points in the conflict, the percent of Catholics and non-Catholics who say the cardinal favors "busing both Negro and white children to achieve racial balance." At the time of the wave 1 survey, 45 percent of Catholics correctly perceive that the cardinal is in favor of busing and 28 percent do not know his position. The percent of Catholics correctly perceiving the cardinal's position jumps to more than 70 percent by the time of the wave 2 survey and to more than 80 percent by the end of the first year of the court order

Table 5.7   Perception of Cardinal Medeiros's Position on Busing

	Percent Saying the Cardinal Is:			
	Opposed	Neutral	Favorable	Don't Know
Catholics:				
Wave 1	10	17	45	28
Wave 2	6	4	74	17
Wave 3	3	4	77	15
Wave 5	6	6	82	6
Non-Catholics:				
Wave 1	13	18	21	49
Wave 2	7	7	62	25
Wave 3	3	4	71	22
Wave 5	3	9	77	12

Note: Question wordings: see Appendix 1, no. 38.
    Data are combined from samples of white residents of six Boston neighborhoods.

Table 5.8   *Respect for the Cardinal and Willingness to Accept Desegregation*

	Percent Saying the School Board Must Take Any Steps to Eliminate Segregation Wave 5	Percent Willing to Support Boycott Wave 5
Level of respect for the statements and policies of the Cardinal Wave 4:		
None, little	41	54
Some, a great deal	64	37

Note: Question wordings: see Appendix 1, nos. 37, 16, 18.

Data are combined from samples of white residents of six Boston neighborhoods.

Data show responses for Catholics personally opposed to busing at the time of the interview.

Patterns shown are significant (.05) when racial prejudice/fear and strength of antibusing opinion are controlled.

(wave 5).[5] In a related question asked in the wave 5 interview, 86 percent of Catholics (and 92 percent of non-Catholics) say they expect Cardinal Medeiros to urge neighborhood residents to comply with Phase 2 of the court order.

Did the Cardinal convert respect for his leadership into support for his views? The data answering this question are shown in table 5.8. If the cardinal was effective using his moral resources to overcome opposition to the court, then those who respect him should be less likely to protest and more likely to favor school board compliance. The survey data show the cardinal had some effectiveness as a moral leader. Those with a great deal of respect for him show a reduced willingness to protest, although the 37 percent in this group who would boycott is still a high number. Those with a great deal of respect show increased support for school board compliance, al-

5. Part of the trend is due to the fact that because of his newness to the city, Bostonians were initially unfamiliar with Cardinal Medeiros's position on most issues and not just his position on busing.

though the 64 percent in this group is far from the level that would be required for a general public mandate.

Conclusion: Religion, Politics, and Desegregation Protest

The Boston Catholic church did not set out to reinforce the antibusing movement. And yet, its final position favoring principled, nonviolent opposition to the court may have had this effect. The church was pushed to this position because strenuous, protracted opposition from the laity, coupled with an inability to ensure consistent support of the court order, meant that a stronger position favoring desegregation was imprudent and unenforceable.

Other evidence, however, suggests that the church, and particularly the cardinal, played a positive role supporting the court order as well. His views favoring desegregation were well publicized, and those respecting his views were more likely to temper their actions. It seems likely that the cardinal and other church leaders abandoned the possibility of leading the public toward acceptance of the court order. The goal of guiding the antibusing movement toward less dangerous, less violent forms of protest was more realistic. The argument that the church's emphasis on principled, nonviolent objection kept the situation from deteriorating further is defensible.

The heat of controversy in Boston brought forth new links between religion and the opponents of desegregation that subsequently have survived and affected American politics. During the Boston conflict a religious doctrine was developed that rejects the principle of social inequality, while justifying opposition to school integration for other reasons.

The argument that state authority should not extend to school enrollment policy because it is "too close to home" was advanced to justify the doctrine of voluntary compliance many times during the Second Reconstruction. John W. Davis, former U.S. representative, solicitor general, Democratic party presidential candidate, and attorney for South Carolina in a companion to the *Brown* case argued:

Is it not a fact that the very strength and fiber of our federal system is local self-government in those matters for which local action is competent? Is it not, of all the activities of government, the one which most nearly approaches the hearts and minds of people—the question of the education of their young? Is it not the height of wisdom that the manner in which that shall be conducted should be left to those most immediately affected by it, and that the wishes of the parents, both white and colored, should be ascertained before their children are forced into what may be an unwelcome contact?

Until the time of the Boston school desegregation controversy, the "too close to home" argument was not socially acceptable. It sounded too much like fear of social equality. The Catholic doctrine of parents' rights to control educational choice, however, allowed parents to reject desegregation that is "too close to home," while not requiring an embarrassing commitment to white supremacy and total apartheid. This was an important step for the development of the antibusing movement in America. Catholic belief also was reinterpreted to provide a further moral basis for the doctrine of voluntary compliance. Religious involvement in the Boston controversy was a small but significant step in the increased involvement of organized religion in American national politics. Some of the implications of this step are discussed in the summary and evaluation of Boston and American racial politics in Chapter 9.

6 | The Politics of Decentralized Enforcement: The Mayor's Role

Local Implementation of National Policy

This chapter analyzes the situation of local public officials as they cope with the conflicting demands of public opinion and the law on desegregation enforcement. Under what circumstances is a public official most likely to strive for smooth implementation of desegregation? Under what circumstances is a public official most likely to yield to public opinion and hinder desegregation?

After finding separate education to be unequal in *Brown,* the Supreme Court ordered a second hearing to determine how desegregation should be enforced. Its 1955 opinion in the second case, referred to as *Brown II,* assigned responsibility for implementation of school desegregation to local levels of the judiciary and to officials serving in local levels of government.[1]

---

1. The Court's opinion in *Brown II* states:

Because these cases arose under different local conditions and their disposition will involve a variety of local problems, we requested further argument on the question of relief. . . .

Full implementation of these constitutional principles may require solution of varied local school problems. School authorities have the primary responsibility for elucidating, assessing, and solving these problems; courts will have to consider whether the action of school authorities constitutes good faith implementation of the governing constitutional principles. Because of their proximity to local conditions and the possible need for further hearings, the courts which originally heard these cases can best perform this judicial appraisal. Accordingly, we believe it is appropriate to remand the cases to those courts.

The decision to rely on local levels of government for decentralized enforcement of the *Brown* decision was made because it was required by the organization of American government and because there was no effective alternative. Federalist features of our government make national supervision of school policy unwieldy. There is, for instance, no national police force that can efficiently ensure compliance with national school policies. Burke Marshall, civil rights chief of the Justice Department during the Kennedy years summarized the problem:

> We do not have a national police force and cannot provide protection in a physical sense for everyone whc is disliked because of the exercise of his civil rights. . . . There is no substitute under the federal system for the failure of local law enforcement responsibility. There is only a vacuum, which can be filled only rarely, with extraordinary difficulty, at monumental expense, and in a totally unsatisfactory fashion.

Supreme Court Justice Felix Frankfurter, during the *Brown* trial, acknowledged the problems that could be posed by community resistance against a more stringent requirement for immediate change:

> The Court would then have to intervene massively . . . to become, so to speak, a national board of education. . . . Nothing could be worse . . . than for this Court to make an abstract declaration and then have it evaded by tricks.

Frankfurter memorably argued that a ringing call for immediate desegregation in public education could be a futile exercise in the "mere imposition of a distant will."

The Supreme Court's acceptance of the principle of decentralized enforcement of *Brown II* is a recognition that local public officials possess resources that are essential for the successful implementation of school desegregation. Local officials mandated by the Court's decision to enact decentralized enforcement include school board members, the local police, other public officials such as the mayor and federal circuit court judges. In the language of Chapter 4, these officials must act as political entrepreneurs to help coordinate the attainment of peaceful desegregation. They must "call attention" to the reasons for compliance and the limited gains that are expected to result from defiance or disobedience. They must use whatever policing or enforcement powers are available to them in an affirmative manner to implement the Court's ruling.

The principle of decentralized enforcement of school desegregation conflicts with another principle of government in America: that local politics should be controlled by a democratic electoral process. The principle of democratic control requires that local officials be sensitive to popular opinion on the policies they pursue. Local officials are therefore faced with a dilemma caused by contradictory definitions of their responsibilities toward desegregation enforcement. The *Brown II* ruling makes desegregation enforcement by local officials a requirement of the law. But the realities of democratic control require local officials to be responsive to popular opinion. Because the policy is so unpopular, local officials who take their role in competitive politics seriously may choose to ignore or even obstruct mandatory school desegregation.

We have already seen that some public officials, such as Louise Day Hicks and John Kerrigan, take actions consistent with local public opinion as they help coordinate opposition to busing in exchange for the rewards of public office and political entrepreneurship. The theory of political entrepreneurship will be further developed in this chapter to analyze the actions of Kevin White, the mayor of Boston during the time of the school desegregation controversy and the public official most directly responsible for local implementation of the federal court's policy on school desegregation.

The Mayor's Office: A General Statement

The mayor's decisions and statements critically affect a city's ability to deal peacefully and successfully with problems of racial conflict (National Advisory Commission on Civil Disorders 1968, pp. 298–299). Whether the resources of communication and opinion leadership are used for or against desegregation significantly affects the amount of conflict in a community (Kirby et al. 1973).

Prior experience in bargaining with neighborhood and community groups provides the mayor's office with considerable knowledge about neighborhood interests, boundaries, and social life. The mayor's willingness to share this information can lead to a more sensitive and realistic plan for school desegregation than is likely to be drawn up by court-appointed experts who are less familiar with neighborhood life (Rossell 1977, p. 260).

The mayor's office has access to a citywide apparatus for coordinating community support for desegregation and community participation in desegregation programs. A powerful and prestigious attention-caller, the mayor publicly shapes constituents' understanding and acceptance of boundaries on their own and each other's behavior. In principle, this can encourage neighborhood representatives to accept more equitable bargains when negotiating and administering school desegregation (Frohlich et al. 1971).

Mayor White's resources as an attention-caller and leader of public opinion are widely recognized in Boston. During the summer after the first year of implementation (wave 5), Boston neighborhood residents were asked which public leader will have the most influence on how parents respond to the Phase II plan. Mayor White was named as the first or second choice by 26 percent of the respondents. Other public leaders receiving significant mention are: Boston School Superintendant Marian Fahey with 24 percent, Boston School Committee Chairman John McDonough with 27 percent, and Judge Garrity with 16 percent.

The mayor's resources include his ability to influence the public because of their respect for him, for his office, and because of their support for him in the past. Overall, 48 percent of the respondents in the Boston neighborhood survey say they have "a great deal" or "some" respect for the statements and policies of the mayor that have to do with "the quality of education in Boston." The percentage is about the same as for Cardinal Medeiros (49 percent), higher than for Judge Garrity (23 percent), but lower than for John Kerrigan (73 percent).

Public respect can be used by the mayor to shape public support for his policies (Neustadt 1960). The number of people who respect the mayor, and who may be willing to tolerate mandatory desegregation because of his support, is much greater than the number who favor this policy on their own. The principle of decentralized enforcement depends, to some extent, on the willingness of the mayor (and other local officials) to use the prestige of office to build a constituency for orderly implementation among community residents who are personally opposed to mandatory desegregation.

Table 6.1   *Public Opinion on Busing and Respect for the Mayor's Leadership*

Opinion on Busing Wave 4	Level of Mayoral Respect Wave 4	Percent of Neighborhood Residents
Opposed	Low	49
Opposed	High	38
Neutral, favor	All levels	13
		100

Note: Question wordings: see Appendix, nos. 5, 37.
   Data are combined from samples of white residents of six Boston neighborhoods.

Table 6.1 shows a rough estimate of the size of the constituency in Boston that might be willing to follow the mayor's leadership on desegregation even when they are personally opposed to the policy. The first group (49 percent) consists of those who are opposed to busing and do not respect the statements and policies of the mayor. The second group (38 percent) is made up of those who personally oppose busing but who say they personally respect the mayor. In the third group are those who favor busing (13 percent).

The second and third groups, together comprising 51 percent, show the constituency that can potentially be mobilized to support the court order because they agree with busing or because they respect the mayor as a local official who is constitutionally responsible for helping implement the policy and may be, therefore, willing to follow his leadership on this matter.[2]

2. The mayor's ability to lead public opinion might depend on a number of other factors as well. Past voting or agreement with the mayor on policies other than desegregation might also increase an individual's willingness to be influenced by mayoral leadership even though the individual is opposed to busing. Someone who voted for the mayor might experience some personal identification with that choice in spite of disagreement over busing. Someone may oppose busing but still be susceptible to the influence of mayoral leadership on this question, because the mayor seems to be the best advocate of his or her interests on other issues. Further research on this topic should be designed to explore the different ways public leaders influence the opinions and actions of their constituencies.

Table 6.2   *The Demand for Public Safety during*
                  Desegregation

	Percent in Agreement
Police Commissioner DiGrazia should deploy large numbers of police to schools where trouble may occur (Wave 5)	88
School officials should suspend any student involved in violence (Wave 4)	79
School officials should ask police to arrest any parent or student involved in violence (Wave 4)	67
School officials should maintain police in schools to handle violence (Wave 4)	68
The mayor should refuse permits for marches and demonstrations that might become violent (Wave 4)	60

Note: Question wordings: see Appendix, nos. 39, 40, 42.
   Data are combined from samples of white residents of six Boston neighborhoods.

Finally, the mayor is able to influence the way the public reacts to desegregation because the mayor is the elected official who ultimately commands the local police.[3] The force and visibility with which local police actions are taken can greatly affect people's perceptions of the threat to safety posed by desegregation and thereby affect the level of conflict a community experiences.[4] There is a great deal of public support for actions by local public officials to keep the process of desegregation orderly and nonviolent. Table 6.2

3. Boston residents are aware of the mayor's constitutional responsibility in this area. On a question asking which public official has the main responsibility for maintaining public safety, 78 percent named the local police commissioner as their first or second choice, followed by 48 percent naming the mayor. The public official receiving the third most frequent mention was the state governor with only 13 percent.
   4. Chapter 4 shows that one of the principal public fears about desegregation is that it is unsafe, and those who regard it as unsafe are more likely to support protest than those who do not.

shows a number of different measures of the demand for public safety. The level of public support is very high for actions by the mayor, the police chief, and other local officials to control violence, including policing the schools (88 percent); suspending students who engage in violence (79 percent); and refusing permits for public demonstrations that may become violent (60 percent).

Even though mayoral resources are crucial, it is rarely the case that a mayor aggressively mobilizes these resources to secure compliance with mandatory desegregation (Orfield 1984; Weatherford 1980; Kirby et al. 1973; Crain et al. 1968). The process of local politics usually makes it an unwise political strategy to do so. Rodgers and Bullock discuss political strategies of local leaders during a desegregation conflict and note, somewhat generally:

> When confronted with an unpopular federal policy demand, local authorities at some point will weigh the costs and benefits associated with compliance. If compliance threatens their political standing, local officials may decide that the utility of the situation favors noncompliance. (1976, p. 53)

The next several paragraphs analyze, systematically, the processes of local politics that make decentralized enforcement such a risky undertaking for community officials. These aspects of the political process include the existence of "ideologically pure" challengers to the mayor, the lack of consistent support for the policy at higher levels of government, and the lack of a sufficient number of "scapegoats" who can absorb some of the opposition.

Coordinators of Opposition

When an incumbent helps coordinate attainment of some public good and there is a significant division of opinion on whether or not the good should be provided, then political entrepreneurs will come forward to challenge the incumbent and the policy. In the theory of political entrepreneurship, these individuals are coordinators of *opposition* to the incumbent's policies (Frohlich et al. 1971, pp. 84–88).

Coordinating opposition involves calling attention to the injustice of the policy, the unfairness of the incumbent, and the need for change. Coordinators of opposition are most likely to gain public support for their position by articulating "consistent" and "ideologically pure" objections to the policy (Frohlich et al. 1971, pp. 103–104). Their incentive is not to promote a balanced discussion of the issues but, rather, to focus attention and emotion on those aspects of the policy that seem to the public to be most unjust. This strategy is most likely to succeed if the incumbent can be portrayed as "extremist" and isolated from the public will.

The careers of Louise Day Hicks and John Kerrigan exemplify the pattern of the ideologically "pure" opponent whose aspirations (and base in the community) do not place a strong premium on obedience to the law. Mrs. Hicks, in her later campaigns for public office, became known by a concise slogan of unmistakable meaning: "Never." Another neighborhood-based activist, Elvira "Pixie" Palladino, was elected to the school board to replace John Kerrigan (who became board president when Louise Day Hicks was elected to the city council). Mrs. Palladino was sworn in while wearing an artificial diamond tiara that spelled, "Stop Forced Busing." She eventually set up her own antibusing organization because of a disagreement with Louise Day Hicks over nominees for the U.S. presidency. Mrs. Hicks backed Henry Jackson; Mrs. Palladino backed George Wallace.

The principal electoral challenge to Mayor White's position also came from the antibusing movement. During the first few months of Phase I, Raymond Flynn, state representative from South Boston, was touted as the "antibusing" mayoral candidate. His signature on the Declaration of Clarification, his challenge to Judge Garrity to restore parents' rights, and his leadership in the movement to repeal the Racial Imbalance Act gave him an impeccably "pure" position on the busing issue. In the election, held after Phase II of Judge Garrity's order began, Mayor White's actual rival was Joseph Timilty, a state senator with a relationship to ROAR that also enabled him to appeal directly to the antibusing vote (Hillson 1977, p. 170).

The existence of opposition leadership is not, in itself, the reason for the hesitancy of local officials to implement desegregation. In any community there will almost always be a division of opinion as to whether or not some public good should actually be provided. Local leaders are usually hesitant to implement desegregation because lack of support for the policy at higher levels of government creates a situation at the local level where coordinators of opposition become especially strong. When this occurs, local leaders are especially susceptible to being portrayed as "extremists" and are especially vulnerable to political challenge.

Lack of Support at Higher Levels of Government

During the *Brown* trial, Kenneth Clark conducted a study on implementation of unpopular social policies. This report, introduced as evidence and published as a special edition of the *Journal of Social Issues* (Clark 1953), argued that successful desegregation requires:

1. a clear and unequivocal statement of policy by leaders with prestige;
2. firm enforcement of the new policy in the face of initial resistance;
3. firm enforcement of the policy against subsequent violations, attempted violations, and incitements to violation; and
4. refusal of local authorities to resort to, engage in, or tolerate subterfuge, gerrymandering, or other devices for evading the principles and the fact of desegregation.

Lack of support for local enforcement of desegregation at higher levels reinforces the political opportunities of those who would coordinate opposition to the policy at lower levels. It provides prima facie evidence, in the public mind, that local officials who implement desegregation are extremist. It provides, at least in the short run, an opportunity for those who articulate rhetorically consistent and ideologically "pure" statements of opposition to present themselves as legitimate heirs to the public will, since they are usually the only visible alternative to the discredited policy of compliance. Those who enforce the law are, in the words of a veteran Arkansas politician, "in the position of a man running for sonofabitch without opposition." In Boston there were few instances of visible support for the desegregation order by higher governmental officials.

In May 1974, one month before Judge Garrity's order, State Representative Flynn and the Boston school board finally were successful in their campaign to have the legislature repeal the state's Racial Imbalance Act. Later that summer, Governor Francis Sargent vetoed the repeal legislation but substituted his own amendments to the RIA removing compulsory busing.

Judge Garrity's ruling, based on federal law, was not affected by the repeal, and then reinstatement, of the RIA. Still, the actions of the legislature and the governor reveal an inconsistent pattern of high-level support for the ruling that made it harder for local officials to implement desegregation. To complicate the issues further, the Phase I plan ordered by Judge Garrity had been devised by the state board of education to implement the RIA before it was repealed, reinstated, and amended. The Phase I plan had been thrown out once by the state legislature, once by the governor, and now was being brought back to life by Federal Court Judge Garrity.

Officials at the state and national levels of Massachusetts government did not articulate consistent support for Judge Garrity's order in their public statements either. A campaign for state governor between liberal Republican incumbent Francis Sargent and liberal Democratic contender Michael Dukakis was in progress at the time of Phase I. Although neither candidate supported the opponents of busing, neither spoke on behalf of the court order (Hillson 1977). In the early weeks of Phase I, Edward Kennedy, U.S. senator from Massachusetts, stated that he understood the feelings of those opposed to busing but repeated his support for Judge Garrity's plan as a means to achieve desegregation. During the course of Phase I, however, Senator Kennedy reduced his number of visits to Boston and rarely spoke about busing (Hillson 1977, pp. 24–25, 131).

The highest level of opposition to Judge Garrity's order came from the White House itself. The national coalition against mandatory desegregation, born in opposition to fair employment practices legislation in the 1940s, reached a new stage of political maturity with the elections of 1966, 1968, and 1972. In the early years after the *Brown* decision, President Eisenhower responded to the pressure of public opposition by saying desegregation should be delayed until public opinion was more favorable. By the time of Judge Garrity's order, the position of the White House was actively solicitous of antibusing opinion.

Rather than merely support delay, President Nixon directed Assistant Attorney General William Rehnquist to draft an antibusing amendment and then, after the Supreme Court's 1971 decision in *Swann*, boldly declared in a message to Congress: "I am opposed to busing for the purpose of achieving racial balance in our schools."

President Ford continued the policy of supporting the opponents of mandatory desegregation while benefiting from divisiveness in the urban Democratic coalition caused by the busing issue. When Mayor White asked for U.S. marshals to help control violent demonstrations, President Ford declared in an October 9, 1974, press conference:

> [Judge Garrity's] decision in that case, in my judgement, was not the best solution to quality education in Boston. I have consistently opposed forced busing to achieve racial balance as to quality education. And therefore I respectfully disagree with the Judge's order. . . . I hope and trust that it's not necessary to call in Federal officials or Federal law enforcement agencies. . . . The marshals, if my information is accurate, are under the jurisdiction of the court, not directly under my jurisdiction. . . . As far as I know, no specific request has come to me for any Federal involvement and therefore I'm not in a position to act.

Scapegoats

A commitment to desegregate by higher levels of government reduces the vulnerability of local officials to the charge of "extremism" by the opposition. Local officials are less vulnerable when there are, in Peltason's term, "scapegoats":

> Some federal judges have failed to recognize that their primary role is to "take the heat." The judge's injunction is required . . . to take the responsibility for ordering desegregation from [local officials]. A judge . . . who fails to understand his duty to serve as a scapegoat, frequently undermines the political situation of the moderates. (1961, pp. 96–97)

Scapegoats reinforce the stability of local politics. It is more difficult for the opposition to portray local officials as "extremist" when there are scapegoats in this role. The charge that local officials favor the law they are enforcing becomes less plausible if local officials can demonstrate that they have no choice. These factors help immunize local officials against challenges from ideologically "pure" opponents. With scapegoats, local officials have a better chance to maintain their standing as "moderates" in the community while enforcing the law.

In the early years after *Brown* the courts did not provide a reliable scapegoat for local officials. The Supreme Court's decision in *Brown II* did not call for immediate compliance. Instead, for reasons discussed in Chapter 2, the Court called for "deliberate" speed in implementation and gave discretion to lower courts and local public officials to find the best mechanical solution to the problem.

Given the flexibility of the instructions from the Supreme Court, the lower courts did not require mandatory desegregation either. Since local judges had such a wide range of choices, they were held personally accountable when they insisted on prompt desegregation. Judges preferred to avoid the isolation and charges of extremism this position would incur:

> These judges . . . can hardly be expected on their own initiative to move against the local power structure. If their instructions from above are ambiguous, the ambiguity will be resolved to conform to the judge's own convictions and the mores of his district. . . . The directions of the United States Supreme Court are not clear and explicit, and this is the crucial problem. (Peltason 1961, p. 13)

In most states the federal circuit courts required only token changes in school board practices or even, in some instances, encouraged continued separation of the races (Peltason 1961; Muse 1964).

The executive branch of government did not support local officials in fulfillment of their legal obligations to enforce desegregation either. In a news conference about a year after *Brown II,* President Eisenhower stated:

> It is difficult through law and through force to change a man's heart. . . . We must all . . . help to bring about a change in spirit so that extremists on both sides do not defeat what we know is a reasonable, logical conclusion to this whole affair.

Two years later, at another news conference, Eisenhower refused to "give an opinion about my conviction about the Supreme Court decisions . . . [although] I might have said something about slower."

President Eisenhower's position lent force to the idea that any citizen, school board, mayor, or district judge acting on the principal of decentralized enforcement was, in fact, an extremist. William O. Douglas, in his posthumous memoir, argues that President Eisenhower's failure to support desegregation deprived local leadership of necessary "political capital" and jeopardized their position:

> If [Eisenhower] had gone to the nation . . . telling the people to obey the law and fall into line, the cause of desegregation would have been accelerated. Ike was a hero and he was worshipped. Some of his political capital spent on the racial cause would have brought the nation closer to the constitutional standards. Ike's ominous silence on our 1954 decision gave courage to the racists who decided to resist the decision ward by ward, precinct by precinct, town by town and county by county.

In several instances state legislatures and governors took positions undermining the position of local officials who favored compliance with *Brown*. Some states passed laws forbidding local officials to desegregate. Other states lodged the authority to administer the schools at higher levels of government where the chance of compliance was nil. These laws, although ultimately unenforceable in light of the *Brown* decree, had a chilling effect on local implementation efforts (Muse 1961; Muse 1964).

In most of the instances studied by Peltason, no one, not even the federal circuit judge, demanded immediate compliance with the law. Peltason's discussion suggests that, in this kind of circumstance, even one official willing to play the scapegoat role will make a difference. In Boston there was at least one scapegoat. By the 1970s the Supreme Court had become much more rigorous in its requirement for immediate desegregation, the executive branch of the federal government had added its authority to the enforcement effort, and Federal Judge Garrity was unambiguous in his requirement for immediate compliance.

In 1964 the Department of Health, Education and Welfare began withholding its funds from school districts that were not meeting racial balance requirements. In 1968 the Supreme Court began taking a harder look at desegregation plans that were not actually producing more racial balance in the schools. In 1971 the Court ruled that a school district, if found guilty, must immediately take action to achieve racial balance and, if necessary, busing was an acceptable means to that end. In 1973, a year before Judge Garrity's decision, the Court ruled for the first time that the *Brown* ruling applied to Northern cities as well. The Supreme Court's position on mandatory desegregation in Boston had become unequivocal.

Judge Garrity's requirement for local officials to assist desegregation was also unequivocal. Having been found guilty in a federal court, the Boston school board was ordered to immediately implement a plan recommended by the Massachusetts state board of education as Phase I of desegregation, and to completely balance the remaining schools in the city the following year as Phase II.

Judge Garrity's unequivocal requirement in Boston weakened the resolve of some to oppose the law. It meant that flagrant actions against desegregation would not escape widespread public attention and that there was a significant chance of prosecution for those engaging in illegal actions. These sanctions were meaningful to Mayor White. During the early years of school desegregation implementation, Mayor White entertained hopes of statewide or national Democratic office. The loss of liberal support among local, statewide, and national leaders in politics and business because of a well-publicized obstructionist approach to Judge Garrity's order would end these hopes.

In spite of Judge Garrity's willingness to take some of the heat, the absence of consistent support for desegregation at higher levels of government compromised the Mayor's ability to consistently and effectively support compliance with the court order. One scapegoat is not enough. A pattern of support for desegregation policy at higher levels of government is also necessary for local officials to be able to be effective in executing their responsibilities under the law.

The Mayor's Strategy for Desegregation

When there is not consistent support for implementing an unpopular policy, officials are usually better off ignoring it, articulating support for the doctrine of voluntary compliance instead, or even providing some kinds of support to those who would obstruct it. In Peltason's words:

> It is politically unrealistic to expect a southern governor, or a southern school board, or even a southern district judge to take a more advanced position on school integration than the President of the United States. . . . An elected southern official who appears to be more of a

civil rights advocate than the President runs a serious political risk of jeopardizing the forces of moderation. If he gets too far out in front—and as the President defined the situation, any stand other than pro-segregation was made to appear daring—he exposes himself [and his allies] to defeat. (1961, p. 49)

Many of the legislators . . . were less emotionally aroused than they publicly proclaimed, but many . . . were afraid their political careers might be jeopardized if they allowed any other legislator to appear to be more dedicated to the preservation of segregation than they. After one representative announced he was "one hundred percent for segregation," another announced he was "a million percent loyal." (1961, p. 238)

The lack of consistent support for desegregation at higher levels of government and the political success of the ideologically "pure" opposition made Mayor White extraordinarily vulnerable to the charge of "extremist support for integration." The mayor responded to his vulnerability by enunciating support for the doctrine of voluntary compliance by encouraging the belief among protesters that their actions might one day be effective and by avoiding actions that would publicly identify his office with the desegregation plan.

Before Judge Garrity's order (wave 1), there was widespread suspicion among opponents of busing (who constituted nearly 90 percent of the community) that Mayor White was an "extremist," out of step with public opinion on crucial issues. Table 6.3 shows the percent of Boston neighborhood residents who believe:

1. Children should attend neighborhood schools.
2. Racial imbalance does not hurt the education of black children.

Table 6.3 also shows the average public perception of the mayor's opinion on each of these issues. In each case the percentage thinking the mayor supports the rationale of the court's decision is higher than the percent supporting that position themselves. A plurality views him as out of step on the question of neighborhood schools and on the issue of whether racial imbalance harms blacks.

Another set of public opinion measures shows that, compared to other local officials, Mayor White is considered to be "soft" on busing. Before Judge Garrity's order (wave 1) only 15 percent of

Table 6.3   *Public Opinion and Perception of the Mayor's Opinion on Desegregation*

Statement	Percent		
	Agree	Disagree	Don't Know
Children should always go to school in their own neighborhood:			
Public opinion	83	11	1
Perception of mayor's opinion	28	47	17
Racial imbalance in the schools hurts the education of black children:			
Public opinion	28	59	4
Perception of mayor's opinion	47	26	18

Note: Question wordings: see Appendix, no. 43.

   Data are combined from sampes of white residents of six Boston neighborhoods.

Boston neighborhood residents believed Mayor White was personally opposed to busing, as opposed to nearly 70 percent who said School Board Chairman John Kerrigan was opposed or even 53 percent who said President Gerald Ford was personally opposed to busing.

Mayor White hoped to counter the charge of "extremism" by using the resources of his office to, in his words, "broker the unpleasant task of implementing a court order" and to lend support to all factions involved in the antibusing conflict.

Perhaps the mayor's most significant contribution to the intensity and duration of the Boston school desegregation controversy was his support for the view that people do not need to follow the court order if they do not want to—i.e., the doctrine of voluntary compliance. On September 9, 1974, the Mayor, in a television speech, stated that:

> People who would boycott schools are asked to weigh the decision carefully, but it is their decision to make. Parents should attend open houses at schools before making a final decision to send or not to send students to school.

The assertion in this statement is, of course, wrong. The United States Civil Rights Commission, in its report on Boston, observed,

> The mayor's position [in this speech] . . . strongly inferred that it was legitimate to boycott schools. It is not. Boycotting schools runs afoul of a panoply of State laws and can result in criminal prosecution. (1975)

With his television speech, the mayor aligned his office with other voices calling for voluntary compliance with the court order and advocating civil disobedience as a last resort. At the time of Mayor White's speech, support for civil disobedience and the doctrine of voluntary compliance had already been publicly supported by organized groups of Catholic clergy in the city (see Chapter 5).

The mayor followed his statement with administrative actions that reduced enforcement of the law. On September 5, 1974, the legal counsel of the Boston Police Patrolmen's Association, in a press release and interview, instructed police that state laws on school trespassing do not require arrests and that court complaints must be sought against protesters on public school property before they can be arrested. This is tantamount to saying protesters and trespassers will not be prosecuted.

The mayor sought to shift responsibility for maintaining order to a higher level of government. In October 1974 he declared it was not possible to guarantee the safety of students in some neighborhoods, and he asked Judge Garrity to assign federal marshals to these areas. Judge Garrity denied the request, but Governor Sargent, on the mayor's request, finally did dispatch more than 400 state and metropolitan police to assume responsibility for public safety in one neighborhood.

Not all of the mayor's actions were in defiance of the principle of decentralized enforcement. In September 1974 he invoked a city crowd control ordinance to disperse groups of three or more persons congregating near public schools. In October he again used his powers of office to ban marches and demonstrations of any kind.

Some of the mayor's public statements encouraged the belief that public protests against the court order might one day be effective. In December 1974 the mayor stated that "citywide busing should not be imposed as long as widespread boycotts and repeated disruptions are still blunting the success of Phase I." Chapter 7 shows that willingness to protest is greatly affected by someone's belief that the action may produce the desired result sometime in the future. By encouraging the belief that the ends of protest might be achieved, the mayor encouraged participation in such actions.

Some of the mayor's public statements also assured the anti-busing public that the significant costs for continuing the struggle against desegregation would be paid. In September 1974 the mayor defended his actions supporting the court order by saying that "the city has exhausted all legal avenues of appeal at a cost of in excess of a million dollars." Later that year, the mayor announced that the city would pay the cost for a Supreme Court appeal of Judge Garrity's decision (Richard, Knox, and Oliphant 1975). These statements ensured that the costs would be paid, thus increasing the confidence of protesters that their cause would continue to mobilize resources successfully. Moreover, the mayor's statements assured that the costs would be borne evenly among city taxpayers, eliminating the fear that others in the community would "take advantage" of one's own support for protest by acting as a "free rider" (Olson 1965).

Not all of the mayor's relations with the media stimulated protest. Access to the media was used to quiet negative publicity about the most sensational aspects of neighborhood resistance. All during the period of conflict, rumors and suspicions were widespread that meetings between Mayor White and local leaders of the media had taken place to agree on guidelines for reporting and "managing" the news. Sensational events, such as mob violence, bus stonings and Ku Klux Klan rallies were to be downplayed. The September 13, 1974, headline of the *Boston Herald American* announced, "Calm Prevails as School Opens," and the *Boston Globe* proclaimed, "Boston Schools Desegregated as Opening Day Generally Peaceful." The *New York Times,* a newspaper presumably not party to the agreed-upon guidelines, described the same scene with the somewhat more volatile headline, "Violence Mars Busing in Boston; Mayor Bans Street Gatherings in South Area."

Thomas Atkins, president of the Boston branch of the NAACP, knew of the behind-the-scenes meetings that resulted in the agreed-upon guidelines. "Political decisions," he recounted, "were made to seduce the media into a 'we will report only positive news' kind of euphoria." The NAACP leader thought the media pact was entered "in good faith" by the communications outlets (Hillson 1977, pp. 33–34).

The mayor initially sought to avoid any involvement of his office with coordinating the design or implementation of the desegregation plan. During the first year of implementation, the mayor's position was that he had not created the Phase I plan and that it was up to the state superintendent of schools to implement it (Richard, Knox, and Oliphant 1975). The mayor's public education effort consisted almost entirely of a series of "coffees" in the homes of persons opposed to busing. There is no public record of the discussion at these meetings.

By the end of the first year, however, following threats by Judge Garrity's court and considerable community conflict, the mayor's office contributed to the design of the Phase II plan (Rossell 1977). In July 1975, the mayor submitted a "Police Utilization Plan" to Judge Garrity which, in the opinion of the U.S. Commission on Civil Rights, contained many of the elements necessary for insuring public safety during the 1975/76 school year.

The Effectiveness of Mayor White's Position

By constitutional criteria, Mayor White failed in his duties. He did not, in the words of the United States Commission on Civil Rights, "support unequivocally the Federal Court's finding of a violation of the Constitution by the Boston School Committee and the court's subsequent orders designed to bring [about a remedy]" (1975). Instead, he tried to shift responsibility for implementing the busing order to higher levels of government, to avoid any personal identification with it, and to provide reassurances to the antibusing movement that their goals might someday be achieved.

But by the criteria of competitive local politics, Mayor White was successful. He avoided a charge of obstruction of justice by Judge Garrity's court. Although frustrated in his attempts to achieve higher elective office, Kevin White remained mayor of Boston for 10 years after Judge Garrity's decision. He won reelection in the contest against State Senator Timilty and succeeded in every campaign after that. In 1984 he finally bowed out of Boston politics, facing charges of corruption, and was succeeded as mayor by State Representative Raymond Flynn.

Was Mayor White's success a result of his policy to "impartially broker" the interests of the parties to the school desegregation con-

Table 6.4   *Perception of the Mayor's Personal Opinion on Busing*

	Percent Saying the Mayor Is:			
Time of Survey	Opposed	Neutral	In Favor	Don't Know Mayor's Opinion
10/73 (Wave 1)	15	15	55	15
4/74 (Wave 2)	16	22	51	11
7/74 (Wave 3)	16	22	50	12
7/75 (Wave 5)	25	25	48	3

Note: Question wordings: see Appendix 1, no. 38.
    Data are combined from samples of white residents of six Boston neighborhoods.

flict? Ironically, his experience in Boston is probably best interpreted as an example of how a local political leader can stay in office even though he is not highly regarded by the antibusing movement. We noted, in connection with table 6.3, that before Judge Garrity's order (wave 1) the mayor was vulnerable to the charge of "extremism" by antibusing candidates. His opinions on the need for a court order, the role of neighborhood schools, and support for busing were believed to be out of step with public opinion by a large proportion of neighborhood residents. In spite of his subsequent actions to distance himself from the conflict by lending support to both sides, the mayor never overcame his vulnerability to the charge of "extremism."

Table 6.4 shows the change in Boston neighborhood residents' perceptions of Mayor White's personal opinion on busing for integration. Before Judge Garrity's order (wave 1 and wave 2), only about 15 percent said the mayor was personally opposed to busing to achieve integration. After more than a year of conflict, and after more than a year of attempting to "broker the unpleasant task of implementing a court order," the percentages changed only slightly. After Phase I (wave 5), only 25 percent said the mayor was opposed to busing and another 25 percent said he was neutral on the issue. Another 48 percent said Kevin White favored busing.

By the end of Phase I (wave 5), more than 75 percent of Boston neighborhood residents believed Mayor White would encourage par-

Table 6.5   *Perception of the Mayor's Actions after the Court Order*

	Percent
The mayor will encourage parents to comply with Judge Garrity's desegregation plan (Wave 5)	76
Mayor White and his staff will comply, openly express approval or work with parents, school officials and students to minimize problems of implementation (Wave 5)	77

Note: Question wordings: see Appendix 1, nos. 34, 35.
    Data are combined from samples of white residents of six Boston neighborhoods.

ents to peaceably comply with Phase II of Judge Garrity's order and that he would put his resources of office to work to achieve that goal. Tha data are shown in table 6.5. The percent who expect the mayor to urge compliance is two to three times higher than the percent who expect a similar message from typical antibusing leaders, such as School Board Chairman John Kerrigan or City Councilwoman Louise Day Hicks.

The survey evidence analyzed here suggests that it was not his position on busing that kept Mayor White in office for 10 years after Judge Garrity's order. Opponents of busing never viewed the mayor as a strong advocate for their interests on this issue. The support he gained from people personally opposed to busing was granted in spite of the mayor's perceived position on mandatory desegregation.

Public Ambivalence about Decentralized Enforcement

Why was the mayor politically successful in spite of his position on the busing issue? The public is deeply ambivalent about what public officials should do during a time of desegregation protest. Public ambivalence creates leeway for local political leaders to take unpopular actions that are legally required while maintaining public support for their incumbency.

The ambivalence of public opinion is reflected in questions that directly address the obligations of public officials under the prin-

Table 6.6   *Public Support for Decentralized Enforcement*

	Percent Agreeing	
	Wave 2	Wave 3
An elected official has more responsibility than an ordinary citizen to obey the law	63	60
Judge Garrity has the right to make decisions people disagree with	39	38

Note: Question wordings: see Appendix 1, nos. 44–47.
     Data are combined from samples of white residents of six Boston neighborhoods.

ciple of decentralized enforcement. About half of the Boston neighborhood residents say public officials ought to fulfill their constitutional responsibilities and about half disagree. The exact percentages fluctuate depending on the question. Illustrative results are shown in table 6.6.

The first row of table 6.6 shows that about 60 percent of Boston neighborhood residents agree with the statement that "an elected official has more responsibility than an ordinary citizen to obey the law." The second row shows that about 40 percent agree with the statement that "Judge Garrity has the right to make decisions people disagree with." The results are quite stable over the two replications of each question (wave 2 and wave 3).

Such public ambivalence means that incumbents who wish to remain in public office during a time of desegregation may be able to do so without having to take an overtly obstructionist position against busing. This is the basis for Ashmore's argument that Arkansas Governor Orval Faubus could have retained his political support without taking the extreme measure of physically obstructing the enrollment of nine black students at Little Rock Central High School:

> [Faubus] was correct, I think, in figuring that [the next governor's] race would require segregationist credentials. But there were less drastic means of obtaining them—as some of his contemporaries in the Upper South demonstrated by denouncing the Supreme Court in the resounding language of the Southern Manifesto and pledging to continue the battle on every legal front. (1982, pp. 259–260)

The lessons from a number of other American cities suggest that as long as an incumbent can make it seem that the idea to desegregate is not his and that he is forced to take action, he will not lose public support by assisting implementation:

> To structure the situation so that desegregation would be more widely accepted in the community, some superintendants quietly advised federal officials about the conditions under which they would comply. Some officials arranged to have the Office of Civil Rights of H.E.W. (OCR) threaten the board with dire consequences if the system was not desegregated. Others passed the word to OCR that they preferred to be sued.
>
> Progressives . . . obeyed OCR sufficiently to avoid severe sanctions but did not make changes that would convince local citizens they were moving faster than necessary. The school board constantly emphasized they were under intense Federal pressure and were only doing what they had to do. (Rodgers and Bullock 1976, pp. 25, 27)

Table 6.7 shows that neighborhood residents who believe local officials are obligated to enforce the law on school desegregation have a higher level of respect for the mayor than those who do not accept the principle of decentralized enforcement. The data in table 6.7 are shown for Boston neighborhood residents opposed to busing at the time of the interview.[5] The top part of table 6.7 shows that busing opponents who think elected officials have more responsibility than the ordinary citizen to obey the law are more likely to support the mayor than those who see no special responsibility. The lower part of table 6.7 shows that those who are personally opposed to busing but who believe Judge Garrity has the right to make an unpopular decision are more likely to support the mayor than those who do not accept the principle of decentralized enforcement.

5. The data in table 6.7 and table 6.8 were also analyzed using a more detailed control for the strength of antibusing opinions to ensure that the measures in these tables possess discriminant validity—i.e., that the predictor variables are not interpretable simply as measures of particularly extreme antibusing opinions. The relationships in these tables were also explored using panel models to study the effects of cross-lag correlations and response instabilities (which might be interpreted in a way that defeats the argument about causal direction advanced here). The conclusions reported in connection with tables 6.7 and 6.8 hold up under these tests.

An example of incumbent leeway is the high level of public support for actions that maintain public order. The public supports actions taken in the name of preserving public safety even though those actions reduce the effectiveness of opposition to an unpopular policy. When Mayor White finally invoked a city ordinance to ban marches and demonstrations, this action was favored by about 60 percent of the residents of Boston neighborhoods. When the public schools opened at the beginning of Phase I, the mayor and the attorney for the Boston Police Patrolmen's Association made statements implying that laws against trespassing and protest on school property would not be enforced. If stronger actions had been taken, the mayor and the police would not have lost public support. Enforcement of the laws against trespass and protest would have been supported by 70 to 90 percent of the residents of Boston neighborhoods. The percentages are shown in table 6.2.

An incumbent who calls attention to the obligation of local offi-

Table 6.7	*Support for Decentralized Enforcement and Respect for the Mayor*	
		Percent with "A Great Deal" or "Some" Respect Wave 4
Opinion on the responsibility of elected officials to obey the law, compared to the average citizen:		
Officials have more responsibility		48
Officials have same or less responsibility		39
Opinion on whether Judge Garrity had the right to make a decision many people disagree with:		
Yes, he did		52
No, he did not		40

Note: Question wordings: see Appendix 1, nos. 45, 47, 37.

Data are combined from samples of white residents of six Boston neighborhoods.

Data show responses of those personally opposed to busing at the time of the interview.

Patterns shown are significant (.05) when racial prejudice/fear and strength of antibusing opinion are controlled.

Table 6.8   *Support for Decentralized Enforcement and*
Willingness to Protest

	Percent in Favor of:		
	Defiance Wave 3	Boycott Wave 3	Neighborhood Action Wave 3
Opinion on the responsibility of elected officials to obey the law, compared to the average citizen:			
Officials have more responsibility	56	59	77
Officials have same or less responsibility	64	64	84
Opinion on whether Judge Garrity has the right to make a decision many people disagree with:			
Yes, he does	37	39	62
No, he does not	71	71	88

Note: Question wordings: see Appendix 1, nos. 45, 47, 14, 15, 17.
   Data are combined from samples of white residents of six Boston neighborhoods.
   Data show responses of those personally opposed to busing at the time of the interview.
   Patterns shown are significant (.05) when racial prejudice/fear and strength of anti-busing opinion are controlled.

cials to obey the law, and the obligation of local courts to demand enforcement of it, may be able to strengthen his or her position against single-issue challengers. Calling attention to the principle of decentralized enforcement may also reduce the level of public protest. People who agree with the principle of decentralized enforcement are less willing to protest than those who do not. The data are shown in table 6.8. Once again, the data are shown for Boston neighborhood residents opposed to busing at the time of the interview.[6]

   6. Further methodological controls, explained in connection with table 6.7, were also examined.

The first part of table 6.8 shows that those who think elected officials have more responsibility than the average citizen are less likely than those who do not to support defiance of the court order, to advocate a school boycott, and to say that it is very important for neighborhood residents to obstruct implementation. The second part of the table shows that those who say Judge Garrity has the right to make a decision many people disagree with are much less likely to support protest than those who do not, for any of the three measures considered.

Conclusion

The conditions outlined by Kenneth Clark regarding when local leadership can most effectively overcome opposition have almost never been met in the history of American school desegregation. Local leaders have almost never had the combination of an unambiguous order for immediate action, a visible scapegoat who can be blamed for the policy, and consistent support for the policy by higher-level officials to help immunize local incumbents against charges of "extremism" and personally favoring mandatory desegregation. Except for a brief period in the 1960s, national political leadership has always been opposed to mandatory desegregation during the Second Reconstruction.

This chapter places the numerous findings from case studies of failures of community leadership in a theoretical context. There is a contradiction between the principle of decentralized enforcement and the principle of local competitive politics which goes to the heart of the explanation of why local leadership frequently finds it preferable to ignore or obstruct implementation of unpopular policies. The principle of local competitive politics means that political entrepreneurs will almost always arise to capitalize on the widespread sense of injustice that is felt and to coordinate opposition to community leaders who support the "extremist" position of compliance with an unpopular law. Support for the law by higher officials in government who are willing to play a "scapegoat" role makes local officials less vulnerable to their ideologically "pure" opponents. The results in Boston show, however, that one scapegoat is not enough—support for the law must be forthcoming from a number of levels and offices in government.

7 | Perception of Public Opinion and Desegregation Protest

Introduction

Solidarity and Mobilization

Americans who oppose desegregation often believe they are part of a conflict between "the people" and "supporters of integration" that has characterized racial politics in this country for more than 100 years. At the heart of the matter is the issue of whether a community has the right to embody its values in the law or whether civil rights take precedence over local mores. The Supreme Court once ruled, in *Plessy v. Ferguson,* that solidarity of community opinion legally prevents the court from barring local-level discrimination:

> So far, then, as a conflict with the Fourteenth Amendment is concerned, [this] case reduces itself to the question whether the statute . . . is a reasonable regulation. . . . In determining the question of reasonableness [a legislature] is at liberty to act with reference to the established usages, customs and traditions of the people, and with a view to the promotion of their comfort. . . . Gauged by this standard, we cannot say that a law which authorizes or even requires the separation of the two races in public conveyances is unreasonable.

The view that majority opinion should determine the rights of the minority was echoed in a memo to Justice Robert Jackson from his clerk William Rehnquist who wrote at the time the *Brown* case was beginning its journey to the Supreme Court:

> To the argument made by Thurgood, not John, Marshall that a major-
> ity may not deprive a minority of its constitutional right, the answer
> must be made that while this is sound in theory, in the long run it is the
> majority who will decide what the rights of the minority are.

School boards once sought to defend themselves with the argument that widespread opposition to desegregation constitutes prima
facie evidence of the reasonableness of their actions. In the 1950
case of *Sweatt v. Painter* the state of Texas produced a public opinion poll showing that most of the people want to maintain segregation. In its final argument in *Brown v. Board of Education,* the state
of Florida produced a poll showing that three-quarters of the "white
leaders" in the state disagree with the *Brown* decision, 30 percent
disagree "violently," and only 13 percent of peace officers intend to
enforce state attendance laws at racially mixed schools.

As Chapters 4 and 5 show, Boston residents were primed to
view the conflict over mandatory desegregation as a contest between
authorities and solidary community opposition. The view that local
autonomy is continually subject to encroachment by the state government, the Protestant establishment, and other "outsiders" was
widespread in Boston. The view that the community cohesively opposes alienation of its rights by state and federal governments was
established as a cultural frame decades before Boston residents
heard of the Racial Imbalance Act or Judge Garrity's order.

A number of scholars have suggested that the extent to which
people believe the community is solidly opposed to mandatory desegregation affects the extent and severity of public reaction when
that policy is implemented. In various case studies it is suggested
that attention-calling, public referenda, special elections, and similar activities allow community residents to develop a well-founded
sense of extensive public opposition to desegregation. As the sense
of solidary opposition increases, so does the daring with which individuals voice their dissatisfaction (Rossell 1983, p. 19; Wirt 1970).

For instance, during the period immediately following the court
order to desegregate the Little Rock public schools, segregationists
were unable to organize much opposition. In the spring of 1957, two
segregationists were defeated by a two-to-one majority when they
tried to unseat incumbent members of the Little Rock Board of Education. Fifty percent of the voters of Little Rock refused to support
even a mild antidesegregation referendum. It was only after orga-

nized attempts by political action groups, public leaders, and community institutions to mobilize against desegregation that segregationist candidates for the school board and other public offices were successful (Peltason 1961; Ashmore 1982; Bates 1962). After more than a year and a half of such activities, the Little Rock school board, after the fall 1958 election, contained three moderates and three segregationists. In this election, a bitter-end segregationist was elevated for the first time to the state supreme court.

The earlier analysis also suggests that one of the reasons mobilization is enhanced by local leaders' statements and prior community organization lies in the impact these factors have on perceptions of group solidarity. Chapter 4 argues that attention-calling increases public perception of the community as a coordinated actor against the injustice of outside authorities. Chapter 5 notes that formal organizations aid mobilization because their established communication links among community residents spread the message that there is a large constituency for protest. Chapter 6 observes that the communication and information resources of the mayor's office significantly shape public expectations regarding the level of public support for desegregation, the level of public compliance, and the likely effectiveness of public opposition.

This chapter explores more directly and precisely how perception of public opposition affects the incentive to protest. Three theories are explored, each one offering a different reason for the relationship between solidarity and mobilization. The Boston survey does not have an elaborate enough design to test the finer points of each and prove that one, rather than another, is the fundamental explanation. Rather, the goal in this chapter is to use each theory to illuminate different aspects of antibusing mobilization.

Perception of Public Opinion and Incentives to Protest: Three Theories

The Spiral of Silence

Noelle-Neumann analyzes the relationship between perception of majority public support and willingness to express one's views on matters of public choice (1974, 1977, 1979; see also Taylor 1982). She finds that those who believe the majority agrees with them, and/ or who believe the majority is tending toward their position, are

more likely than others to be willing to publicly express their opinion. This theory is labeled the "spiral" of silence because of a tendency among those who believe they are in the minority to become
less and less likely to advance their views.

The theme of intimidation by the majority is common in historical analyses of American racial politics. W. J. Cash, writing of the
South during the period before the Civil War, notes the progressive
social isolation of the moderates:

> The defense of slavery not only eventuated . . . in a taboo on criti-
> cism; in the same process it set up a ban on all analysis and inquiry. . . .
> In a world in which patriotism to the South was increasingly the first
> duty of men, in which coolness about slavery was accounted treason,
> [detachment] was next to impossible. (Cash 1941, p. 101)

Martin Luther King wrote of the same phenomenon occurring more
than 100 years later. The spiral of silence not only eliminates the
appearance of divisions of opinion among whites but also, by doing
so, minimizes the opportunity for a coalition to form between blacks
and white moderates:

> As a result of the Citizens Councils' activities most white moderates
> in the South no longer feel free to discuss in public the issues involved
> in desegregation for fear of social ostracism and economic reprisals.
> What channels of communication had once existed between whites
> and Negroes have thus largely closed. (King 1958)

Virginius Dabney, editor of the Richmond *Times-Dispatch* spoke
ominously of the "thunderous silence" of his friends and colleagues
on Southern newspapers. George Washington Cable's 1890 lament
on this subject was titled *The Silent South*.

As a tool for understanding intimidation in racial politics, the
theory of the spiral of silence is quite valuable. But as a tool for
explaining the relationship between perception of public opinion
and willingness to protest, the spiral of silence is quite limited. The
theory explains why people *do not* express themselves when they
think they are in the minority. In the smallest, daily kinds of interactions with one's neighbors and associates—i.e., in the realm where
ideas about race become fashionable or unfashionable—the spiral
of silence may explain why integrationist ideas cease to be ex-

pressed and why segregationist ideas acquire their apparent grip on the popular imagination.

The theory does not explain, however, why those who believe they are in the majority may be *more* likely to act. One could argue that the reason some people express their views is the opposite of the reason others do not—perhaps an absence of fear of isolation. But this is not an adequate explanation. Absence of fear is not a sufficient motivational basis for action. The next two theories offer a positive motivational basis for the relationship between perception of public opinion and willingness to protest.

Reinforcing versus Dividing Community Cleavage

Gamson et al. argue that the likelihood of joining a protest depends, to some extent, on how a person believes the community to be divided (1982). Two patterns of community cleavage are depicted in figure 7.1. The symbol "P" stands, in the terminology of Gamson et al., for "potential challengers." In the present context, these would be the residents of a community facing a court order. The symbol "A" stands for "authorities," those mandating desegregation. Gamson et al. argue that those who believe there is a reinforcing cleavage have a greater incentive to protest than those who believe there is a dividing cleavage.

In the "reinforcing" pattern, the courts (and others who support integration) are on one side of the line and the residents of the community are on the other. Perception of a reinforcing cleavage makes protest more likely because it helps establish a collective, group identity. A sense of group solidarity means that people do not think it likely that the "outsiders" will be able to co-opt "loyalists" within the group. Divisions are not expected to become strong within the community. People's loyalties to individuals and institutions in the group motivate actions on behalf of the group:

> [Perception of a reinforcing cleavage] promotes a sense of social solidarity and collective identification. The encounter contains a "we" and a "they," and the salient cleavage operates to encourage participants to see things in these terms. Mobilization for collective action operates partly through the loyalty people feel to a group with which they identify. A reinforcing pattern helps to activate such loyalties and thereby facilitates mobilization. (Gamson et al. 1982, p. 78)

1. A Reinforcing Cleavage

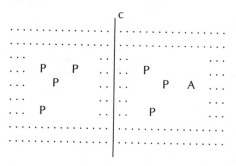

2. A Dividing Cleavage

Figure 7.1. Possible cleavage patterns: two ideal types. c = social cleavage; A = authorities; P = potential challengers. (Drawing based on Gamson et al. 1982, p. 78.)

In the "dividing" pattern, the salient cleavage separates the participants into one set that includes the courts and some community residents favoring desegregation, and another set that includes other community residents opposing desegregation. Someone who believes there is a dividing cleavage is less likely to protest than someone who thinks there is a reinforcing cleavage, because the sense of group identity does not develop; there is a clearly recognized possibility of a coalition between some members of the community and the advocates of desegregation; and, therefore, there is less reason to believe protest activities will be successful:

The dividing pattern is the most difficult and intractable context for [mobilization]. Here, the salient cleavage divides people into a set that includes the authority and some potential challengers, and another set that includes the rest of the potential challengers. This greatly enhances the possibility of a split developing among potential challengers, in which a loyalist faction emerges in support of compliance. Potential challengers are highly vulnerable to efforts by authorities that stimulate internal division, paralyzing the ability of the group to act collectively. Furthermore, there is no easy basis for building collective identification. To achieve this, challengers must rely on more immediate, situational bonds among participants. (Gamson et al. 1982, p. 149)

Solidarity and the Ability to Impose Costs

Albert Hirschman has written a short book about collective action which suggests that the reward a person expects from joining a protest is directly proportional to the cost he or she believes can be imposed on authorities (1970). He argues that in situations of community conflict the higher the proportion who are believed to be protesting, the greater the cost an individual expects can be imposed by his joining the protest. Therefore, the higher the proportion believed to be protesting, the greater the expected reward to the individual from joining. By these rules of rational calculation and reward-based incentive, the decision to take part in antibusing protest is most likely to occur when someone believes the community is unanimously or predominantly opposed to desegregation.[1]

Hirschman's model assumes that each person who is opposed to busing has an impression of how the community is reacting to it. Each person's impression of the relationship between the imposition of an unpopular public policy and the extent of public opposition to it can be represented on a graph like figure 7.2 (based on appendix A of Hirschman's book).

This figure represents the impressions two different people have of how the community is reacting to school desegregation. The *x*-

---

1. Hirschman's model is a specialized version of a cost/benefit model. It is analyzed in this chapter because it is concerned with the effect of perceived public opinion on the incentives for participation—the topic of this chapter—and not because it is concerned with costs and benefits per se. The more conventional model for analyzing costs, benefits, and social movement participation is discussed in Chapter 8.

a) Public Reaction Comparatively Inelastic

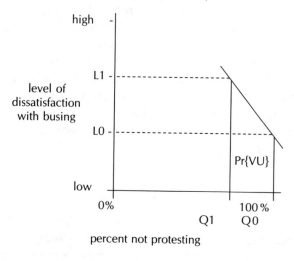

b) Public Reaction Comparatively Elastic

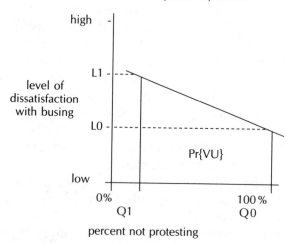

Figure 7.2. Graphs showing perceived public reaction and likelihood of protest. Pr{VU} = The likelihood an individual will protest. (Drawing based on Hirschman 1970, p. 130.)

axis of figure 7.2a represents the percent expected *not* to protest school desegregation; $Q0$ is the percent not protesting before the court order, 100 percent.[2] $Q1$ is the percent expected not to protest after the court order. The percent who are believed to protest is therefore ($Q0 - Q1$).

The y-axis represents the amount of dissatisfaction a person experiences with the "proponents of integration." The level before busing is $L0$; the level after court-implemented desegregation is $L1$. As Y increases on the graph, the level of dissatisfaction increases.

The dependent variable in the analysis, the likelihood that an individual will protest, is represented as the region labeled $Pr\{VU\}$. It is assumed that the likelihood of action is a function of the level of dissatisfaction and the percentage of others expected to protest. When many are protesting, the individual believes that significant costs are quite likely to be imposed on authorities and that joining the action can significantly increase those costs.

Given an individual's level of dissatisfaction, the proportion expected to protest depends on the slope of the line relating the level of dissatisfaction (L) to the percent protesting (Q). The slope of this line is what Hirschman calls the "quality-elasticity of demand" (1970, p. 130), an individual's sense of the volatility of public opinion. It is his or her estimate of the extent of community conflict likely to erupt as a result of a given level of dissatisfaction with busing.

The importance of the perceived volatility of public response can be seen by comparing part *a* with part *b* in figure 7.2. Both represent individuals who have the same level of dissatisfaction with busing. A person who believes he is in the minority or that there is a dividing cleavage perceives a low elasticity of public response. This person is represented in figure 7.2a. The proportion engaging in protest as a result of the court order ($Q0 - Q1$) is believed to be relatively small. The likelihood that the community can impose significant costs on authorities or that an individual can contribute in a significant way is therefore believed to be low. The region labeled

2. Rossell (1983) notes that antibusing protests almost never occur in a community before the time of a court order, even though antibusing feeling may be widespread before that time and there is a widespread expectation that a court order will be issued.

$Pr\{VU\}$, showing the likelihood that this individual will engage in illegal protest, is comparatively small.

A person who believes he is in the majority or that there is a reinforcing cleavage perceives a high elasticity of public response. This is represented in figure 7.2b. This person believes the proportion engaging in illegal protest as a result of the court order ($Q0 - Q1$) is relatively high. The likelihood that the community can impose significant costs on authorities and that an individual can contribute in a significant way is therefore believed to be high. The region $Pr\{VU\}$, corresponding to the likelihood of participating in illegal action, is also comparatively large.

What, exactly, do people consider when judging the costs likely to be imposed by community protest and the value of joining? There is a difference between nonpublic goods and public goods in the kinds of costs created for authorities. There is no simple "unit" cost for each person who decides to stop "buying" and to start protesting against school desegregation. The costs of this kind of action, especially its illegal varieties, are borne by those responsible for the day to day operation of the schools, the police, and other community institutions.

Despite there being no simple "unit rule" relating public opposition to the difficulties (i.e., costs) that can be placed in the way of school desegregation implementation, there is no doubt that Boston residents were aware that costs were associated with protest actions. Mayor White repeatedly requested funds and police from other jurisdictions to defray the costs of enforcing public order during the time of protest. On several occasions he publicly discussed the financial burden brought on the city and the school district by having to cope with public resistance to school desegregation (Richard, Knox, and Oliphant 1975).[3]

In this situation, where higher costs are known to be associated

3. Not only are community residents likely to be aware of a modified unit rule relating protest to cost, but social science scholarship uses this equation to explain the power of social movements. Crain et al. (1968) and Oberschall (1973) argue that one of the resources of the American civil rights movement in the 1960s was the ability to create organizational costs and unfavorable publicity for public policymakers in Southern states. Lipsky (1968) makes the general argument that a movement's ability to generate protest is a political resource. Coleman (1971) makes the same argument emphasizing the need to create a link in the public mind between organizational costs and unpopular organizational policies.

with higher levels of public opposition, Hirschman's model elegantly describes the reward-based relationship between perceived levels of public opposition and a person's willingness to protest.

The Role of Media

Each theory analyzed here relies significantly, albeit indirectly, on effects of mass media and mass communications. Each theory analyzes how *perceived* opinions *perceived* alignments of the community against "outside" forces, and *perceived* levels of opposition in the community affect the willingness of individuals to take part in protest actions. Media have a potentially significant role in shaping these perceptions.

Each theory points to a different way the media might influence perceptions and, thereby, affect the level of mobilization in a community. In the spiral of silence, the principal impact of the media is on the perception of the opinions of one's neighbors. With Gamson's theory, the principal impact of media would be on people's perceptions of an alignment of the community against unjust, "outside" authorities. In Hirschman's theory, the primary influence of media would be on perceptions of the proportion of the community already mobilized and the net costs and benefits that might follow from joining in.

The theories and research reported here show a number of significant ways that media effects on mobilization might be conceptualized and studied. The Boston survey was not designed principally as a media analysis. The analyses here suggest, however, that media effects can significantly reinforce community tendencies to mobilization.

Perception of Opinion and Desegregation Protest: Empirical Findings

Public Opinion about Public Opinion

The independent variable in each of the three theories is the same—i.e., the general perception of public disagreement with (and reaction to) desegregation. Table 7.1 shows the results for a number of measures of people's perceptions of community opinion and neighborhood action during the time of the Boston school

Table 7.1   *Perception of Public Opinion and Public Action against Desegregation*

	Wave 1	Wave 2	Wave 3	Wave 4	Wave 5
Percent saying opposition is dominant opinion for neighbors (actual: 95% opposed)	94	98	98		96
Average percent of neighbors believed to agree with Judge Garrity (actual: 16% agree)			15%		
Average percent believed to be boycotting in early fall 1974 (actual: 12% boycott)				19%	
Perceived trend in the school boycott:					
Percent "increasing"				19	
Percent "no change"				45	
Expected future trend in the boycott:					
Percent "increase"				26	
Percent "no change"				59	
Average percent believed boycotting in 1974/1975 school year (actual: 27% boycott)					33%
Expected future trend in the boycott:					
Percent "increase"					52
Percent "no change"					36
Percent of neighbors expected to resist, defy, openly oppose, or avoid Phase I			65		
Percent of neighbors believed to have defied, demonstrated against, avoided, interfered with, or worked against Phase I				79	
Percent of neighbors expected to avoid, demonstrate against, openly oppose, or create problems to hinder Phase II					75

Table 7.1 *(continued)*

	Wave 1	Wave 2	Wave 3	Wave 4	Wave 5
Percent saying preference for separation of the races is the dominant opinion among neighbors	61				58

Note: Question wordings: see Appendix 1, nos. 48–58.
   Data are combined from samples of white residents of six Boston neighborhoods.
   Data show responses of those opposed to busing at the time of the interview.

desegregation controversy. Neighborhood residents who perceive widespread opposition to the court order, a reinforcing pattern of community conflict and/or an elastic public response to busing, are those who say:

1. Public opinion is predominantly opposed to busing.
2. The percent boycotting the public schools is high and/or increasing.
3. Their neighbors will work to resist or avoid the court order.

The first row of table 7.1 shows that in each wave nearly 100 percent of the respondents in the Boston sample have the impression that public opinion in their neighborhood is predominantly opposed to two-way busing to achieve school desegregation. The second row of table 7.1 shows people's perception of neighborhood support for Judge Garrity's decision. People were asked to estimate the proportion of their neighbors agreeing with the court order. The second row of table 7.1 shows that during the time of the wave 3 interview, the average of these estimates is 15 percent.

The next five questions in table 7.1 deal with the topic of school boycotts. The third row shows that during the beginning months of Phase I (wave 4) residents of the Boston neighborhoods estimate that, on average, 19 percent of their neighbors are not sending their children to public school regularly. During this same time, 19 percent say the level of boycott participation has been increasing since the beginning of the school year (see row 4 of table 7.1) and 26 percent say the school boycott will become even more extensive (see row 5). During the summer after Phase I (wave 5), residents of the Boston neighborhoods estimate, on average, that 33 percent of their neighbors had not sent their children to public school regularly (row 6). Fifty-two percent expect the boycott will increase during the next school year (row 7).

The next three questions in table 7.1 have to do with the perception respondents have of their neighbors' actions regarding the court order. Just before the beginning of Phase I (wave 3), 65 percent say their neighbors will "resist," "defy," "openly oppose," or "find a way around" the court order (row 8). By the end of the first few months of Phase I (wave 4), 79 percent of the respondents say their neighbors are actually participating in "demonstrations," "defiance," "interference," "avoidance," or are "actively working to reverse the Phase I decision" (row 9). This level of perceived neighborhood reaction remains steady. At the end of the 1974/75 school year (wave 5), 75 percent say their neighbors will engage in a similar inventory of actions to hinder implementation of the Phase II plan (row 10).

Perception of Opposition and Mobilization

Each of the three theories offers a different explanation of the relationship between perceived support for one's point of view and willingness to protest. According to the spiral of silence, those who believe they are in the minority fear social isolation and so do not risk exposing themselves to the disapproval of their neighbors. According to the theory advanced by Gamson et al., someone who believes the public is strongly opposed to a policy tends to perceive a reinforcing cleavage. This activates group loyalties and increases the salience of any past conflicts between insiders and outsiders as a way of understanding the issue. According to Hirschman's theory, the higher the proportion believed to oppose a policy, the more certain an individual is that protest can impose significant costs on authorities, and therefore the more likely an individual is to join.

During the period of time spanned by the wave 1 to wave 4 surveys—from before Judge Garrity's order until the beginning of Phase I—the pattern is strongly in the direction predicted by each theory. Perception of the strength of public opposition to busing is strongly, monotonically related to people's willingness to protest. Data from the wave 1 interviews are shown in table 7.2.

Table 7.2   *Perceived Public Opposition and Willingness to Protest, Wave 1*

	Percent Willing to Support Defiance	Percent Willing to Support Boycott
Perceived level of opposition to busing among neighbors:		
Very strongly opposed	61	48
Less strongly opposed	47	25
Neutral, favorable	37	27

Note: Question wordings: see Appendix 1, nos. 48, 14, 15.

Data are combined from samples of white residents of six Boston neighborhoods.

Data show responses of those personally opposed to busing at the time of the interview.

Patterns shown are significant (.05) when racial prejudice/fear and strength of antibusing opinion are controlled.

The percentages in table 7.2 and in the next two tables are for respondents opposed to busing.[4] In principle, analyses could be done to show the effect of perceived community opinion on willing-

4. Data are analyzed separately for antibusing respondents for a number of reasons. Most important, it is necessary to control for the fact that one's opinion on busing is related to one's perception of the level of antibusing sentiment in the community. This phenomenon, known as the "looking glass" effect, is well documented in the literature on pluralistic ignorance and the theory of the spiral of silence. Second, it is necessary to establish the discriminant validity (Cronbach 1971) of the measures of perceived public opinion and willingness to publicly voice one's views against busing. It is necessary to show that perception of public opposition and willingness to take part in antibusing actions are not simply measures of extreme antibusing opinion.

The relationships in tables 7.2, 7.3, and 7.4 were initially analyzed using a more detailed measure of the intensity of antibusing opinion as well as a number of other measures of racial prejudice (see Chapter 3). At all levels of intensity and at all levels of prejudice, there is a strong relationship between perception of community opinion and willingness to take part in antibusing actions.

Panel analyses were also performed to determine whether the conclusions hold up when adjustments are made for "cross-lagged" effects and instability of response. Although any such procedure cannot, in principle, determine the direction of a causal relationship (Duncan 1969, 1972, 1975), the pattern of coefficients in the panel models shows that the strongest effects are the ones suggested by the findings as they are presented in tables 7.2, 7.3, and 7.4.

ness to act on behalf of the court order. Given the sample size, however, there are too few probusing respondents to do so.[5]

The first column in table 7.2 shows the percent saying they would encourage defiance of the court order if they were members of the Boston school board. We recall from table 4.8 that, overall, 57 percent of the Boston neighborhood residents opposed to busing say they would. The first column in table 7.2 shows how this measure of willingness to protest is related to perceived levels of public opposition to busing. As the perceived level of public opposition diminishes, so does willingness to defy the court.

The second column in table 7.2 shows a similar result for the percent saying they would support a school boycott if they were members of the Boston school board. Again, we recall from table 4.8 that, overall, 43 percent say they would. Table 7.2 shows that willingness to support a school boycott is also strongly related to the level of perceived public opposition to busing during this stage of the controversy. Among those who believe the public is "very strongly opposed" to busing, 48 percent support the boycott. As the perceived level of public opposition diminishes, support for the boycott does as well.

Table 7.3 shows the relationships for the measures asked in the wave 3 interviews. The questions analyzed in the first two columns are wave 3 replications of the wave 1 measures examined in the previous table—support for school board defiance and support for a school boycott. The third column introduces a third measure. Respondents were asked how frequently they discuss "the issue of racial balance in the Boston public schools with other people in [the] neighborhood." Since the analysis in table 7.3 is limited to people who, at the time of wave 3, say they are personally opposed to busing, it seems safe to argue that the third column of table 7.3 shows the proportion willing to discuss antibusing views with their neighbors. At the time of the wave 3 survey, 41 percent of the Boston residents opposed to busing say they talk "frequently" or "very frequently" with their neighbors about the busing issue. This measure is one of the "low-level," "everyday" indicators of sen-

5. This is unfortunate because one of my earlier studies finds that the effect of perceived support for one's views is sometimes different for those who are actually in the majority than for those actually in the minority (Taylor 1982).

sitivity to public opinion that is central to tests of the theory of the spiral of silence.

Table 7.3 shows the effect of three different measures of perceived public support on willingness to protest and on frequency of discussing antibusing views with the neighbors. The first measure of public perception—perceived severity of opposition to busing—is

Table 7.3   *Perceived Public Opposition, Protest and Expression of Antibusing Views, Wave 3*

	Percent Willing to Support Defiance	Percent Willing to Support Boycott	Percent Discussing Opinions Frequently or Very Frequently with Neighbors
Perceived level of opposition to busing among neighbors:			
Very strongly opposed	64	63	47
Less strongly opposed	40	48	15
Neutral, favorable	33	48	10
Perceived percent of neighbors agreeing with Judge Garrity:			
0%	76	75	56
10%, a few	59	62	41
25% or more	47	45	28
Expected action of neighbors regarding the court order:			
Antagonistic	63	65	46
Neutral, favorable	52	51	32

Note: Question wordings: see Appendix 1, nos. 48, 49, 55, 14, 15, 59.

   Data are combined from samples of white residents of six Boston neighborhoods.

   Data show responses of those personally opposed to busing at the time of the interview.

   Patterns shown are significant (.05) when racial prejudice/fear and strength of antibusing opinion are controlled.

the wave 3 replication of the measure of public perception analyzed in the previous table. The second measure of public perception in table 7.3 asks respondents to estimate the proportion of their neighbors who "agree with Judge Garrity's decision." The third measure asks respondents what they "think most people in [the] neighborhood will actually do in the next two months [i.e., July and August] in response to Judge Garrity's decision [and in preparation for Phase I implementation]." Those classified as "perceiving public opposition" are the ones who say their neighbors will take steps to "resist," "reverse," or "get around" the decision.[6]

For each of the three dependent measures the pattern in table 7.3 is the same: the more a person perceives public opinion or public action to be opposed to busing, the more willing a person is to take part in antibusing actions and to talk with the neighbors about his or her antibusing views. Perception of public opposition to Judge Garrity's order is, perhaps, the strongest predictor (of the measures in table 7.3) of willingness to take part in antibusing actions. Among those who say none of their neighbors agree with Judge Garrity, 76 percent say they would favor defiance, 75 percent say they would support a school boycott, and 56 percent say they discuss the busing issue frequently or very frequently with their neighbors. As the perceived level of neighborhood support for Judge Garrity's decision increases, there is a substantial reduction in the percent willing to take part in such actions. This pattern is the same for any combination of the three measures of perception and the measures of willingness to take part in antibusing actions or express antibusing views shown in table 7.3.

The data from waves 1–4, without exception, confirm the three theories discussed in this chapter. Those who see support for their views in the social environment, those who see a reinforcing cleavage, and those who think that protest is widespread are all more

6. One might ask why the measures of public perception in table 7.3 are not also used in table 7.2 (and not identical with the ones in table 7.4). The second and third measures of public perception in table 7.3 could not have been asked in earlier waves because Judge Garrity had not yet announced his decision. The nature of issues and events continually evolves during a community crisis. Because of this the questions asked in panel studies of community conflict must change, even though it is desirable for many reasons to have repeated measures asked in exactly the same way from one wave to the next.

Table 7.4   *Perceived Public Opposition, Protest and Expression of Antibusing Views, Wave 5*

	Percent Willing to Support Boycott	Percent Discussing Opinions Frequently or Very Frequently with Neighbors
Perceived level of opposition to busing among neighbors:		
Very strongly opposed	46	68
Less strongly opposed	31	54
Neutral, favorable	46	18
Percent of neighbors believed to have boycotted during 1974/1975:		
45% or more	49	73
15%–44%	44	71
14% or less	43	57
Expected action of neighbors regarding the court order:		
Antagonistic	48	69
Neutral, favorable	29	51
Expected future trend in the school boycott during 1975/1976:		
Increase	49	85
No change	31	51
Decrease	54	71

Note: Question wordings: see Appendix 1, nos. 48, 53, 54, 57, 16, 60.

Data are combined from samples of white residents of six Boston neighborhoods.

Data show responses of those personally opposed to busing at the time of the interview.

Patterns shown are significant (.05) when racial prejudice/fear and strength of antibusing opinion are controlled.

likely to support protest against desegregation than those who do not. The data from the wave 5 interviews, shown in table 7.4, also tend to support the three theories, although not completely. As before, findings are shown for Boston neighborhood residents personally opposed to busing at the time of the current interview.

The second column in table 7.4 shows the percent saying they "frequently" or "very frequently" talk with their neighbors about "how the events of the past year have affected the quality of the Boston schools." This is the wave 5 replication of the measure of frequency of discussion analyzed in the previous table (wave 3). The difference between wave 3 and wave 5 in overall percentages suggests that the frequency of discussing antibusing views went up during the Phase I protest. The change in question wording, however, requires some note of caution about this conclusion.[7]

The second column of table 7.4 shows that the frequency of discussing antibusing opinions with the neighbors is highest for those who believe the neighbors are "very strongly opposed" to busing, for those with very high estimates of the proportion of neighbors participating in the school boycott, and for those expecting their neighbors to take antibusing actions during Phase II. These findings support the three theories. Other evidence in table 7.4, however, is inconsistent with them.

The percent discussing their antibusing opinions with the neighbors is especially high for those who expect increased support for the boycott during Phase II, but it is also especially high for those who expect decreased support. This suggests a pattern of rearguard action.[8] During the late stages of the antibusing conflict, willingness to express antibusing views is especially high for those who think

7. The conclusion seems justifiable, however. An increase in likelihood of expressing one's opinion was not found for those personally neutral toward, or in favor of, the court order. In the third wave, 28 percent said they discussed the issue frequently or very frequently with their neighbors. In wave 5, the level was about the same, 27 percent. A potential response effect attributable to changed question wording would be unlikely to affect these groups differentially.

8. The term "rearguard" is relative. The first four waves of the Boston panel survey are "early" measures with respect to the timing of the data collection but not with respect to the history of the school desegregation controversy in Boston. As noted in Chapter 2, the wave 1 survey reflects public opinion after more than 10 years of civil rights activity and after a state-mandated busing plan was already ordered.

the trend is in their favor, but it is also especially high for those who think their opinions are against the trend.

Other evidence in table 7.4 also illustrates a rearguard pattern. The percent supporting the school boycott is especially high for those who expect increased boycotting, but it is also especially high for those who expect a decrease in neighborhood boycott participation. Likewise, the percent in favor of the boycott is especially high for those who perceive "very strong" neighborhood opposition to busing, but it is also especially high for those who think their neighbors are neutral or positive on busing.

Why should there be a rearguard pattern? The wave 5 interviews were conducted after the first year of court-ordered desegregation was complete. During this time, boycotts and defiance had been contained by public authority, and the threat of receivership had been announced (but not yet implemented) by Judge Garrity. Evidence presented in the next chapter shows that by the time of the wave 5 interviews most Boston neighborhood residents had given up on the idea of delaying desegregation. The rearguard pattern in table 7.4 is evidence of support for a lost cause during the final stages of a conflict. This phenomenon contradicts the three theories of mobilization analyzed here and suggests that the three theories are most applicable during earlier stages of a community conflict.

On the Accuracy of Public Perceptions

Misperception of the direction of public opinion is referred to as pluralist ignorance (Merton 1968; Allport 1924; Krech and Crutchfield 1948; Isenberg 1980). This phenomenon is important for studies of mobilization, because people may be willing to protest based on their perceptions of community opinion but, because of pluralistic ignorance, may be greatly mistaken in that perception. Survey studies of the accuracy of public assessments of public opinion agree that misperception is, in certain circumstances, widespread. Fields and Schuman (1976) and O'Gorman (1975, 1976, 1979) report quite high levels of public misperception of community opinion, particularly with regard to matters of racial politics and racial preferences.

The figures in table 7.1 show, however, that Boston residents have a quite accurate picture of the level of opposition to busing and the court order during the time covered by these surveys. The first two rows of table 7.1 show that about 95 percent say community opinion is predominantly opposed to two-way busing and that only a small percentage favor Judge Garrity's order. About 85 to 90 percent of neighborhood residents actually are opposed to busing during this period. To assess the accuracy of the perception of community opposition to Judge Garrity's order (row 3), people were asked whether they themselves were for or against the court's decision. At the time of the wave 3 interview, 16 percent agree with the court: a result quite close to the average percent perceived to agree with Judge Garrity, 15 percent.

Public estimates of boycott participation are also quite accurate. Neighborhood residents estimate, on average, a boycott participation rate of 19 percent at the beginning of Phase I and a rate of 33 percent by the end of the first year. Public school enrollment was actually down 12 percent during the first few months of Phase I and down 27 percent by the end of the 1974/75 school year. With respect to the boycott, the only figure that might be called inaccurate is the high percent expecting more extensive participation during the next school year, which, in fact, did not happen.

There are no objective standards for measuring the accuracy of the last three measures of perceptions shown in table 7.1. Survey analysts are loath, for a number of reasons, to inquire too deeply about participation in protest actions that are a violation of the law. Therefore, we cannot tell if the percent believed to be participating in such action is too high or too low.

Why is the apparent level of pluralistic ignorance lower in the Boston data than in other surveys having to do with some of the same topics? Some of the previous research is based on national surveys conducted during times of relative racial calm, compared to the situation in Boston in the mid-1970s (e.g., O'Gorman 1975, 1976, 1979). It may be that communication patterns are more dense and better informed during times of community crisis, thus leading to more accurate perceptions of public opinion and public action. A second reason may be that these studies ask about private behavior ("would your neighbors allow their children to play with children of another race") and general feelings ("are your neighbors generally for or against separation of the races") rather than about public behavior (protests) and opinions on concrete political issues (the court order). The high levels of pluralistic ignorance about racial issues found in other surveys may not characterize the situation in more geographically concentrated areas when detailed questions are asked about (1) public opinion regarding local issues that have been a matter of controversy for some time; and (2) public participation in particular actions, such as school boycotts, where information regarding neighbors' actions may have been a topic for coverage by mass media.

Interestingly, one question asked in the Boston survey is more like the general questions used in the earlier studies of pluralistic ignorance, and it shows a higher level of public misperception of public opinion. The eleventh row of table 7.1 shows that about 60 percent say their neighbors are predominantly in favor of separation of the races. The findings reported earlier show that belief in separation of the races is actually the minority opinion in these neighborhoods—favored by only 5 to 10 percent. It may be that perceptions of public opinion on racial matters are accurate for questions about implementation of minority rights (where public opinion is generally opposed) but not for questions regarding endorsement of general principles about racial equality (where public opinion is generally tolerant).

The one question that does show mistaken impressions of the majority view also has little relationship to willingness to protest. This suggests that only minimum gains can be achieved by attempts to "shape" perceptions of public opinion in a way that varies too greatly from reality. Unfortunately, not enough questions are included in the Boston survey to determine if this is a general pattern.

Conclusion

In *Brown II*, the Supreme Court allowed that "a variety of obstacles" justified delay by local officials in implementing desegregation. The court did not, however, recognize public opinion as a valid reason for delay:

> It should go without saying that the vitality of these constitutional principles cannot be allowed to yield simply because of disagreement with them.

The argument that public opposition justifies delay was specifically tested in the Little Rock case and found unacceptable:

> In the summer of 1958 the Little Rock School Board [argued that] the illegal interference by Arkansas officials and the consequent disorder had created such chaotic educational circumstances that they felt entitled to resegregate. [The Federal Circuit Judge] agreed. But . . . the court of appeals reversed . . . saying that to yield to the contention that disorder justifies resegregation would be to enthrone official lawlessness. . . . The formal position of the judges is that the attitude of the community toward desegregation is irrelevant. A judge is to act "uninfluenced by private and public opinion as to the desirability of desegregation." The Supreme Court in the Little Rock case held that opposition in a community, even violence, does not justify a board in refusing to desegregate the schools . . . or authorize a judge to refuse an injunction. (Peltason 1961, pp. 47, 132.

In spite of unfavorable legal precedent, opponents of desegregation still search for evidence of the extensiveness of public opposition, and school boards still introduce that evidence into federal court hearings on desegregation. Such actions, of course, have no legal standing. They do, however, provide vivid public documentation of widespread community opposition to busing and may prolong the period of public conflict.

Public Opinion and the Mobilization of Discontent

The three explanations in this chapter of the relationship between perception of opinion and willingness to protest are not mutually exclusive. A person's belief in the elasticity of public response is probably related to his or her belief about the extent to which the current community conflict follows "historical" lines of cleavage. An excitable public is likely to be aroused again by a court order. A person's sense of the level of arousal of the "excitable" public is also proportional to his or her sense of the social harm that is done by the court order. This sense of harm is, of course, subject to manipulation by media, authorities, and other sources of information. The theory of the spiral of silence explains how, in the end, dissent from the majority view against busing can become locked out because of intimidation, frustration, and, finally, loss of interest.

The findings in this chapter suggest that, for peaceful implementation, it is important for community leaders to actively discourage and discredit opposition to integration. Efforts should be made to preserve and publicize diversity of opinion in a community. Attempts should be made to build coalitions on the desegregation issue in a new way so that busing does not seem like a new version of the "same old conflict." If these actions are not taken, it becomes more likely that the dynamics of compliance will not be smooth. Instead, the more or less practical, sometimes "rational" choices of most individuals will encourage the development of an antagonized community with a sense of its identity as such. Busing opponents will join protests that seem likely to inflict harm. Intolerance for desegregation will eventually be reinforced by a weakened resolve among allies of the court to even pursue their argument publicly.

8 | On the Goals of
Antibusing Protest

Costs and Benefits

Rodgers and Bullock argue that the decision to protest against mandatory desegregation is a function of the costs and benefits people expect:

> Citizens obey most laws because they perceive that the utilities of compliance outweigh the utilities of noncompliance. However, when citizens perceive the utilities of the situation favor disobedience, they break the law. The individual's values and expectations . . . determine how he calculates the net pleasure/pain which he expects to result from a particular act. (1976, p. 3)

Their exploration of the relation between costs, benefits, and protest is not, however, rigorous. They do not report evidence showing the likelihood of success, the likelihood of repression, and how these factors affect the likelihood of protest.

The findings in this book show that the cost/benefit approach, at least as we normally think of it, needs to be substantively modified before it is a useful framework for analyzing protest against mandatory desegregation. Antibusing protest is not motivated by a sense that it will end mandatory desegregation in the near future. Those who do think the short-term goal is attainable—an immediate end to busing—are no more likely to favor protest than those who do not. The absence of a link between the expectation of success and a willingness to protest suggests, by conventional cost/benefit reasoning, that antibusing protest is not rational, goal-oriented behavior.

The failure of Rodgers and Bullock's model is not so much due to the irrationality of antibusing protesters as it is to the way "bene-fits," and to some extent "costs," are normally defined by social re-searchers. Michael Schwartz, in a careful and rewarding discussion, argues that unless social researchers study the way costs and benefits are perceived by community residents, formal models of rational protest will be of limited utility (1976, pp. 135–144). Schwartz's discussion focuses on the distinction between accurate versus inac-curate perception of benefits and suggests that motivation for pro-test which is tied to some expectation of benefit should be consid-ered rational, whether or not the expectation is accurate.

The summary of goals of antibusing protest in this chapter adds another dimension to Schwartz's argument. My analysis of the sur-vey data indicates that the issue of rational versus irrational protest is not related to the accuracy of perceptions so much as it is related to the nature of the goal expected to be attained by collective action. Only a small number of Boston neighborhood residents mistakenly believe their efforts are likely to bring about an end to busing. Yet, at least during the intense periods of conflict, many Boston residents believe some good will come from protesting even though the bene-fits cannot be specifically named and the time frame for achieving them is indefinite.

The belief that antibusing protest is valuable even though the na-ture and timing of the benefits cannot be fully specified is encour-aged by:

1. Public leaders who suggest that court orders can be reversed, without specifying exactly when or how this will happen.
2. Public leaders who encourage neighborhood residents to im-pose costs on the police and on the school system by sug-gesting that these costs increase the chance busing will end.
3. Statements by representatives from the executive branch of the federal government holding out the hope that it might provide tangible assistance to the antibusing movement.
4. A tendency for external support for most social movements to increase as displays of public conflict continue.

Support for Protest, Uncertainty about Results

The Boston survey shows that neighborhood residents are nearly unanimous in their support for legal challenges and legislative efforts aimed at neutralizing Judge Garrity's order. These findings are shown in table 8.1. Before Judge Garrity's order (wave 1), 73 percent of those opposed to busing support attempts to repeal the Racial Imbalance Act (RIA), and 80 percent support efforts to pass a constitutional amendment against busing. After the court order, the level of support for the antibusing amendment rose to 89 percent, 84 percent support an appeal of the court order to the Supreme Court, 88 percent favor congressional legislation limiting the use of busing, and 76 percent favor legislation limiting the power of judges to implement policies in this area.

The Boston survey also shows that a majority of neighborhood

Table 8.1   *Support for Legal Challenges to Judge Garrity's Order*

	Wave 1	Wave 3
Percent favoring efforts to repeal the Racial Imbalance Act	73	
Percent favoring efforts to pass a constitutional amendment against busing	80	89
Percent favoring appeal of Judge Garrity's decision to the Supreme Court		84
Percent favoring efforts to pass national legislation to limit busing		88
Percent favoring efforts to pass national legislation to limit power of courts to order busing		76

Note: Question wordings: see Appendix 1, nos. 61–66.
    Data are combined from samples of white residents of six Boston neighborhoods.
    Data show responses of those personally opposed to busing at the time of the interview.

residents supported, at one time or another, civil disobedience and other illegal actions to slow implementation of Judge Garrity's order. (The data were presented in Chapter 4, table 4.8). Before the court order (wave 1), just over 40 percent of those opposed to busing supported the school boycott. By the time of the court order (wave 3), support for the boycott rose to 60 percent.[1] During the early stages of the conflict (waves 1–3), between 50 and 60 percent supported school committee defiance of the court order, and almost 80 percent said the most important thing for their neighbors to do when the first year of desegregation begins is to resist or evade the court order.

The results in table 8.2 show, in a number of ways, that Boston neighborhood residents do not expect their protest actions to bring about an end to busing anytime soon. Before the court order (wave 2), 37 percent said the federal court would find the school board not guilty. Only about one-third of those opposed to busing believed the Supreme Court would actually overturn Judge Garrity's decision. Almost all said it was "impossible" or "extremely difficult" to reverse an unpopular court decision. More than half said a court can "make people go along with" unpopular decisions most of the time or all of the time. And finally, even a year before Judge Garrity's decision (wave 1), only 39 percent of those opposed to busing said it could be delayed indefinitely. By the time of the court order (wave 3), the level of optimism fell to 14 percent, and by the end of the first year of implementation (wave 5), only 6 percent said Phase II could be delayed.

Why is public willingness to support legal and illegal action against Judge Garrity's order so high if the effect of these actions on reversing public policy is expected to be so low?

Indefinite Benefits and Protest Actions

Frohlich and Oppenheimer argue that a variety of measures of the expected gain from voting, such as whether it will do "some good," should be analyzed in studies of political rationality. All-or-nothing

1. Table 4.8 suggests that after the first year (wave 5) the level of support for the boycott declines to near 40 percent. However, the wave 5 measure is substantially different in wording from the wave 1 and wave 3 measures, so this conclusion may not be warranted.

Table 8.2   *Pessimism About the Benefits From Challenging Judge Garrity's Order*

	Wave 1	Wave 2	Wave 3	Wave 4	Wave 5
Percent saying a federal court would find the school board not guilty		37			
Percent saying the Supreme Court will reverse Judge Garrity's decision				35	
Opinion on difficulty of reversing an unpopular judicial decision:					
Impossible/extremely difficult		50	53	59	
Difficult		42	40	38	
Easy		8	7	3	
Opinion on how often courts can make people go along with unpopular decisions:					
All of the time		10			
Most of the time		42			
Sometimes		37			
Rarely		9			
Percent saying busing can be delayed indefinitely	39	18	14	6	6

Note: Question wordings: see Appendix 1, nos. 67–74.

    Data are combined from samples of white residents of six Boston neighborhoods.

    Data show responses of those personally opposed to busing at the time of the interview.

measures, such as whether one's vote will alter the outcome of the election, do not capture the full measure of indefinite benefits people expect from voting (1978 pp. 97–116).

    Their observations apply to political actions other than voting as well. The survey measures in table 8.2 are not the right questions for measuring the benefit expected from taking part in a community conflict. Questions like the ones in table 8.2 show a high degree of hopelessness (and are not correlated with willingness to protest) because they ask about the chance for a complete victory in the immediate future. The public is aware that the chance any individual action will bring an end to desegregation is actually quite small.

This does not mean, however, that antibusing actions have no expected benefits. Protests against mandatory desegregation occur when neighborhood residents believe "some kind of good" is likely to come from such actions "some time in the future." When analyzing the "benefits" motivating participation in desegregation protest, it is the expectation of unspecifiable gain in an indeterminate time frame that most importantly affects people's motivations and not the belief that an action can bring about an end to busing.

What are some protest activities that are supported because they might yield indefinite benefits? What is the basis for the belief that these benefits may, in fact, be realized?

Litigation, Legislation, and Delay

Beginning in the 1960s, the Boston school board ignored the requirements of the Racial Imbalance Act (RIA) and the United States Department of Health, Education and Welfare to racially balance the public schools. Instead, the school board persisted in segregative actions and challenged all attempts to implement the RIA or HEW guidelines with litigation.

The school board's tactics did not stop desegregation plans from being drawn up or enacted. Noncooperation and litigation, however, first delayed and then reduced the scope of desegregation actually implemented at each stage of the process. Although the board did not achieve a complete victory, it produced limited benefits for neighborhood residents supporting its actions. For instance, the school board chose to litigate rather than cooperate with the state commissioner of education in developing the 1972 plan to implement the RIA. The plan subsequently proposed by the state commissioner left out large sections of the city. It happened that Judge Garrity's Phase I order was based on this plan. Therefore, a number of neighborhoods did not experience desegregation during the first year of Judge Garrity's order.

Defiant actions by local authorities frequently delay implementation of unpopular policies. The procedure for federal enforcement

of desegregation requires the assumption that local officials are acting in good faith. The actions of local officials cannot be overturned
without due process. Thus, public "segregation academies" were
known to be illegal but were approved anyway by Arkansas Governor Orval Faubus and the state legislature because they would force
time-consuming legal tests (Peltason 1961, p. 194). Eugene Cook,
attorney general of the state of Georgia, referred to such practices
and admitted, "We might as well be candid. Most of the laws will be
stricken down by the Courts in due course" (Irving 1957). One segregationist in the Georgia state legislature, reflecting on the assumption of good faith and due process, noted happily, "As long as we
can legislate, we can segregate."

State legislators from Boston neighborhoods organized bills to
repeal the RIA every year from 1966 onward. These actions, as
well, were ultimately rewarded with compromise, confusion, and
a meaningful symbol for rallying further public opposition to the
court order.

The state legislature finally did repeal the RIA in May 1974, one
month before Judge Garrity's order. Governor Francis Sargent vetoed the repeal at the end of the summer but amended the law to
eliminate compulsory busing. Judge Garrity's decision, based on the
Constitution, was legally affected by these actions. However, the
conflicting interpretations of the law created frustration and confusion.[2] In addition, Judge Garrity's Phase I order itself became con-
fusing because it was the plan designed by the state commissioner of
education before the repeal and subsequent modification of the RIA.

State Congressman Richard Finnigan explained that the purpose
of the RIA "repealer" was to call attention to the extent of public
opposition to desegregation and to influence subsequent Supreme
Court decisions:

> It wouldn't have any legal bearing [on the court order] . . . I would say
> that the legislature in repealing the RIA, I would hope that the Federal
> courts might take a second look at what is happening in the area of
> forced busing. (U. S. Commission on Civil Rights 1975, p. 158)

---

2. A similar event took place in Little Rock, Arkansas. In April 1959 the state
supreme court sustained the plan to close the schools and create publicly supported
"segregation academies." The decision had no legal significance in the face of the
contrary federal decisions, but politically it served to confuse the situation.

In this case as well, an action against Judge Garrity's order is supported because it can potentially yield a benefit (which cannot be fully specified) at some indefinite time in the future.

Imposing Costs on Authorities

Protest against Judge Garrity's order was encouraged by the belief that doing so might create a situation so costly for authorities that the policy of mandatory desegregation would be abandoned. Before Judge Garrity's order, school board defiance had already created a situation where the necessary funds might not be available to implement desegregation:

> The development of any overall school desegregation training plan was affected by HEW's freeze on the Emergency School Assistance Act and other Federal Funds which was brought about because of the Federal district court finding of discrimination and which lasted until January 1975. (Richard, Knox, and Oliphant 1975)

After the beginning of Phase I, a well-publicized effect of the boycott was to reduce class sizes in the public schools, which reduced the amount of state aid to the district, ultimately limiting the number of days the school district could be open during the year.

Mayor White, in a number of public statements during Phase I and Phase II, suggested that the cost of busing could not be absorbed in the city budget, which was already overextended because of the need to maintain order (Hannon 1980). Other statements by the mayor as well, documented in Chapter 6, suggested that the disturbance caused by the conflict over busing in Phase I was too great to allow the rest of Judge Garrity's plan to proceed on schedule.

Eliciting External Support

In the 1960s the executive branch of the federal government provided external support for the civil rights movement that resulted in significant progress:

> The crucial actions that implemented the Supreme Court's mandate for desegregated schools . . . emanated from the national Congress and the Executive. . . . The shift in power was accomplished by the pas-

sage of the Civil Rights Act of 1964 and its enforcement by the Department of Health, Education and Welfare. New procedures required HEW certification of desegregation before federal monies were available for a school district. The Attorney General was authorized to initiate suits in behalf of Negro children for the desegregation of school districts. (Vines 1970, pp. 255–266)

During the first years of Judge Garrity's order, Boston residents were encouraged in the belief that the executive branch would eventually provide tangible support for the antibusing cause. President Ford stated in a press conference just after the beginning of Phase I that he was "against forced busing to achieve racial balance as to quality education." In a press conference at the beginning of Phase II, Vice-President Rockefeller announced he would work for a constitutional amendment against busing. The Ford administration publicized its deliberations with the U.S. attorney general and solicitor general to find a strategy for appealing Judge Garrity's order that could be joined by the federal government (Hillson 1977, p. 257).

There is substantial historical justification for the belief that high-level support for the aims of the antibusing movement can forestall or nullify a court order. In the 1950s and 1960s state governments delayed mandatory desegregation by forbidding compliance. In some cases local officials were required to litigate. In Texas local officials were subject to fine and imprisonment and local school districts would lose state financial aid if any desegregation occurred without first a favorable vote in a public referendum. After Nixon's election in 1968, support for mandatory desegregation by the executive branch of government ended and, instead, steps were taken to delay or derail desegregation in a number of American cities (Panetta and Gall 1971). For instance, in 1968 HEW initiated 28 certification reviews. In 1969, the first Nixon year, the number dropped to 16, in 1970 to 15, in 1971 to 11, in 1972 to 9, in 1973 to 1, and in 1974 to zero.

For many busing opponents, visible conflict in the community sustains hope that tactical and/or financial support from others might one day be forthcoming. The suggestion of executive-level support is one example of a promise that antibusing protesters believe might one day be delivered "if only we can hold out long enough." In a memorable analysis, McAdam shows that the early successes of the civil rights movement led to significantly greater contributions of tactical and financial support from sources originally uninvolved with the conflict. In McAdam's words, "external support, far from triggering insurgency, is actually a product of it" (1982, p. 148). The same dynamics apply to protest activities against desegregation. Alabama Senator Sam Englehardt noted that the Montgomery bus boycott "made" the white-supremacist Citizens Councils:

> The bus boycott made us. Before [they] stopped riding the buses, we had only eight hundred members. Now we have thirteen thousand to fourteen thousand in Montgomery alone.

Indefinite Costs: Nonenforcement of the Law

In some cases local leaders suggest that violations of the law will not be punished and that other impediments to protest will be removed. These are not, technically speaking, indefinite benefits motivating desegregation protest. They are, rather, suggestions that costs that might otherwise chill support for protest might not be suffered. The removal of negative incentives can also increase the likelihood of engaging in political action (Oliver 1980).

One of the reasons for the extended period of conflict over school desegregation in Little Rock, Arkansas, is believed to be nonenforcement of the law by federal and local officials. In Little Rock, the Department of Justice refused to seek an injunction to restrain segregationist protest. This action had curbed violence and disorder in other, similar cities. By the time the court order was imminent, Arkansas Governor Orval Faubus believed that under no circumstances would federal officials become involved in implementation (Peltason 1961, pp. 53, 165).

Federal enforcement of civil rights law was not vigorous in Boston either. On September 11, 1974, a great deal of public attention was drawn to the fact that William Gardner, criminal lawyer from the Department of Justice, arrived in Boston to process civil rights complaints. Within 30 days, Attorney General Saxbe dispatched five more prosecutors to Boston to prepare civil rights cases. Between September and December 1974, however, federal investigations resulted in only 11 prosecutions. As of August 1975 there had been five convictions, one acquittal, two dismissals on government motion and three still pending trial.

Finally, there was a sense that even Judge Garrity's court might be lax and forgiving. Federal and state aid to the schools had more than once been withdrawn and then restored by court order in spite of few tangible signs of cooperation by the school board. Judge Garrity threatened the school board with a finding of contempt of court for several months. The threat was finally enforced on December 22, 1974, but then reversed shortly thereafter (January 8, 1975) in spite of the failure of the school board to act in accordance with the judge's instructions (Richard, Knox, and Oliphant 1975).

Indefinite Costs: Safety in Numbers

Chapter 7 shows that those who believe desegregation protest is widespread are more likely themselves to support those actions. One of the reasons for this relationship, not discussed in the previous chapter, is that people may believe there is "safety in numbers"—i.e., if protest is widespread, the chance of negative sanctions falling on any individual taking part is quite low.

Granovetter argues that individuals vary in the level of safety they require before entering a protest (1978). Each person has a "threshold," defined as the proportion of the group he would have to see join before he would feel safe in doing so as well. Granovetter's model shows how the expected benefit and the perceived "safety" of the situation combine to determine whether someone joins a collective protest or not. During a strike, for instance, the potential cost of being one of a small number of strikers is high, especially for those in a vulnerable employment situation (1978, p. 1423).

Financial Costs Proportioned Equally

Collective action can fail because potential participants are uncertain that the costs of acting will be proportionally allocated among all who benefit. Each individual is better off allowing the others to pay the costs of acting, while benefiting from the result as a "free rider."

Mayor White and school board members, as political entrepreneurs, coordinated community expectations that legal costs would be paid and that they would be paid by each member of the community. During the first week of desegregation, Mayor White declared on local television, "The city has exhausted all legal avenues of appeal at a cost of in excess of a million dollars" (Richard, Knox, and Oliphant 1975). On December 19 of that year, School Committee Chairman Kerrigan announced an appeal of Judge Garrity's order to the Supreme Court. Ten days later Mayor White, in a press release, announced the city's intention to pay the costs of the Supreme Court appeal.

Summary: Leadership and the Goals of Protest

It is not necessary to explicitly encourage illegal actions to create a situation where a high proportion of the community is willing to break the law. Public officials and media contribute to the sense that antibusing protest is an effective lever against authority by calling attention to the indefinite benefits of protest, by suggesting that civil disobedience is a personal matter, by coordinating the payment of legal costs, and by suggesting there is "safety in numbers." Such efforts to influence perceptions of costs and benefits can make both legal and illegal protest actions seem worthwhile. Such actions once prompted Warren Burger, then circuit judge for the U.S. Court of Appeals for the District of Columbia to declare in 1958:

> The desegregation orders have led some reckless and irresponsible men in high places to think they can aid and abet defiance of laws they do not like without seeming to realize that this would encourage others to defy the laws.

Protests end when opponents of desegregation become convinced that the indefinite benefits of such actions will not actually materialize. Since many of the hoped-for benefits were sustained by the rhetoric, promises, and posturing of antibusing leaders, it is often the case that these leaders are also repudiated when a community desegregates.

Although the public, at one level, would like to believe that the promises of antibusing leaders can be fulfilled and that mandatory desegregation is not necessary, there is also a great deal of uneasiness about the role of local leadership in antibusing mobilization. A survey taken after a court order to desegregate the central city and suburban school districts in Detroit finds that about two-thirds of whites and about 80 percent of blacks agree that "political candidates have blown the busing issue out of proportion." Between 50 and 60 percent of whites (and more than 90 percent of blacks) believe that "most black and white children would do fine in school together if adults didn't stir up the situation."

Three years after implementation of Phase I of desegregation in Boston, Louise Day Hicks, John J. Kerrigan, and Pixie Palladino were all voted out of office. In this same election John Bryant, the first black school board member, was elected. In the fall of 1981, three white moderates and two liberal blacks captured all five seats on the school board.

Conclusion

The United States has been hesitating between two worlds—one dead, the other powerless to be born. War brought an older order to an end but as usual force proved unequal to founding a new one.

Supreme Court Justice Robert Jackson
February 1954

9 | The Boston Conflict: Summary and Evaluation

The cause of controversy in Boston was not disagreement over whether there should be any integration at all in the public schools. Incentive programs and voluntary action had produced a level of integration in the Boston public schools before Judge Garrity's order that was higher than the level in a number of American cities after compliance with a court decree. The issue was whether school desegregation would be mandatory.

The conflict in Boston was one of the first Northern tests of the doctrine of voluntary compliance. Judge Garrity's order was announced in June 1974, only months after the Supreme Court ruled, for the first time, that a Northern city could be required to desegregate its public schools (*Keyes vs. Denver, Colorado School District No. 1,* 1973).

In a legal sense, the experience in Boston proved that the doctrine of voluntary compliance does not apply in the North, as it does not apply in the South. In Boston a reluctant mayor, a reluctant state governor, and a reluctant federal executive were forced into an irrevocable commitment of police powers to implement mandatory desegregation. These actions affirmed that the powers of the state would be used, if necessary, to enforce compliance with mandatory desegregation in Northern cities.

This chapter summarizes the first significant, protracted Northern challenge to the doctrine of voluntary compliance for American racial politics since that time. It begins with a review of some of the factors contributing to the extended conflict in Boston, based on the findings in earlier chapters, and then follows with a brief recitation of changes in Boston and in the Boston public schools that have occurred since the time of the events analyzed here. It concludes with a discussion of the impact of the Boston school desegregation controversy on American racial politics since the 1970s.

Patterns of Conflict: A Summary

The conflict in Boston showed that whites oppose mandatory desegregation in the North as well as in the South, in the 1970s as well as in the 1950s. The motives for resistance have changed, however, since the 1950s. Chapter 3 shows that the public is no longer strongly opposed to the principle of integration and accepts small amounts achieved on a voluntary basis.

The resistance in Boston was focused on the issue of mandatory versus voluntary compliance. Chapters 3 and 4 show that white resistance to mandatory desegregation is rooted in fears of minority concentration and in the belief that, as a social policy, mandatory desegregation is unfair, unjust, and likely to produce social harm. Fear of minority concentration and the injustice frame are the perceptions that currently justify, or, in Myrdal's term, "rationalize" antibusing protest. They provide explanations, in contemporary terms and in everyday language, for the applicability of the doctrine of voluntary compliance. Boston is a vivid national symbol of widespread white support for this doctrine—the view that discrimination is illegal but that desegregation is not mandatory.

The conflict in Boston illustrates the kinds of circumstances where opponents of desegregation are most likely to be successful in mobilizing their communities against busing. Most communities, after all, do not experience the kind of conflict Boston did, even though public support for the doctrine of voluntary compliance, fear of minority concentration, and perception of the injustice of busing are likely to be as great. The chapters in Part Two of this book examine a number of reasons why the conflict over mandatory desegregation was particularly strong in Boston (and, by implication, less so in other American cities where the rationalizations for the doctrine of voluntary compliance may have been as widely held).

In most places the opponents of desegregation do not become organized until just before or just after an order to comply:

> Organized opposition seems to have occurred when desegregation began or was imminent. Before it became obvious that desegregation

was about to occur, whites apparently saw no need to oppose the process demonstrably since school officials were thwarting federal objectives successfully. By the time whites did organize, it was a rear guard action just before or after dual schools were eliminated. (Rodgers and Bullock 1976, p. 43)

In places where the opposition does become organized, it tends to dissipate quickly:

> Kirby et al. (1973) and Rossell (1978b) find that demonstrations begin after the decision to desegregate has been made. . . . They rarely occur before a decision has been made because the information costs are too great, and they seldom persist past the year in which the plan is implemented because the likelihood of success is low. (Rossell 1983, pp. 20–21)

In Boston, however, the antibusing movement was better organized and better supplied with resources than similar movements in other cities. As several chapters in this book note, the long history of state versus local control of city government divided the community in a way that was reproduced at the time of the desegregation struggle. A number of antibusing leaders developed political careers and were elevated to public office during the years preceding the busing conflict because of their support for local as opposed to "outside" control of governmental policy. Other antibusing leaders achieved power and political office during the conflict on the strength of their ability to add to and otherwise exploit public dissatisfaction over the "alienation" of community control by the state government and Judge Garrity's federal court.

Unlike the pattern in most other cities, considerable resources for mass communication, organization, and attention-calling were available to the antibusing movement. Some of these resources came from the political office held by antibusing leaders. As Chapter 4 notes, the positions on the school board and city government held by prominent antibusing leaders provided a type of neighborhood "precinct" organizational base for the antibusing movement. Judge Garrity never was able to close off access to these organizational resources.

Other resources came from community organizations that were successfully co-opted into the antibusing movement. Chapter 5 analyzes the strains on Catholic church leadership produced by conflict with the laity over desegregation policy. At first, these strains caused the church to be unable to maintain a consistent probusing position in its organizational hierarchy. Ultimately, the need to avoid protracted conflict with the laity led to a position of public support by a number of church officials for principles of civil disobedience and the doctrine of voluntary compliance.

The existence of a well-heeled, well-organized, ideologically "pure" opposition put the mayor and other local leaders charged with enforcing Judge Garrity's order in a political bind. As Chapter 6 notes, American political institutions provide easy means for retribution against public leaders who do not implement the will of the majority—even when that will is contrary to the requirements of the law. There is no explicit constitutional safeguard that local leaders who enforce an unpopular law will be returned to office in the next election. Local political leaders risk prosecution if they do not enforce an unpopular law and an end to their political career if they do. Those who choose to enforce the law have the best chance to stay in office if they explain their actions as necessary to ensure public safety and otherwise minimize the appearance of agreement with the policy. The task of local enforcement is also easier when there is consistent support for the policy at higher levels of government. In Peltason's language, someone must be willing to take a "scapegoat" role. In Boston, even though Judge Garrity played this role, support for desegregation was not consistent enough across other levels of government to provide adequate support for local leaders charged with enforcing the policy. Chapter 6 illustrates how inconsistent support for the law by officials at all levels of government, coupled with a divided constituency, created a situation where Boston Mayor Kevin White joined other community leaders speaking on behalf of the doctrine of voluntary compliance.

Finally, two "microanalytic" theories, which explain some of the "macro" effects discussed so far, are considered in Chapters 7 and 8. Chapter 7 explores the relationship between awareness of community opposition and willingness to protest. When people believe that community mobilization is widespread, then they themselves are more willing to join in protest. Statements by public leaders, the media, and other "influentials" that call attention to the widespread community opposition or the conflict between "the people versus the authorities" on the issue increase the perception that a busing opponent is in the majority and that something may be gained from protesting.

Chapter 8 addresses the theory of costs, benefits and "rational" protest. In Boston, public leaders encouraged the view that protest would be worthwhile even if it would not bring an end to the court order. The success of the antibusing movement in stalling and over-turning previous mandates for desegregation fueled the view among Boston residents that something like that might happen again if the opponents of busing could create enough disorder and otherwise "hold out long enough." The result is that during the time of most intense conflict, many Boston residents believed that antibusing pro-test would be worthwhile even though a much smaller (and declining proportion) believed that the court order could be delayed.

The public reacts to the perceived costs and benefits of protest. From the point of view of an economic theory of protest, however, the most significant finding may be that there is a great deal of in-definiteness about the public's view of the expected benefits of pro-test. Many people favor protest because they expect it will do some good, but most of them are unable to say precisely which benefits are likely to be realized from protest, or the time frame in which such benefits might be expected. Actions by local leaders that pro-duce "small antibusing victories" (such as successfully delaying the threat of receivership), statements calling attention to past in-stances of successful defiance, and current public disorder (when it is perceived as widespread) all fuel the belief among busing oppo-nents that protest is worthwhile, other indications to the contrary notwithstanding.

The Aftermath in Boston: A Brief Note

This book analyzes the events just preceding and just following Judge Garrity's order. Some discussion of events since the middle 1970s, however, is important for appreciating how the Boston school conflict has affected American racial politics since then. During the time of Judge Garrity's receivership (which ended September 4, 1985), many changes in enrollment, administration and educational quality in the Boston public schools have ensued. This chapter be-gins with a recitation of a few of the most salient facts. Any attempt at a full discussion of these topics would, of course, raise methodological and historical issues worthy of a separate book-length manuscript.

Judge Garrity's order was followed by the largest proportional change in the pattern of public school enrollments of any Northern school system undergoing desegregation. In 1974 the public school enrollment of 93,647 included 53,593 whites, 31,963 blacks, and 8,091 others. Ten years later there were 57,400 students, including 15,257 whites, 27,400 blacks, and 14,743 of other heritage.

Why did enrollment changes of such great magnitude follow Judge Garrity's order? Comparative studies show that the enrollment change experienced by a city undergoing desegregation depends on a number of factors:

> [These factors] include whether the plan affects only the central city or includes the entire metropolitan area, the size of the minority student population, the proportion of the white student population assigned to schools outside their neighborhoods and busing distance. After implementation, white loss begins to level out and busing distance ceases to be a factor. (Rossell and Hawley 1983, p. 6)

Some of the factors leading to the extensive enrollment changes in Boston include the type of plan implemented; the fact of extended conflict over the plan; idiosyncrasies of the historical, religious, and demographic setting of the school desegregation issue in Boston; and patterns of demographic change and migration in the metropolitan area that would have caused changes in enrollment with or without Judge Garrity's order.

The extraordinary enrollment change in the Boston public schools is partly explained by the high proportion of Catholics in the city (see Chapter 5), which makes it likely that there is a high capacity in the parochial school system to absorb transfer students. Many white families are able to avoid the court order by enrolling their children in private or parochial schools. Today, ten years after Judge Garrity's order, a majority of Boston's white school-age children, 19,637 of them, attend nonpublic schools.

The extraordinary enrollment change is also partly due to the violence and disorder of the conflict. Rossell analyzes the results from a number of cities and shows that, controlling for other relevant factors, the amount of white enrollment loss is strongly related to the amount of protest against desegregation (1978b). The comparatively high turnover in enrollment may be due to the fact that Boston remained in active conflict for a much longer time than any other city undergoing school desegregation since the 1960s.[1]

Some of the extraordinary enrollment change in Boston is explained by the limited nature of the plan implemented by Judge Garrity. As discussed in earlier chapters, the mayor, the school board, and other local officials did not help design the plan implemented by Judge Garrity. The Phase I order, designed by the State Office of Education, sought to minimize busing. But, in the words of two court-appointed experts, it was "short on providing for practical remedies involving race relations, curriculum and instruction, and the content of participation" (Dentler and Scott 1981, p. 46). The plan was less sensitive to questions involving neighborhood differences, the appropriate pairing of schools, and similar matters than it would have been if local school and neighborhood actors had helped in the design.

Perhaps the most significant limitation on Judge Garrity's plan, however, is that it did not extend beyond the boundaries of the central city. It is more difficult to peacefully implement desegregation and to avoid enrollment loss with a "central city only" plan (Orfield 1978). The exemption of suburban whites, the extensive enrollment in private and Catholic schools, and the flow of middle class whites out of the central city area make mandatory desegregation the kind of political issue where economic status determines whether or not someone is affected by the policy:

> An integration program that excludes middle-class whites on the edge of the city and in the suburbs while involving only students from working class and poor backgrounds, is to involve a group of white students most threatened by racial change and least able to handle it. This is especially so if the program seeks to minimize busing and thus integrate black and white schools within close proximity. The Boston desegregation effort should be instructive in this regard. (Rist 1980, p. 127)

1. Daily attendance rates were affected by the extensiveness of the conflict. During the first year of implementation, sharp drops in school attendance followed adult street disturbances (Richard, Knox, and Oliphant 1975).

It may be that the most violent reactions to mandatory desegregation occur where the unevenness of implementation is most extreme. Those closest to the conflict say this was the reason for the protracted defiance in Little Rock:

> [Faubus] saw, correctly, that when the plan worked through to its conclusion the affluent whites in the suburbs would be largely exempt from integrated schools while the working-class whites in the downtown section would have to send their children to class with blacks. (Ashmore 1982, p. 261)

In spite of an extraordinary amount of protest, extraordinary changes in enrollment, a uniquely well-organized opposition, and a limited plan, Judge Garrity's order produced significant changes in the quality of education for those who remained in the Boston public schools. These changes should not be lost sight of when evaluating the Boston experience.

Judge Garrity's intervention forced self-examination and public accountability on a school system that was not functioning well. In the words of Gregory Anrig, former Massachusetts commissioner of education:

> [Boston] was a poorly run school system for blacks and whites with overcrowded classes, small numbers of students going to college and a teaching force that was very provincial. Now, [after the court order] teachers and principals are more diverse and achievement levels have gone up.

Those who stayed in the public school system have received a better education than would have been the case without the court order. According to John Bryant, who in 1977 became the first black elected to the Boston School Committee:

> The school system was in such a state of decline that what happened, in essence, was that the court order set up mechanisms whereby all schools were monitored, not just for integration but also for the quality of academic programs.

The court required changes that effectively upgraded the curriculum, quality, and even safety of the Boston public schools. Under the court order, standardized curricula were developed. Previously, there was no assurance that children in the same grade in different schools studied the same material. Now educational objectives for each grade level have been listed and performance criteria established for evaluation. Between 1974 and 1984, daily attendance rose from 82 percent to 86 percent, and the proportion of graduates going on to further education increased from 41 percent to 62 percent. The racial tension and occasional violence that marked the first two or three years of desegregation subsided. There is, however, no precise way to measure the change in school safety because no security force existed before 1974 and incidents were never recorded.

Several of the educational changes required by the court had national significance as well. The court order provided an early showcase for the concept of magnet schools, allowing students to choose schools that offer programs in specialized areas, such as the arts or the sciences. The order requiring school officials to match schools with corporations and universities became a harbinger of business and university collaboration with public education (*New York Times,* 28 December 1984). The matching requirement ultimately resulted in the "Boston compact," under which 316 local firms have agreed to hire city high school graduates. These features of the Boston plan have been adapted by other school systems in setting up desegregation plans (*Christian Science Monitor,* 15 November 1984).

Boston and American Racial Politics

The events in Boston reshaped calculations affecting antibusing politics on the national scale. The opponents of mandatory desegregation "lost" the Boston school conflict, but they have become more powerful since then. The link between Boston and American racial politics since the middle 1970s is the topic of the final section of this book.

Before Judge Garrity's order there already was a conservative coalition of Republicans and Southern Democrats organized to oppose mandatory desegregation (see Chapter 2). This coalition aided the opponents of desegregation in Boston by promising support for an antibusing amendment and by passing legislation to limit the authority of federal agencies to affirmatively pursue desegregation. In fact, opposition to busing became the rationale for attacks by the coalition on most of the civil rights legislation passed in the 1960s.

The resistance in Boston has become a symbol unifying Northern whites with the other members of this coalition. Boston is "the North's most publicized desegregation case" (*New York Times,* 28 December 1984).[2] For years Little Rock, Arkansas, stood as the symbol of white resistance to a sort of integration—mandatory or voluntary—in the public schools. Now Boston is the symbol of white resistance.

The resistance of Northern whites to mandatory desegregation and their receptiveness to the message of conservative Republicans and white Southerners has weakened the base of the Democratic party coalition and is currently a force for realignment in national party politics. In the South there was once a time when one party dominated politics because it was "the institutional incarnation of the will to white supremacy" (Cash 1941, p. 132). American tolerance for voluntary forms of integration makes it unlikely that this will happen again. Nonetheless, the coalition of Southern Democrats, conservative Republicans and other Northern whites has gained considerable political advantage by associating itself with opposition to busing and support for the doctrine of voluntary compliance.

Most studies show that opinions on busing and mandatory desegregation do not significantly predict presidential voting choice among white Americans. These findings are often interpreted as evidence that issues of race and mandatory desegregation do not significantly affect national politics. These studies, however, underestimate the importance of racial issues. Americans tend to vote for the political party they believe best serves their general interest and the party they say they "belong to" (Page 1978). Busing and mandatory desegregation are issues that affect people's views on these "intervening" causes of political support. Black Americans now vote nearly unanimously for Democratic party presidential candidates. A majority of white Americans have not done so since the 1960s, and in the South a majority have not done so since the 1940s (Nie, Verba, and Petrocik 1976).

The issues of busing and mandatory desegregation affect the national political process in other ways as well. The threat of minority electoral status has caused the Democratic party to reevaluate its platform. The current indications are that the party will avoid these

2. Content analyses of national news media show that most of the coverage on busing has been limited to Boston and one or two other cities (Orfield 1978).

issues. If so, busing and mandatory desegregation will become "organized out of politics" (Schattschneider 1960, p. 71) and will not provide a basis for major party competition. The ability to pursue desegregation or other changes in race relations through electoral means will then become severely limited.

White opposition to mandatory desegregation in the North, symbolized by the Boston experience, united culturally disparate groups in a national coalition. As a result, liberal support for desegregation as well as for other social causes has diminished, at least for the time being.

Conservative Republican and conservative Southern opposition to mandatory desegregation arises from a religious and historical context that is quite different from, and quite at odds with, the more liberal, "humanistic" orientation of white Northern society. Neoconservative culture more strongly endorses evangelical religious belief, the use of force in social relations, and the "right to life" than does the climate of opinion in Northern cities. Neoconservative culture also believes that "alien" influences and unpatriotic challenges to national security are more imminent than do the residents of Northern cities. The issues were clarified more than 100 years ago by J. H. Thornwell, Presbyterian minister and eventually president of the College of South Carolina:

> The parties in this conflict are not merely abolitionists and slave-holders—they are atheists, socialists, communists, red republicans, jacobins on one side, and the friends of order and regulated freedom on the other. In one word, the world is the battleground—Christianity and atheism the combatants; and the progress of humanity the stake.

Opposition to busing and mandatory desegregation unites white Northerners with the neoconservative coalition even though white Northerners do not strongly endorse most of the other items on the social and cultural agenda of their newfound partners. But neoconservative political strength makes it prudent for white Northerners to tolerate, and occasionally support extension of, the neoconservative agenda in spite of its unpopularity.

In the summer of 1984 Senators Howard Baker, Daniel Moynihan, Claiborne Pell, Thomas Eagleton, and Orrin Hatch sponsored legislation to fund mathematics and science programs in the public schools and to finance magnet schools in cities undergoing desegregation. The act also makes illegal any use of the funds to teach "secular humanism." Section 509 of the act states:

> Grants under this title may not be used for consultants, for transportation, or for any activity which does not augment academic improvement, or for courses of instruction the substance of which is secular humanism.

To most adherents of neoconservatism and the religious right, "secular humanism" has a fairly general meaning. To quote the *New York Times:*

> It stands for everything they [the new right] are opposed to, from atheism to the United Nations, from sex education to the theory of evolution to the writings of Hemingway and Hawthorne.

Senator Hatch, who wrote the paragraph into the bill, explained its meaning: "I'm tired of seeing the dumbing down *[sic]* of textbooks and schools to ignore all reference to religion and patriotic values." With this guidance from Congress on the definition of secular humanism, the Department of Education in January 1985 proclaimed it to mean whatever local school authorities determined it to mean (*New York Times,* 22 February 1985).

One Nation, Two Worlds

Racial understanding is not something Americans are born with. It is something that needs to be pursued, sometimes as a matter of policy. In the words of Martin Luther King:

> A productive and happy life is not something that you find; it is something that you make. And so the ability of Negroes and whites to work together, to understand each other, will not be found ready made; it must be created by the fact of contact. (1967, p. 28)

The 1954 Supreme Court decision in *Brown v. Board of Education* recognizes an obligation to pursue racial contact as a matter of public policy. Specifically, local officials are required to take action to end segregation that came about for illegal reasons. To paraphrase Supreme Court Justice Robert Jackson, one world, based on white supremacy, is dead. The Court's 1954 decision, he hoped, would help bring the next world to life.

Today few Americans argue that racial integration is unnecessary, but few argue that affirmative steps should be taken to achieve this goal. Today white Americans, for the most part, favor desegregation when the number of blacks is small and the changes are voluntary rather than planned. Most whites believe that this is the only effective, legal way to solve the problem.

The arguments against mandatory desegregation have a remarkable historical consistency. More than 100 years ago in the *Civil Rights Cases* of 1883, the Supreme Court ruled against "favoritism":

> Sooner or later there must be some stage in the progress of [the Negro's] elevation when he takes the rank of mere citizen and ceases to be the special favorite of the laws, and when his rights . . . are to be protected by the ordinary means by which other men's rights are protected.

Five generations later, Morris Abram, recently appointed vice-chairman of the United States Commission on Civil Rights, echoed the argument. He wrote that favoritism, affirmative action, and other forms of "reverse discrimination" produce unintended negative consequences and are, in any account, unconstitutional:

> Civil rights have a unique meaning in this country. Elsewhere, in some of those societies where engineering a certain distribution of wealth and goods is part of the state's mission, people have economic rights— the right to housing, health care, and other goods. But civil rights have a different meaning in this country. We live in a constitutional democracy built not on the proposition that each [individual] has a fundamental entitlement to a particular piece of the economic pie, but rather on the concept that it is up to each individual to compete for economic goods, constitutionally protected from interference by guarantees of equal protection under the law, due process, the Bill of Rights and, most fundamentally, the ballot. (Abram 1984)

Abram believes that incremental, voluntary action will solve the problem:

> It may not be fashionable to counsel patience, but patience is necessary. We must acknowledge the historical fact that the progress of a

group, once barriers are removed, does indeed take time. Of course, we could accomplish more with greater speed if we were willing to take more drastic measures, turning our backs on the Constitution. But we dare not do that. (1984)

Mandatory requirements to desegregate are not only unpopular, they are sometimes extraordinarily difficult to implement. This book illustrates the political processes that are unleashed when local officials are required to implement an unpopular policy, when opposition to the policy is well-organized and when there is a widespread belief that public opposition can bring about some kind of relief in the future. Mandatory desegregation is most likely to "fail" when legal requirements and/or local implementation procedures reduce the pressure on local officials for immediate compliance and empower the opposition by recognizing the legitimacy of its voice (see Hochschild 1984).

The difficulty of desegregation, in fact, proves Abram's argument. The forces impeding desegregation are as much a part of American political life as the Constitution or the ballot. Indeed, much of the strength of the antibusing movement has come, directly or indirectly, from the rights of speech, religion, association and assembly guaranteed in the Constitution, and from the power of voting enfranchisement. A mandatory requirement to desegregate challenges interests of individuals that are protected by the traditions and doctrines of our government. But Supreme Court Justice Jackson's point is, I believe, that even though the old world of white supremacy is dead, without a requirement to desegregate the procedures of American society and politics make the next world insufficiently powerful to be born.

Appendix: Wordings for Questions Used in the Boston Survey

Opinions on Busing and Racial Integration

1. Many public officials and groups have made a variety of statements concerning racial issues. I'm going to read some of these statements to you, and for each please tell me whether you strongly agree, agree, disagree or strongly disagree with it. (Wave 5)

Blacks should not push themselves where they are not wanted.

White people have the right to keep blacks out of their neighborhood, and blacks should respect that right.

2. How strongly would you object if a member of your family wanted to bring a black friend home to dinner? Would you object strongly, mildly or not at all? (Wave 5)

3. Would you, yourself have any objection to sending your children to a school where 10 percent of the children are Negro? (Wave 1)

[IF NO] Where 25 percent of the children are Negro?

[IF NO] Where 50 percent of the children are Negro?

[IF NO] Where more than 50 percent of the children are Negro?

4. Speaking in general terms, do you favor racial integration, separation of the races or something in between? (Waves 1, 5)

5. One approach to achieving racial balance in the schools is to bus both Negro and white children from one school district to another school district. In general, do you favor or oppose busing both Negro and white children to achieve racial balance? (Waves 1, 2, 3, 4, 5)

6. On the whole, do you personally favor or oppose Judge Garrity's decision concerning segregation in Boston's public schools? (Wave 3)

Alternatives to Judge Garrity's Plan

7. As a member of the school committee, how strongly would you support or oppose a proposal that expands the open enrollment program so that more Negro families who wanted to could send their children to white schools with empty seats? (Wave 1)

8. During the last few months, other approaches have been proposed which would reduce the number of racially imbalanced schools in Boston. I am going to read five of these proposals to you. If you were a member of the Boston School Committee, how strongly would you support or oppose these proposals? . . .

A proposal that would establish excellent schools in Negro neighborhoods in order to attract more white students for the purpose of achieving racial balance? (Wave 3)

9. As a member of the school committee, how strongly would you support or oppose a proposal that requires a change in school district boundaries so that as many schools as possible are racially balanced but keeps busing of Negro and white children within each district to a minimum? (Wave 1)

10. During the last few months, other approaches have been proposed which would reduce the number of racially imbalanced schools in Boston. I am going to read five of these proposals to you. If you were a member of the Boston School Committee, how strongly would you support or oppose these proposals? . . .

A proposal that requires a change in school district boundaries so that as many schools as possible are racially balanced but keeps busing of Negro and white children within each district to a minimum? (Wave 3)

11. As you probably know, Judge Garrity has ordered the School Committee to submit to him on Dec. 16 a plan to desegregate schools throughout Boston beginning in Sept. 1975. We would like to know how strongly you support or oppose each of the following proposals which may or may not be part of the plan. . . .

A proposal that would make major changes in school district boundaries throughout the city which would eliminate segregation in all schools with as little busing as possible. (Wave 4)

12. As a member of the school committee, how strongly would you support or oppose a proposal that requires racially balancing all high schools by busing older children from one area to another, but does not require busing of elementary school children? (Wave 1)

13. A different approach is to reduce the number of racially imbalanced schools by busing only Negro children to every white school in Boston, but not to bus any white children. In general, do you favor or oppose the busing of only Negro children to every white school in Boston in order to reduce the number of racially imbalanced schools? How strongly do you (FAVOR/OPPOSE) busing of only Negro school children to every white school in Boston—very strongly, strongly, moderately, or just slightly? (Waves 1, 2, 3)

Willingness to Protest

14. As a member of the Boston School Committee, would you encourage other members of the School Committee to defy the court order? (Waves 1, 2, 3)

15. If you were a member of the Boston School Committee, how strongly would you favor or oppose school boycotts by white parents to protest any change in the racial balance of white schools? (Waves 1, 3)

16. I'm going to read you a list of actions which public officials might consider taking this fall when the Phase II plan is implemented. I'd like you to evaluate each of these actions using the scale [on this card.] "+3" means you feel the action definitely should be taken this fall. "−3" means you feel the action definitely should not be taken this fall. (Wave 5)

The Boston School Committee encourages parents to participate in school boycotts this fall. To what extent do you feel this action should or should not be taken?

17. Now that Judge Garrity has made his decision, which of the actions listed [on this card] do you personally think is the most important thing other people in the neighborhood should do: openly resist; work to reverse; find ways to get around it; quietly comply; comply and openly express agreement; participate actively in groups that support it; help organize groups to make sure school desegregation works this fall. (Wave 3)

18. Many public officials have made a variety of statements concerning racial issues. I'm going to read some of these statements to you, and

for each please tell me whether you strongly agree, agree, disagree or
strongly disagree with it. . . . (Wave 5)

The Boston School Committee must take whatever steps are necessary to eliminate all aspects of segregation in the Boston public
schools.

School Board Culpability

19. Do you think that there are many, some, only a few, or no racially imbalanced public schools in Boston? (Waves 2, 3)

20. Do you think that recent Boston School Committees have been
completely, partially, or not at all responsible for the existence of racially
imbalanced schools in Boston? (Waves 2, 3)

21. Regardless of how you feel about the decision as a whole, we
would like to know your opinion on specific aspects of Judge Garrity's
decision. I will read 8 statements made by Judge Garrity in his decision.
Please look at this card. The top of the ladder, +3, would mean that
you strongly agree with Judge Garrity's statement, and the bottom of the
ladder, −3, means that you strongly disagree with the statement. Please
give me a number which represents your feelings about each statement.
(Wave 3)

The Boston School Committee intentionally maintained a segregated
school system that affected students, teachers and faculties throughout the entire city.

22. Many public officials and groups have made a variety of statements concerning racial issues. I'm going to read some of these statements to you, and for each please tell me whether you strongly agree,
agree, disagree or strongly disagree with it. (Wave 5)

The Boston School Committee intentionally maintained a segregated
school system.

Social Harms Caused by the Court Order

23. There has been a lot of discussion about violent incidents which
have occurred between students in the school since Judge Garrity's school
desegregation plan went into effect this September. Do you think this will

be an extremely serious, a somewhat serious, or only a minor problem for the Boston public schools this year? (Wave 4)

24. Next year, do you think violence in Boston public schools will be an extremely serious problem, a somewhat serious problem, or only a minor problem? (Wave 5)

25. Research has shown that white student test scores often decrease when they attend desegregated schools. (True or False) (Wave 2)

26. Many public officials have made a variety of statements concerning racial issues. I'm going to read some of these statements to you, and for each please tell me whether you strongly agree, agree, disagree or strongly disagree with it. (Wave 5)

> White students' test scores often decrease when they attend desegregated schools.

Alienation of Rights by the Court Order

27. I'm going to mention several areas of school policy. For each one, please tell me how much influence you think parents should have on how public schools are run compared to how much influence they have now. What about which schools students are assigned to? Would you say parents have far too much influence, too much influence, about the right amount of influence, too little influence, or far too little influence in that area? (Wave 3)

28. I'm going to mention several areas of school policy. For each one, please tell me how much influence you think parents have on how public schools are run compared to how much influence they should have. What about which schools students are assigned to? Would you say parents have far too much influence, too much influence, about the right amount of influence, too little influence, or far too little influence in that area? (Wave 5)

29. Here is a list of well-known public figures, some of whom have commented on racial imbalance in Boston's public schools. I'm going to read five statements that have been made and you tell me for each statement who on the list would agree, who would disagree, who would neither agree nor disagree, and also tell me whether you would agree or disagree with each statement. (Wave 1)

> Children should always go to school in their own neighborhood.

30. I'm going to read four statements. Please tell me for each statement whether you strongly agree, agree, disagree or strongly disagree
with it. (Wave 3)

Children should always go to school in their own neighborhood.

31. Many public officials and groups have made a variety of statements concerning racial issues. I'm going to read some of these statements to you, and for each please tell me whether you strongly agree,
agree, disagree or strongly disagree with it. (Wave 5)

Children should always go to school in their own neighborhood.

32. Some people think that certain groups have more influence than
they are entitled to, when public officials make decisions about busing
school children to achieve racial balance. Others think these same groups
have less influence than they are entitled to. Let's say that the top of this
ladder, +4, represents those groups that have much more influence than
they are entitled to; the bottom of this ladder, −4, represents those
groups that have much less influence than they are entitled to; and the
middle of the ladder, 0, represents those groups which have just about as
much influence as they are entitled to. Where on this ladder would you
place . . . (Wave 1)

People in your neighborhood.

You, yourself

33. Some people think that certain groups have more influence than
they are entitled to, when public officials make decisions about busing
school children to eliminate segregation. Others think these same groups
have less influence than they are entitled to. Let's say that the top of this
ladder, +4, represents those groups that have much more influence than
they are entitled to. The bottom of the ladder, −4, represents those
groups that have much less influence than they are entitled to. The middle
of the ladder, 0, represents those groups which have just about as much
influence as they are entitled to. Where on this ladder would you place
. . . (Wave 5)

People in your neighborhood.

You, yourself

Awareness of Actions and Statements of Leaders

34. During the coming school year, certain public officials and groups may express opinions on whether parents should comply with or defy Judge Garrity's Phase II school desegregation plan. I am going to read you some of the names of these officials and groups, and I'd like you to rate them according to how strongly they will encourage parents to comply with or defy Judge Garrity's Phase II plan. "+4" on the scale means you think they will encourage parents to comply, and "−4" means you think they will strongly encourage parents to defy. Now, how would you rate . . . (Wave 5)

Mayor Kevin White

City Councilor Louise Day Hicks

School Committeeman John Kerrigan

Cardinal Medeiros

35. What actions [on this card] do you think Mayor White and his staff will take when Judge Garrity's plan goes into effect this September: defy even if they may go to jail; participate in demonstrations to protest the plan; find ways to get around the plan; create problems in implementing the plan; comply; openly express disapproval; work with parents, school officials, and students to try to minimize problems that accompany desegregation. (Wave 5)

Demand for Transfer to Parochial Schools

36. I'm going to read you a list of actions which public officials might consider taking this fall when the Phase II plan is implemented. I'd like you to evaluate each of these actions using the scale [on this card.] "+3" means you feel the action definitely should be taken this fall. "−3" means you feel the action definitely should not be taken this fall. . . . (Wave 5)

Cardinal Medeiros removes all restrictions on the admission of students to parochial schools in Boston.

Respect for Statements and Policies of Leaders

37. In the last years, many public officials have made important statements and policies that affect the quality of education in both Boston and suburban schools. We would like to know how much in general you

respect the statements and the policies made by some of these public officials. . . .

Would you say you have a great deal of respect, some respect, very little respect or no respect at all for the statements and policies that have been made by [list of leaders] in the last years? (Wave 4)

Cardinal Medeiros

Mayor Kevin White

Perception of Leaders' Positions on Busing for Integration

38. The top of this ladder, number +4, represents the position extremely favorable to busing both Negro and white children to achieve racial balance. And the bottom of the ladder, number −4, represents the position extremely opposed to busing both Negro and white children to achieve racial balance. Where on this ladder would you place . . . (Waves 1, 2, 3, 5)

Cardinal Medeiros

Mayor White

The Demand for Public Safety

39. I'm going to read you a list of actions which public officials might consider taking this fall when the Phase II plan is implemented. I'd like you to evaluate each of these actions using the scale [on this card.] "+3" means you feel the action definitely should be taken this fall. "−3" means you feel the action definitely should not be taken this fall. . . . (Wave 5)

On the first day of school, Police Commissioner DiGrazia deploys large numbers of police to any schools where trouble might occur.

The state Board of Education strictly enforces the state truancy laws if large numbers of students fail to attend public schools this fall.

When school opens, President Ford sends more federal marshals to Boston to help implement Judge Garrity's Phase II plan.

Judge Garrity prohibits any group from organizing demonstrations to protest the Phase II desegregation plan.

40. What method do you think school officials should use to reduce violent incidents between children in the schools? Should they . . . (Wave 4)

Immediately suspend for at least two weeks any student involved in the violent incident.

Ask police to arrest any parent or student involved in any violent incident.

Regularly maintain an adequate number of police inside the schools to handle such violent incidents.

41. As you know, some parents are still not sending their children to public school. What do you think would be the best way to handle this? Should the school department strictly enforce the state's compulsory attendance law? (Wave 4)

42. I'm going to read actions which were proposed by public officials in the last few months. I'd like to know what you thought about each action when it was proposed by the public officials. (Wave 4)

Do you think Governor Sargent should or should not have mobilized the National Guard in case they were needed in Boston?

Do you think President Ford should or should not have sent federal troops to Boston to help implement a federal school desegregation order?

Do you think the Mayor should or should not have refused permits for marches and demonstrations when he thought violence might take place?

Beliefs about Desegregation, Perception of Mayor's Opinion

43. Here is a list of well-known political figures, some of whom have commented on racial imbalance in Boston's public schools. I'm going to read five statements that have been made and you tell me for each statement who on the list would agree, who would disagree, who would neither agree nor disagree, and also tell me whether you would agree or disagree . . .

Racial imbalance in schools hurts the education of Negro children.

Children should always go to school in their own neighborhood.

Support for the Principle of Decentralized Enforcement

44. Compared to the ordinary citizen, how much responsibility does an elected official have to comply with a court decision he disagrees

with: more responsibility, the same responsibility or less responsibility? (Wave 2)

45. Compared to the ordinary citizen, how much responsibility does an elected official have to comply with Judge Garrity's decision, even if the public official disagrees with the decision: more responsibility, the same responsibility or less responsibility? (Wave 3)

46. Do you think that courts have the right to make decisions which many people disagree with? (Wave 2)

47. Do you think that Judge Garrity had the right to make a decision which many people in Boston might disagree with? (Wave 3)

Perception of Neighborhood Opinion and Action against Desegregation

48. The top of this ladder, number +4, represents the position extremely favorable to busing both Negro and white children to achieve racial balance. And the bottom of the ladder, number −4, represents the position extremely opposed to busing both Negro and white children to achieve racial balance. Where on this ladder would you place other parents in your neighborhood? (Waves 1, 2, 3, 5)

49. In your opinion, how many people in your neighborhood agree with Judge Garrity's decision: almost all, about three fourths, about half, about one quarter or only a few? Categories coded: 90, 75, 50, 25, 10 and 0 percent; "none" volunteered. (Wave 3)

50. Approximately what percent of the parents in your neighborhood would you say are sending their children to school on a regular basis? (Wave 4)

51. [Asked after previous question:] Do you think the percentage has increased, remained the same or decreased since the beginning of school in September? (Wave 4)

52. [Asked after previous question:] Do you think the percentage will increase, remain the same or decrease in the remainder of the school year? (Wave 4)

53. Last year, approximately what percentage of the parents in your neighborhood sent their children to public schools on a regular basis? (Wave 5)

54. [Asked after previous question:] Do you think this percentage will increase, decrease or remain about the same when the Phase II desegregation plan goes into effect this September? (Wave 5)

55. What do you think most people in your neighborhood will actually do in the next two months in response to Judge Garrity's decision [of actions listed on this card]? Openly resist; work to reverse the decision; find ways to get around the decision; quietly comply even if they disagree; comply and openly express agreement; participate actively in groups that support it; help organize groups to make sure school desegregation works in the fall. (Wave 3)

56. What actions [of those listed on this card] do you think most parents in your neighborhood took when Judge Garrity's school desegregation plan went into effect this September? Defied; participated in demonstrations protesting the plan; worked to reverse the plan; found ways to get around the plan; attempted to interfere with successful implementation of the plan; quietly accepted the plan even if they disagreed with it; complied and openly expressed agreement; supported the plan and encouraged parents, school officials and students to work together so that school desegregation would go as smoothly as possible. (Wave 4)

57. What actions [of those listed on this card] do you think most parents in your neighborhood will take when Judge Garrity's Phase II school desegregation plan goes into effect this September? Defy; participate in demonstrations to protest the plan; find ways to get around the plan; create problems that hinder implementation; comply even if they disagree; openly express disapproval; openly express approval; work with parents, school officials and students to try to minimize the problems that accompany desegregation. (Wave 5)

58. In your opinion, how many people in your neighborhood would you say are in favor of separation of the races: at least 90 percent of them; about 75 percent; about 50 percent; about 25 percent; or less than 10 percent? (Waves 1, 5)

Frequency of Discussing Opinions

59. Do you discuss the issue of racially balancing the Boston public schools with other people in your neighborhood? [IF YES] How often do these discussions take place? Would you say very frequently, frequently, occasionally or infrequently? (Wave 3)

60. In the past month or so, how frequently have you talked with people about how the events of the past year have affected the quality of education in the Boston public schools? Would you say very frequently, frequently, occasionally, hardly ever or not at all? (Wave 5)

Support for Legal Challenges to Judge Garrity's Order

61. For the last 10 years, Boston has faced periodic crises concerning the concentration of Negro children in certain schools. If you were a member of the Boston School Committee, how strongly would you favor or oppose repealing the State Racial Imbalance Act, which requires that no more than half the students in the school should be Negro—would you strongly support repealing the act, support repeal, oppose repeal or strongly oppose repeal? (Wave 1)

62. For the last 10 years, Boston has faced periodic crises concerning the concentration of Negro children in certain schools. If you were a member of the Boston School Committee, how strongly would you favor or oppose an amendment to the United States Constitution that would prohibit court-ordered busing of school children from one school district to another in order to achieve racial balance? (Wave 1)

63. As a member of the Boston School Committee how strongly would you support or oppose the following antibusing amendment to the U.S. Constitution: no public school student because of his race, creed or color should be assigned or required to attend a particular school? (Wave 3)

64. As a member of the School Committee, how strongly would you support or oppose an appeal of Judge Garrity's decision to the U.S. Supreme Court? (Wave 3)

65. As a member of the School Committee, how strongly would you support or oppose legislation currently being considered by Congress that would prohibit court-ordered busing from one school district to another? (Wave 3)

66. Do you think that Congress should pass legislation that would limit the power of federal judges and the U.S. Supreme Court to make decisions concerning school desegregation?

Pessimism about the Immediate Benefits of Protest

67. Do you think that a Federal Court would find the Boston School Committee guilty of running a segregated school system in violation of

the U.S. Constitution? Would you say definitely yes, most likely yes, most likely no or definitely no? (Wave 2)

68. Do you think the Federal Court of Appeals or the U.S. Supreme Court will overturn or uphold Judge Garrity's school desegregation ruling? (Wave 4)

69. Do you think it would be practically impossible, extremely difficult, difficult or relatively easy to reverse a court decision which many people disagree with? (Wave 2)

70. If many people in Boston disagree with Judge Garrity's decision, how difficult will it be to reverse it: extremely difficult, difficult or relatively easy? (Waves 3, 4)

71. In the past few years, Federal and state courts have made decisions in such areas as prayer in public schools, the rights of criminals, obscene books and films, and abortion, which many people have not agreed with. How often do you think the courts have been able to make people go along with these decisions even though many people disagree with them? Would you say all of the time, some of the time or rarely? (Wave 2)

72. Do you think the day will ever come when both Negro and white children will be bused from one school district to another in Boston to achieve racial balance? (Waves 1, 2, 3)

73. Do you think the Boston School Committee will ever submit a desegregation plan that Judge Garrity will ever accept? [IF YES] When do you think that plan will actually be implemented? Do you think it will be in the next school year, 2 to 3 years from now, in the distant future or never? (Wave 4)

74. How likely do you think it is that any parents or public officials will be able to delay implementation of the Phase II plan? Is it very likely, somewhat likely or not at all likely? (Wave 5)

Bibliography

Abney, F. G. "Factors Related to Negro Voter Turnout in Mississippi." *Journal of Politics* 37:1057–1063, 1974.

Abram, M. "What Constitutes a Civil Right?" *New York Times Magazine,* 10 June 1984.

Abrams, C. *Forbidden Neighbors: A Study of Prejudice in Housing.* New York: Harper, 1955.

Abrams, R. "Not One Judge's Opinion: Morgan v. Hennigan and the Boston Schools." *Harvard Educational Review* 45:5–16, 1975.

Allport, F. *Social Psychology.* New York: Houghton-Mifflin, 1924.

Allport, G. *The Nature of Prejudice.* Boston: Addison-Wesley, 1954.

Armor, D. "The Evidence on Busing." *Public Interest* 28:90–126, 1972.

Armor, D. "White Flight and the Future of School Desegregation." Pp. 215–226 in W. Stephan and J. Feagin (eds.), *School Desegregation: Past, Present and Future.* New York: Plenum, 1980.

Ashmore, H. *The Negro and the Schools.* Chapel Hill: University of North Carolina, 1954.

Ashmore, H. *The Other Side of Jordan: Negroes Outside the South.* New York: Norton, 1960.

Ashmore, H. *Hearts and Minds: The Anatomy of Racism from Roosevelt to Reagan.* New York: McGraw-Hill, 1982.

Balbus, I. "The Concept of Interest in Pluralist and Marxian Analysis." *Politics and Society* 1:151–177, 1971.

Barnes, S. and M. Kaase. *Political Action.* Beverly Hills, Calif.: Sage, 1979.

Baron, H. "The Demand for Black Labor: Historical Notes on the Political Economy of Racism." *Radical American* 5:1–46, 1971.

Bartley, N. *The Rise of Massive Resistance.* Baton Rouge: LSU Press, 1969.

Bartley, N. and H. Graham. *Southern Politics and the Second Reconstruction.* Baltimore, Md.: Johns Hopkins University Press, 1975.

Bates, D. *The Long Shadow of Little Rock.* New York: McKay, 1962.

Berman, W. *The Politics of Civil Rights in the Truman Administration.* Columbus: Ohio State University, 1970.

Blalock, H. "Percent Nonwhite and Discrimination in the South." *American Sociological Review* 22:677–682, 1957.

Bobo, L. "Whites' Opposition to Busing: Symbolic Racism or Realistic Group Conflict." *Journal of Personality and Social Psychology* 45: 1196–1210, 1983.

Bonacich, E. "Advanced Capitalism and Black/White Race Relations in the United States: A Split Labor Market Interpretation." *American Sociological Review* 41:34–51, 1976.

Brink, W., and L. Harris. *Black and White.* New York: Simon and Schuster, 1967.

Brooks, T. *Walls Come Tumbling Down: A History of the Civil Rights Movement.* Englewood Cliffs, N.J.: Prentice-Hall, 1974.

Buell, E. *School Desegregation and Defended Neighborhoods: The Boston Controversy.* Lexington, Mass.: Lexington, 1982.

Bullock, C. "The Election of Blacks in the South: Preconditions and Consequences." *American Journal of Political Science* 19:727–739, 1975.

Carter, Hodding, III. *The South Strikes Back.* Garden City, N.Y.: Doubleday, 1959.

Cash, W. *The Mind of the South.* New York: Vintage, 1941.

Cataldo, E., M. Giles, and D. Gatlin. *School Desegregation Policy.* Lexington, Mass.: D.C. Heath, 1978.

Center for National Policy Review. "School Segregation and Residential Segregation: A Social Science Statement." Pp. 231–247 in W. Stephan and J. Feagin (eds.), *School Desegregation: Past, Present and Future.* New York: Plenum, 1980.

Clark, K. "Desegregation: An Appraisal of the Evidence." *Journal of Social Issues* 9:(entire issue), 1953.

Clark, K. *Prejudice and your Child.* Boston: Beacon Press, 1959.

Clotfelter, C. "Urban School Desegregation and Declines in White Enrollment: A Re-examination." *Journal of Urban Economics* 6:352–370, 1979.

Coleman, J. *Community Conflict.* New York: Free Press, 1957.

Coleman, J. *Resources for Social Change: Race in the United States.* New York: Wiley, 1971.

Coleman, J., J. Kelly, and S. Moore. "Trends in School Segregation." Paper no. 722-03-01. Washington D.C.: Urban Institute, 1975.

Crain, R. "Why Academic Research Fails to Be Useful." Pp. 31–45 in F. Levinsohn and B. Wright (eds.), *School Desegregation: Shadow and Substance.* Chicago: University of Chicago, 1976.

Crain, R., M. Inger, G. McWorter, and J. Vanecko. *The Politics of School Desegregation*. Chicago: Aldine 1968.

Crain, R., and R. Mahard, "School Racial Composition and Black College Attendance and Achievement Test Performance." *Sociology of Education* 51:81–101, 1978.

Cronbach, L. "Test Validation." Pp. 443–507 in R. Thorndike (ed.), *Educational Measurement*. Washington D.C.: American Council on Education, 1971.

Cusick, P., Gerbing, D., and Russell, E. "The Effects of School Desegregation and Other Factors on 'White Flight' from an Urban Area." *Educational Administration Quarterly* 15:35–49, 1979.

Daniel, J. "Negro Political Behavior and Community Political Socioeconomic Structural Factors." *Social Forces* 47:274–280, 1969.

Davis, J. "Extending Rosenberg's Technique for Standardizing Contingency Tables." *Social Forces* 62:679–708, 1984.

Davis, J., and T. Smith. *General Social Survey Cumulative Codebook: 1972–1983*. Storrs, Conn.: Roper Public Opinion Research Center, 1983.

Davison, W. P. "The Public Opinion Process." *Public Opinion Quarterly* 22:1, 1957.

Dentler, S., and M. Scott. *Schools on Trial: An Inside Account of the Boston Desegregation Case*. Cambridge, Mass.: Abt Books, 1981.

Dolbeare, K., and P. Hammond. *The School Prayer Decisions*. Chicago: University of Chicago Press, 1971.

Downs, A. *An Economic Theory of Democracy*. New York: Harper 1957.

Doyle, B. *The Etiquette of Race Relations in the South*. Chicago: University of Chicago Press, 1937.

Drake, S., and H. Clayton. *Black Metropolis*. New York: Harper, 1963.

Duncan, O. D. "Some Linear Models for Two-Wave, Two-Variable Panel Analysis." *Psychological Bulletin* 72:177–182, 1969.

Duncan, O. D. "Unmeasured Variables in Linear Models for Panel Analysis." Pp. 36–82 in *Sociological Methodology 1972*. San Francisco: Jossey-Bass, 1972.

Duncan, O. D. "Some Linear Models for Two-Wave, Two-Variable Panel Analysis, with One-Way Causation and Measurement Error." Pp. 285–306 in H. Blalock (ed.), *Quantitative Sociology*. Chicago: Aldine, 1975.

Dye, T. "Urban School Segregation: A Comparative Analysis." *Urban Affairs Quarterly* 2:141–165, 1968.

Elster, J. "Rationality, Morality and Collective Action." Unpublished MSS, Department of Political Science, University of Chicago, 1984.

Erbe, B. "On the Politics of School Busing." *Public Opinion Quarterly* 41:113–117, 1977.

Fields, J., and H. Schuman. "Public Beliefs about the Beliefs of the Public." *Public Opinion Quarterly* 40:427–48, 1976.

Fligstein, N. *Going North*. New York: Academic, 1981.

Franklin, J. *Reconstruction: after the Civil War*. Chicago: University of Chicago Press, 1961.

Frey, W. "Black In-Migration, White Flight and the Changing Economic Base of the Central City." *American Journal of Sociology* 85:1396–1417, 1980.

Friedman, D. *White Militancy in Boston*. Lexington, Mass.: D. C. Heath, 1973.

Frohlich, N. and J. Oppenheimer. *Modern Political Economy*. Englewood Cliffs, N. J.: Prentice-Hall, 1978.

Frohlich, N., J. Oppenheimer, and O. Young. *Political Leadership and Collective Goods*. Princeton, N.J.: Princeton University Press, 1971.

Gamson, W. *Power and Discontent*. Homewood, Ill.: Dorsey Press, 1968.

Gamson, W. *The Strategy of Social Protest*. Homewood, Ill.: Dorsey Press, 1975.

Gamson, W., B. Fireman, and S. Rytina. *Encounters with Unjust Authority*. Homewood, Ill.: Dorsey Press, 1982.

Gatlin, D., et al. "Policy Support within a Target Group: The Case of School Desegregation." *American Political Science Review* 72:985–995, 1978.

George, A. "Political Leadership and Social Change in American Cities." *Daedalus* 97:1194–1217, 1968.

Gerlach, L., and V. Hine. *People, Power, Change: Movements of Social Transformation*. New York: Bobbs-Merrill, 1970.

Giles, M. "School Desegregation and White Withdrawal: A Test of the Tipping Point Model." Unpublished MSS., Department of Sociology, Florida Atlantic University, Boca Raton, Fla., 1977. Mimeo.

Giles, M., and D. Gatlin. "Mass Level Compliance with Public Policy: The Case of School Desegregation." *Journal of Politics* 42:722–746, 1980.

Giles, M., D. Gatlin, and E. Cataldo. "Racial and Class Prejudice: Their Relative Effects on Protest against School Desegregation." *American Sociological Review* 41:280–288, 1976.

Glazer, N. *Affirmative Discrimination*. New York: Basic, 1975.

Glynn, C., and J. McLeod. "Implications of the Spiral of Silence Theory for Communications and Public Opinion Research." In *Political Communications Yearbook*. Beverly Hills, Calif.: Sage, 1984.

Goldman, P. *Report from Black America*. New York: Simon and Schuster, 1970.

Graglia, L. "From Prohibiting Segregation to Requiring Integration." Pp.

69–96 in W. Stephan and J. Feagin (eds.), *School Desegregation: Past, Present and Future.* New York: Plenum, 1980.

Granovetter, M. "Threshold Models of Collective Behavior." *American Journal of Sociology* 83:1420–1443, 1978.

Greeley, A. "School Desegregation and Ethnicity." Pp. 133–155 in W. Stephan and J. Feagin (eds.), *School Desegregation: Past, Present and Future.* New York: Plenum, 1980.

Greeley, A., W. McCready, and K. McCourt. *Catholic Schools in a Declining Church.* Kansas City, Mo.: Sheed and Ward, 1976.

Handlin, O. *Boston's Immigrants.* New York: Atheneum, 1959.

Hannon, J. *The Catholic Church and School Desegregation in Boston.* M.A. thesis, Department of Sociology, University of Wisconsin, Madison, 1980.

Harris, E. "Prejudice and Other Social Factors in School Segregation." *Journal of Negro Education* 37:440–443, 1968.

Henri, F. *Black Migration.* Garden City, N.Y.: Doubleday, 1975.

Higginbotham, A. *Race and the American Legal Process.* New York: Oxford University Press, 1978.

Hillson, J. *The Battle of Boston.* New York: Pathfinder, 1977.

Hirschman, A. *Exit, Voice and Loyalty.* Cambridge, Mass.: Harvard, 1970.

Hirschman, A. *Shifting Involvements.* Princeton, N.J.: Princeton University Press, 1982.

Hochschild, J. *The New American Dilemma: Liberal Democracy and School Desegregation.* New Haven, Conn.: Yale University Press, 1984.

Hollander, S., and L. Scarpa. "A Note on the Perception of Race." *Public Opinion Quarterly* 36:606–607, 1972.

Irving, Florence. "Segregation Legislation in the South." *New South* (February 1957).

Isenberg, D. "Levels of Pluralistic Ignorance Phenomena: The Case of Receptiveness to Interpersonal Feedback." *Journal of Applied Social Psychology* 10:457–467, 1980.

Jackman, M. "General and Applied Tolerance: Does Education Increase Commitment to Racial Change?" *American Journal of Political Science* 22:302–324, 1978.

Jencks, C. "Busing: The Supreme Court Goes North." Pp. 14–26 in N. Mills (ed.), *The Great School Bus Controversy.* New York: Columbia Teachers College, 1973.

Johnson, R. *The Dynamics of Compliance.* Evanston, Ill.: Northwestern University Press, 1967.

Katz, E., and P. Lazarsfeld. *Personal Influence.* New York: Free Press, 1955.

Kelley, J. "The Politics of School Busing." *Public Opinion Quarterly* 38:23–29, 1974.

Kesselman, L. *The Social Politics of FEPC: A Study in Reform Pressure Movements.* Chapel Hill: University of North Carolina, 1947.

Key, V. O. *Southern Politics.* New York: Vintage, 1949.

Killian, L. *The Impossible Revolution.* New York: Random House, 1975.

Kinder, D., and D. Sears. "Symbolic Racism versus Racial Threats to the Good Life." *Journal of Personality and Social Psychology* 40:414–431, 1981.

King, M. L. *Stride toward Freedom: The Montgomery Story.* New York: Harper, 1958.

King, M. L. *Where Do We Go from Here: Chaos or Community?* Boston: Beacon, 1967.

King, M. L. *Why We Can't Wait.* New York: Harper, 1963.

Kirby, J. *Black Americans in the Roosevelt Era: Liberalism and Race.* Knoxville: University of Tennessee Press, 1980.

Kirby, D., T. Harris, R. Crain, and C. Rossell. *Political Strategies in Northern School Desegregation.* Lexington, Mass.: D. C. Heath, 1973.

Kluger, R. *Simple Justice: The History of Brown v. Board of Education.* New York: Vintage, 1975.

Kmenta, J. *Elements of Econometrics.* New York: Wiley, 1971.

Krech, D., and R. Crutchfield. *Theory and Problems of Social Psychology.* New York: McGraw-Hill, 1948.

Lawrence, D. "14th Amendment Unlawfully Adopted." *New Orleans Times-Picayune,* 9 February 1959.

Lawson, S. *Black Ballots: Voting Rights in the South.* New York: Columbia University Press, 1976.

Lazarsfeld, P. "The Use of Panels in Social Research." *Proceedings of the American Philosophical Society* 42:405–410, 1948.

Levin, M. *The Alienated Voter.* New York: Holt, Rinehart and Winston, 1960.

Levy, F. *Northern Schools and Civil Rights.* Chicago: Markham, 1971.

Lipsky, M. "Protest as a Political Resource." *American Political Science Review* 62:1144–1158, 1968.

Lubell, S. *White and Black: Test of A Nation.* New York: Harper and Row, 1964.

McAdam, D. *Political Process and the Development of Black Insurgency 1930–1970.* Chicago: University of Chicago, 1982.

McConahay, J. "Self-Interest versus Racial Attitudes as Correlates of Anti-busing Attitudes in Louisville: Is It the Buses or the Blacks?" *Journal of Politics* 44:692–720, 1982.

McConahay, J., and J. Hough. "Symbolic Racism." *Journal of Social Issues* 32:23–45, 1976.

Mahard, R., and R. Crain. "Research on Minority Achievement in Desegregated Schools." Pp. 103–125 in C. Rossell and W. Hawley (eds.), *The Consequences of School Desegregation.* Philadelphia: Temple University, 1983.

Matthews, D., and J. Prothro. "Stateways versus Folkways: Critical Factors in Southern Reactions to Brown v. Board of Education." Pp. 139–156 in G. Dietz (ed.), *Essays on the American Constitution.* Englewood Cliffs, N. J.: Prentice-Hall, 1964.

Matthews, D., and J. Prothro. *Negroes and the New Southern Politics.* New York: Harcourt, 1966.

Mays, B., and J. Nicholson. *The Negro's Church.* New York: Arno Press and the *New York Times,* 1969.

Merton, R. *Social Theory and Social Structure.* New York: Free Press, 1968.

Mills, N. "Busing: Who's Being Taken for a Ride?" Pp. 3–13 in N. Mills (ed.), *The Great School Bus Controversy.* New York: Columbia Teachers College, 1973.

Mills, R. *Justice Delayed and Denied: HEW and Northern School Desegregation.* Washington D.C.: Center for National Policy Review, 1974.

Moon, H. *Balance of Power: The Negro Vote.* Garden City, N. Y.: Doubleday, 1948.

Mosteller, F., H. Hyman, P. McCarthy, E. Marks, and D. Truman. *The Pre-Election Polls of 1948.* New York: Social Science Research Council, 1949.

Mottl, T. "The Analysis of Countermovements." *Social Problems* 27: 620–635, 1980.

Muller, E. *Aggressive Political Participation.* Princeton, N. J.: Princeton University Press, 1979.

Mumford, L. "White Flight from Desegregation in Mississippi." *Integrated Education* 11:12–26, 1973.

Muse, B. *Virginia's Massive Resistance.* Bloomington: Indiana University Press, 1961.

Muse, B. *Ten Years of Prelude.* New York: Viking, 1964.

Myrdal, G. *An American Dilemma.* New York: Parthenon, 1944.

NAACP Legal Defense and Educational Fund. "It's Not the Distance, It's the Niggers." Pp. 322–356 in N. Mills (ed.), *The Great School Bus Controversy.* New York: Columbia Teachers College, 1973.

National Advisory Commission on Civil Disorders. *Report of the National Advisory Commission on Civil Disorders.* New York: Bantam, 1968.

Neustadt, R. *Presidential Power.* New York: Wiley, 1960.

Newman, D., N. Amidei, B. Carter, W. Kruvant, D. Day, and J. Russell. *Protest, Politics, and Prosperity*. New York: Academic Press, 1978.

Nevin, D., and R. Bills. *The Schools That Fear Built*. Washington, D.C.: Acropolis, 1976.

Nie, N., S. Verba, and J. Petrocik. *The Changing American Voter*. Cambridge, Mass.: Harvard, 1976.

Noelle-Neumann, E. "The Spiral of Silence: A Theory of Public Opinion." *Journal of Communication* 24:43–51, 1974.

Noelle-Neumann, E. "Turbulences in the Climate of Opinion: Methodological Applications of the Spiral of Silence." *Public Opinion Quarterly* 41:143–158, 1977.

Noelle-Neumann, E. "Public Opinion and the Classical Tradition: A Reevaluation." *Public Opinion Quarterly* 43:143–156, 1979.

Oberschall, A. *Social Conflict and Social Movements*. Englewood Cliffs, N. J.: Prentice-Hall, 1973.

O'Gorman, H. "Pluralistic Ignorance and White Estimates of White Support for Racial Segregation." *Public Opinion Quarterly* 39:313–320, 1975.

O'Gorman, H. "White and Black Perceptions of Racial Values." *Public Opinion Quarterly* 43:48–59, 1979.

O'Gorman, H., with S. Garry. "Pluralistic Ignorance: A Replication and Extension." *Public Opinion Quarterly* 40:449–458, 1976.

Oliver, P. "Rewards and Punishments as Selective Incentives for Collective Action: Theoretical Investigations." *American Journal of Sociology* 85:1356–1375, 1980.

Olson, M. *The Logic of Collective Action*. Cambridge, Mass.: Harvard University Press, 1965.

Orfield, G. *The Reconstruction of Southern Education*. New York: Wiley, 1969.

Orfield, G. *Must We Bus*. Washington D.C.: Brookings, 1978.

Orfield, G. "Public School Desegregation in the United States, 1968–1980." Washington D.C.: Joint Center for Political Studies, 1983.

Orfield, G. "Lessons of the Los Angeles Desegregation Case." *Education and Urban Society* 16:338–353, 1984.

Page, B. *Choices and Echoes in Presidential Campaigns*. Chicago: University of Chicago Press, 1978.

Panetta, L., and P. Gall. *Bring Us Together: The Nixon Team and the Civil Rights Retreat*. Philadelphia: Lippincott, 1971.

Parkman, H. "The City and the State." In E. Herlihy (ed.), *Fifty Years of Boston*. Boston: Boston Tercentenary Committee, 1932.

Pearce, D. "Deciphering the Dynamics of Segregation: The Role of Schools in the Housing Choice Process." Unpub. MSS, Department of Political Science, Catholic University, 1980.

Peltason, J. *Fifty-Eight Lonely Men: Southern Federal Judges and School Desegregation.* Urbana: University of Illinois, 1961.

Peterson, P. *School Politics Chicago Style.* Chicago: University of Chicago Press, 1976.

Pettigrew, T., and E. Q. Campbell. "Faubus and Segregation: An Analysis of Arkansas Voting." *Public Opinion Quarterly* 24:436–447, 1960.

Pettigrew, T., and M. Cramer. "The Demography of School Desegregation." *Journal of Social Issues* 15:61–71, 1959.

Pettigrew, T., and R. Green. "School Desegregation in Large Cities: A Critique of the Coleman 'White Flight' Thesis." *Harvard Educational Review* 46:1–53, 1976.

Pettigrew, T., J. Ross, and T. Crawford. "Bigotry in Boston: Mrs. Hicks and Her Supportors." In T. Pettigrew, *Racially Separate or Together.* New York: McGraw-Hill, 1971.

Pettigrew, T., E. Useem, C. Normand, and M. Smith. "Busing: A Review of 'The Evidence.'" *Public Interest* 30:88–118, 1973.

Pinard, M. *The Rise of a Third Party.* Englewood Cliffs, N.J.: Prentice-Hall, 1971.

Piven, F., and R. Cloward. *Poor People's Movements.* New York: Vintage, 1979.

Preston, M., L. Henderson, and P. Puryear. *The New Black Politics.* New York: Longman, 1982.

Raffel, J. "Political Dilemmas of Busing." *Urban Education* 9:375–395, 1977.

Raper, H. *The Tragedy of Lynching.* New York: Arno and the *New York Times,* 1969.

Ravitch, D. *The Great School Wars.* New York: Basic, 1974.

Richard, R., R. Knox, and T. Oliphant. "The First Year." *Boston Globe* 25 May 1975, pp. A1–A24.

Rist, R. "School Integration: Ideology, Methodology and National Policy." *School Review* 84:417–430, 1976.

Rist, R. "On the Future of School Desegregation." Pp. 117–131 in W. Stephan and J. Feagin (eds.), *School Desegregation: Past, Present and Future.* New York: Plenum, 1980.

Rodgers, H., and C. Bullock. *Law and Social Change.* New York: McGraw Hill, 1972.

Rodgers, H., and C. Bullock. *Coercion to Compliance.* Lexington, Mass.: D. C. Heath, 1976.

Rosenberg, M. "Test Factor Standardization as a Method of Interpretation." *Social Forces* 41:53–61, 1962.

Ross, I. *The Loneliest Campaign: The Truman Victory of 1948.* New York: New American Library, 1968.

Ross, J. "Research Design and Sample: Multi-Wave, Quasi-Experimental Field Study." Chicago: National Opinion Research Center, 1976.

Ross, J., and W. Berg. *I Respectfully Disagree with the Judge's Order.* Lexington, Mass.: Lexington, 1981.

Ross, J., T. Crawford, and T. Pettigrew. "Negro Neighbors—Banned in Boston." *Transaction* 3:13–18, 1966.

Ross, J., R. Vanneman, and T. Pettigrew. "Patterns of Support for George Wallace: Implications for Racial Change." *Journal of Social Issues* 36:69–91, 1976.

Rossell, C. "The Mayor's Role in Implementing School Desegregation." *Urban Education* 12:247–270, 1977.

Rossell, C. "School Desegregation and Community Social Change." *Law and Contemporary Problems* 42:133–183, 1978a.

Rossell, C. "The Effect of Community Leadership and Mass Media on Public Behavior." *Theory into Practice* 8:131–139, 1978b.

Rossell, C. "Desegregation Plans, Racial Isolation, White Flight and Community Response." Pp. 13–57 in C. Rossell and W. Hawley (eds.), *The Consequences of School Desegregation.* Philadelphia: Temple University, 1983.

Rossell, C., and W. Hawley. "Desegregation and Change." Pp. 3–12 in C. Rossell and W. Hawley (eds.), *The Consequences of School Desegregation.* Philadelphia: Temple University Press, 1983.

Rubin, L. *Busing and Backlash.* Berkeley: University of California, 1972.

Rubin, L. "White against White: School Desegregation and the Revolt of Middle America." Pp. 67–83 in F. Levinsohn and B. Wright (eds.), *School Desegregation: Shadow and Substance.* Chicago: University of Chicago, 1976.

Ruchames, L. *Race, Jobs and Politics.* New York: Columbia University Press, 1953.

Rule, J. and C. Tilly. "Political Process in Revolutionary France: 1830–1832." Pp. 41–85 in J. Merriam (ed.), *1830 in France.* New York: New Viewpoints, 1975.

Salmon, C., and F. G. Kline. "The Spiral of Silence Ten Years Later." In *Political Communication Yearbook,* 1984.

Sandburg, C. *Abraham Lincoln, The Prairie Years: Vol. 2.* New York: Harcourt, 1926.

Sarratt, R. *The Ordeal of Desegregation.* New York: Harper and Row, 1966.

Schattschneider, E. E. *The Semisovereign People.* Hinsdale, Ill.: Dryden Press, 1960.

Schuman, H., and S. Presser. *Questions and Answers in Attitude Surveys.* New York: Academic, 1981.

Schuman, H., C. Steeh, and L. Bobo. *Racial Attitudes in America: Trends and Interpretations.* Unpub. MSS., Department of Sociology, University of Michigan, Ann Arbor, 1983.

Schwartz, M. *Radical Protest and Social Structure.* New York: Academic, 1976.

Sears, D., C. Hensler, and L. Speer. "Whites' Opposition to Busing: Self-Interest or Symbolic Politics?" *American Political Science Review* 73:369–384, 1979.

Sears, D., R. Law, T. Tyler, and H. Alden. "Self-Interest vs. Symbolic Politics in Policy Attitudes and Presidential Voting." *American Political Science Review* 74:670–684, 1980.

Shorter, E., and C. Tilly. *Strikes in France, 1830–1968.* London: Cambridge University Press, 1975.

Sniderman, P. *A Question of Loyalty.* Berkeley: University of California, 1981.

Snow, D., L. Zurcher, and S. Ekland-Olson. "Social Networks and Social Movements: A Microstructural Approach to Differential Recruitment." *American Sociological Review* 45:787–801, 1980.

Stephen, A. "Integration and Sparse Negro Populations." *School and Society* 81:133–135, 1955.

Stinchcombe, A., M. McDill, and D. Walker. "Is There a Tipping Point in Racially Changing Schools?" *Journal of Social Issues* 25:127–136, 1969.

Stinchcombe, A., and D. G. Taylor. "On Democracy and School Integration." Pp. 157–186 in W. Stephan and J. Feagin (eds.), *School Desegregation: Past, Present and Future.* New York: Plenum, 1980.

St. John, N. *School Desegregation: Outcomes for Children.* New York: Wiley, 1975.

Sundquist, J. *Politics and Policy: The Eisenhower, Kennedy and Johnson Years.* Washington D.C.: Brookings, 1968.

Taeuber, K., G. Orfield, and others. "School Segregation and Residential Segregation: A Social Science Statement." Pp. 227–247 in W. Stephan and J. Feagin (eds.), *School Desegregation: Past, Present and Future.* New York: Plenum, 1980.

Taylor, D. G. "Housing, Neighborhoods and Race Relations: Recent Survey Evidence." *Annals of the American Academy* (January 1979).

Taylor, D. G. "Pluralistic Ignorance and the Theory of the Spiral of Silence: A Formal Analysis." *Public Opinion Quarterly* 46:311–335, 1982.

Taylor, D. G. "A Formal Model for Neighborhood Investment." Chap. 6 in R. Taub, D. G. Taylor, and J. Dunham, *Paths of Neighborhood Change.* Chicago: University of Chicago Press, 1984a.

Taylor, D. G. "Estimating Standardized, Regression-Adjusted Scores with the General Linear Model." Appendix 3 in R. Taub, D. G. Taylor, and

J. Dunham, *Paths of Neighborhood Change.* Chicago: University of Chicago Press, 1984b.

Taylor, D. G. "A Revised Theory of Racial Tipping." Chap. 7 in R. Taub, D. G. Taylor, and J. Dunham, *Paths of Neighborhood Change.* Chicago: University of Chicago Press, 1984c.

Taylor, D.G., P. Sheatsley, and A. Greeley. "Attitudes toward Integration." *Scientific American* 238:42–49 1978.

Taylor, D. G., and A. Stinchcombe. "The Boston School Desegregation Controversy." Chicago: National Opinion Research Center, 1977.

Tilly, C. *From Mobilization to Revolution.* New York: Addison-Wesley, 1978.

Tipton, J. *Community in Crisis.* New York: Columbia Teachers College, 1953.

Treiman, D. "Status Discrepancy and Prejudice." *American Journal of Sociology* 71:651–664 1966.

United States Commission on Civil Rights. *Desegregating the Boston Schools: A Crisis in Civic Responsibility.* Washington, D.C.: Government Printing Office, 1975.

United States Commission on Civil Rights. *Fulfilling the Letter and Spirit of the Law.* Washington, D.C.: Government Printing Office, 1976.

United States Department of Health, Education, and Welfare. "General Statement of Policies under Title VI of the Civil Rights Act of 1964 Respecting Desegregation of Elementary and Secondary Schools," reprinted in *Guidelines for School Desegregation,* Hearings before the special subcommittee on the judiciary, 89th Cong., 2d sess., 1966.

United States Department of Justice. *Report of the Community Relations Service to Senators Brooke and Javits.* Washington D.C.: *Congressional Record,* June 26, 1976.

Useem, B. "Solidarity Model, the Breakdown Model and the Boston Anti-Busing Movement." *American Sociological Review* 45:357–369, 1980.

Useem, B. "Local vs. Cosmopolitan Conflict in School Desegregation Protest." Unpub. MSS., Department of Sociology, University of Illinois, Chicago, 1984.

Vanfossen, B. "Variables Related to Resistance to Desegregation in the South." *Social Forces* 47:39–44, 1968.

Vines, K. "Epilogue: 1970." In J. Peltason, *Fifty-Eight Lonely Men: Southern Federal Judges and School Desegregation.* Urbana: University of Illinois Press, 1970.

Vose, C. *Caucasians Only.* Berkeley: University of California Press, 1959.

Washington, J. *Black Religion, the Negro and Christianity in the United States.* Boston: Beacon Press, 1964.

Watters, P. *Down to Now: Reflections on the Civil Rights Movement.* New York: Pantheon, 1971.

Weatherford, S. "The Politics of School Busing: Contextual Effects and Community Polarization." *Journal of Politics* 42:747–765, 1980.

Weber, M. *On Law in Economy and Society,* ed. M. Rheinstein. New York: Simon and Schuster, 1967.

Weinberg, M. *Desegregation Research: An Appraisal.* Bloomington, Ill.: Phi Delta Kappa, 1968.

Weinberg, M. "The Relationship between School Desegregation and Academic Achievement: A Review of the Research." *Law and Contemporary Problems* 39:241–270, 1975.

Weinberg, M. *A Chance to Learn: A History of Race and Education in the United States.* New York: Cambridge University Press, 1977.

Wirt, F. *Politics of Southern Equality.* Chicago: Aldine, 1970.

Woodward, C. V. *The Strange Career of Jim Crow: Third Revised Edition.* New York: Oxford University, 1974.

Zolberg, A. "Moments of Madness." *Politics and Society* (Winter 1972): 183–207.

Index

233